VIDEO GAME OPTIMIZATION

BEN GARNEY AND ERIC PREISZ

Course Technology PTR

A part of Cengage Learning

COURSE TECHNOLOGY
CENGAGE Learning™

Australia • Brazil • Japan • Korea • Mexico • Singapore • Spain • United Kingdom • United States

COURSE TECHNOLOGY
CENGAGE Learning

Video Game Optimization
Ben Garney and Eric Preisz

Publisher and General Manager,
Course Technology PTR:
Stacy L. Hiquet

Associate Director of Marketing:
Sarah Panella

Manager of Editorial Services:
Heather Talbot

Marketing Manager:
Jordan Castellani

Senior Acquisitions Editor:
Emi Smith

Project and Copy Editor:
Marta Justak

Technical Reviewer: Jeffrey T. Kiel

Interior Layout Tech: MPS Limited,
A Macmillan Company

Cover Designer: Mike Tanamachi

Indexer: BIM Indexing and
Proofreading Services

Proofreader: Kezia Endsley

For product information and technology assistance, contact us at
Cengage Learning Customer & Sales Support, 1-800-354-9706

For permission to use material from this text or product,
submit all requests online at **cengage.com/permissions**

Further permissions questions can be emailed to
permissionrequest@cengage.com

NVIDIA® is a registered trademark of NVIDIA Corporation. ATI™ is a
trademark of Advanced Micro Devices. Quake® is a registered trademark
of id Software, Inc. V-Tune™ is a trademark of Intel Corporation. All other
trademarks are the property of their respective owners.

All images © Cengage Learning unless otherwise noted.

Library of Congress Control Number: 2008931077

ISBN-13: 978-1-59863-435-8

ISBN-10: 1-59863-435-6

Course Technology, a part of Cengage Learning
20 Channel Center Street
Boston, MA 02210
USA

Cengage Learning is a leading provider of customized learning
solutions with office locations around the globe, including Singapore,
the United Kingdom, Australia, Mexico, Brazil, and Japan. Locate your local
office at: **international.cengage.com/region**

Cengage Learning products are represented in Canada by Nelson
Education, Ltd.

For your lifelong learning solutions, visit **courseptr.com**

Visit our corporate website at **cengage.com**

Printed in the United States of America
1 2 3 4 5 6 7 12 11 10

To my mother, who taught me to write.
To my father, who taught me to program.

—Ben Garney, Feb 1, 2010

To my wife and son, whose support made this book possible.
To my mom, whose drive inspires me.
To Ben, who not only provided the voice and content,
but also drove the book's completion during
my move, job change, and appendectomy.

—Eric Preisz, Feb 1, 2010

ACKNOWLEDGMENTS

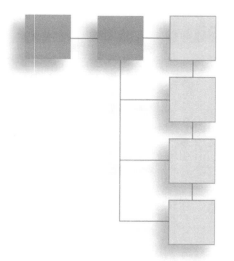

Video Game Optimization started when Eric had the opportunity to teach a class on optimization at Full Sail University's game development program and thought the subject might be interesting to more than just students. We want to acknowledge Full Sail for their support of the book.

Emi Smith of Cengage Learning was receptive to Eric's book proposal, and she supported us along the rocky road to completion. Our editor, Marta Justak, showed her mettle by working long hours, taking our rough drafts and turning them into professional, proofread and edited chapters. Thank you, Emi and Marta!

Jeff Kiel of NVIDIA, our tech editor, has caught a remarkable number of factual errors, and he has actively contributed to making the book more useful and comprehensible. Arzhange Safdarzadeh of Intel helped make Chapters 8, 9, and 10 a reality by writing early drafts and doing a lot of the groundwork. Grant Skinner (gskinner.com) kindly let us reference his ActionScript 3 performance tests.

We want to thank Deborah Marshall of GarageGames and Nate Beck of TLD Studios for reviewing drafts of the book and offering their feedback. Paul Lindburg and his team at Intel provided feedback and shared our work at their conference events. And Michael Abrash not only gave feedback, but also hosted Eric for a quick visit while in Seattle. Thank you all for your involvement, honest criticisms, and thoughtful opinions.

This book would not be in your hands without Jay Moore's involvement. Before he signed on to do the book, Eric knew he needed a co-author. And Jay, who is a consummate networker, knew just the right guy. Thank you, Jay!

Over the two years we have spent working on this book, we are confident that we've lost at least one name from our notes. Therefore, thank you to everyone we didn't mention here. Your contribution is much appreciated.

Finally, we have to acknowledge the community of talented optimizers who have shared their experience, research, and knowledge in books, papers, and on Internet pages. We stand on the shoulders of giants.

ABOUT THE AUTHORS

Eric Preisz is the Director of Torque at InstantAction (formerly GarageGames). Eric's video game optimization work experience grew from his passion for the topic and the opportunity to teach the subject at Full Sail University where he was a department chair and course director. His development background includes engine and game development for companies and organizations such as Disney, NASA, the Department of Defense, and others.

Ben Garney works at PushButton Labs, where he is the lead developer on the PushButton Engine, an open source Flash game framework. Before he got into Flash game development, Ben spent five years at GarageGames, working on Torque engine technology. During that time, he helped ship several games, most notably *Marble Blast Ultra* on the Xbox 360.

CONTENTS

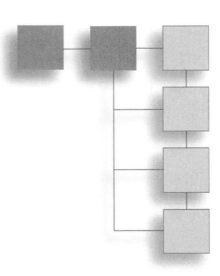

Chapter 4   **Hardware Fundamentals. 57**

INTRODUCTION

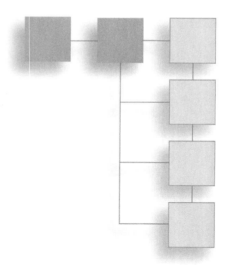

Optimizing is a game of trade-offs.

There are many anecdotes, articles, and books about optimizing in specific scenarios. Sometimes, these include hard numbers; if so, it's usually for hardware that is several years old. Often, the discussion is very specific, such as optimizing memory copies for a specific chip, and the advice is frequently hard to apply for a project that needs to run well on a wide variety of hardware.

Video Game Optimization is a discussion of optimization from theory to practice. It is our hope that, even as hardware architectures come and go, the basic lessons of optimization will remain useful to you.

In addition to covering the abstract, we also measure real-world performance of different techniques using a performance test harness. Binaries and source code are included, so that when you are on new hardware, you can run the harness and get the "lay of the land" for that hardware's performance characteristics.

What You'll Find in This Book

This book teaches you what you need to know to be an effective optimizer. To optimize effectively, you must:

- Recognize how instructions are processed.

- Know how memory is accessed.

- Understand how to use hard drives, network interfaces, and graphics cards efficiently.

- Be acquainted with system architecture, whether you are dealing with a PC, a console, or a cell phone.

- Be able to reliably measure where time and other resources are being used in the course of execution.

In addition to discussing these topics, we also include a practical perspective in the form of the performance test harness.

One of the hardest parts of optimizing quickly is developing a good intuition as to what solutions to apply when. We have developed a performance test harness. For most performance situations in this book, we have written short tests and included charts of their performance on our test systems. By seeing how different variables affect performance, it becomes easier to decide what implementation might be fastest.

Of course, you will still need to measure and benchmark, but having an idea of the directions you can go means you might find something fast enough in one or two iterations instead of three or four.

The code for the test harness is open source and available freely online, so that you can run the tests on your own hardware and adjust your approaches accordingly. Visit http://perftestharness.googlecode.com/ for instructions on how to download the harness.

Who This Book Is For

We have written this book for three kinds of people:

- **Students:** You're taking a class on performance programming. This book is set up to be used as a textbook for such a course. One of the authors taught the optimization course at Full Sail using material that led to the creation of this book.

- **Professional programmers on a deadline:** You're writing a game. You're a pretty good programmer, but performance isn't what it should be, and you need to get the game up fast. There are no miracle solutions, but if you can make it through the first few chapters of this book, you'll be able to effectively take on your performance problems.

- **Optimization gurus:** You already know a thing or two about optimization. You've been around the block a few times. You're going to get the most out of the latter portions of this book, which focus on measured performance from the test harness and hardware details. Depending on your background, the high-level sections on benchmarking may be useful as well—many people who are good at low-level optimization forget to look at the big picture.

But what if you are not a game developer? Good optimization techniques are applicable nearly everywhere. This book also emphasizes optimizing applications that use both CPU and GPU, and in that light, there are several other areas that face similar problems:

- **Modeling, simulation, and training:** Governments and military organizations have great interest in using video game technology to support modeling, simulation, and training. Successful projects such as *Virtual Battlefield 2*, *America's Army*, and the use of engines such as Unreal, support the belief that video games, as a medium, can provide superior solutions at an affordable rate.

- **Virtual worlds and collaboration:** Industries around the world are using video game technology to accommodate group collaboration for engineering or social gatherings, such as virtual meetings.

- **GPGPU:** Standing for "General Purpose GPU," this interesting field uses GPUs to increase the performance of certain stream-friendly algorithms. In some cases, researchers have increased the performance of algorithms 50 times over their CPU implementations.

How This Book Is Organized

This book is divided into two broad parts. The first part extends from Chapter 1 through Chapter 5, and it covers the foundations. In this segment of the book, we discuss the theory of optimization, show how to optimize in the context of a project, detail what makes a good benchmark, discuss the optimizer's tools, and present an atlas of the modern computer as it relates to optimization.

The second part extends from Chapter 6 through Chapter 16. Most importantly, we discuss optimizing the CPU (Chapters 6 and 7) and optimizing the GPU (Chapters 8 through 10). The remaining chapters cover networking (Chapter 11), mass storage (Chapter 12), concurrency (Chapter 13), console (Chapter 14), managed languages (Chapter 15), and GPGPU (Chapter 16).

In addition, the performance test harness, which contains all the performance tests we discuss in the book, can be found at <http://perftestharness.googlecode.com/>.

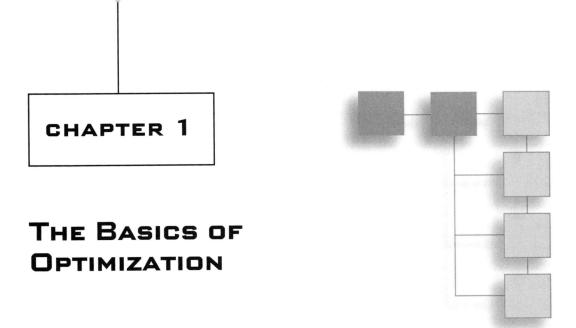

CHAPTER 1

THE BASICS OF OPTIMIZATION

Wikipedia defines "optimization" as the process of modifying a system to make some aspect of it work more efficiently or use fewer resources. But why optimize your code?

Each game has a certain fixed amount of computing resources available to it. Within that world of possibility, the developer must create a compelling experience. Market forces dictate that it must be as good an experience as possible.

When you optimize your code, you are increasing the amount of work you are able to do per unit of computational power and maximizing your efficiency. By optimizing your CPU and GPU usage, you can add more polygons, more pixels, more physics, more AI, more responsiveness, more immersion—leading to more fun and better visuals, the elements that help make and sell revolutionary video games.

Optimization should always be done holistically. Look at the big picture first and then drill down until you find the specific problem that is slowing your application. When you don't optimize holistically, you risk fruitless optimizations. Many beginner optimizers start by choosing the exact lines they want to speed up, without considering the big picture. Deadlines are tight, and you can't afford to waste time optimizing every line.

The optimization process is simple. Start by looking at the whole system. Find a situation that consistently exhibits bad performance. That done, measure where resources (such as computing power or memory) are being used. Take steps to reduce them. Finally, measure again to see if you have improved the situation sufficiently. If it is good enough, you are done. Otherwise, find the next performance problem and start all over again.

A good optimizer uses a wide variety of techniques to perform this process. Don't worry—the next few hundred pages are all about how to get performance wins quickly, reliably, and sanely by focusing on a repeatable process.

Let's start by discussing, at a high level, the contents of this book and the why, where, and when of optimization.

The Optimizer's Mantra

1. **Benchmark:** Create a repeatable example of a problem situation.

2. **Measure:** Establish a baseline of memory and compute resource usage.

3. **Detect:** Find the part of the program that is mis-using the resources (memory/computation).

4. **Solve:** Change how the program works to improve resource usage.

5. **Check:** Determine if there was an improvement through measurement.

6. **Repeat:** Do the process over and over again until you hit your performance goals.

Getting to Better Optimization

Anyone can follow the basic optimization process and eventually get a game to run faster. You could even write a program to randomly change one line of your source code and only keep the changes that increase your frame rate. A beginner optimizer who chooses lines to optimize without regard for the big picture works this way. However, this type of optimization will fall short of the efforts of a good optimizer.

The goal is to help you, a software developer, become a great optimizer. You'll find that experience, skill, and knowledge are necessities. You will also need to use your intuition and your patience. Optimization is a crucial step to building compelling games.

Unlike a random code-rewriting program, any developer will approach a performance problem with a few ideas about what might solve it. For instance, if you see a loop is running a million times and causing the game to run slowly, you might try to reduce the number of iterations. If your knowledge of the algorithm prevents it from entering the loop at all, surely the application will go faster.

Using your intuition involves assumptions. The downfall of novice optimizers is that they do not know the assumptions under which they are operating. Their intuition misleads them. They may assume, for example, that inline code always makes it run faster, or that garbage collection is always slower than manual memory allocation. The expert optimizer understands his assumptions, and he knows when to question them—and better still, realizes that he is fallible and must build assumptions based on measurements and analysis

The difference between a novice and master chess player isn't how quickly they move their pieces. The difference is that the master chess player immediately identifies the key details of the situation. Both players try to look several moves ahead, but the master only thinks about the moves that will likely lead to victory.

In optimization, there are a million different things you can do to speed up your code. A beginner will struggle because he has to try a lot of approaches, and may not hit on the things most likely to give big performance wins.

On the other hand, good optimizers are able to quickly identify the three or four things that will make the biggest difference, measure their effects, and choose the best from among them.

The major goal of this book is to get you into the position of being an experienced optimizer as quickly as possible. We will do this in a few ways:

- **Performance tests:** Every optimization book and article includes a lot of little cryptic code snippets with timing information, usually recorded on the authors' systems. In our experience, the authors are generally developing on a cutting-edge 486DX and the numbers are completely useless for your Core 2 Quad development system and Centrino target system. We'll include a performance test harness with this book, and every performance claim we make is backed by hard data. In five years when everyone has 128-core terahertz systems, all you have to do is rerun the tests to see what the performance picture is for your hardware right then.

- **Theoretical understanding:** We will discuss the fundamentals of performance. How are things perceived as fast or slow, responsive or lagging? How does measurement work? What are the properties of code in the context of performance?

- **Practical knowledge:** Being able to write 3D graphics code is a specialized skill. Making it fast is another issue entirely. We'll cover the background you need in order to ask such questions as "What is fast on this hardware?" and we'll give you the answers for a typical PC circa 2010.

Performance Test Harness

The test harness bundled with this book can be downloaded at http://code.google.com/p/perftestharness. It is a lightweight framework for running performance tests. Every performance graph and code snippet from the book is included.

The purpose of this harness is to give you a realistic performance picture. Every optimizer has assumptions, such as "random memory access is slower than linear access" or "accessing a lot of data is slower than accessing a little data," but very few can say how *much* slower or if this assumption applies to the current situation. By comparing simple performance scenarios, you can get a sense of what the relative performance trade-offs are. Knowing this, you will know how much of an improvement a change to your code can give you, and when it's worth it to switch from one technique to another.

In the process of writing and reviewing these performance tests, many of our own performance assumptions have been challenged.

We should also discuss some of the things that this book will *not* cover. There are an infinite number of things to know, and the best resources are focused. Therefore, this book will not teach you about the following areas:

- You will *not* learn how to write assembly, but we will discuss when to appropriately use or understand assembly to optimize your game.

- This book is *not* a game design algorithm book. Although we will certainly be discussing game algorithms, we will not be giving you an exhaustive review on which game algorithm is suitable from a game design perspective. We will, however, use game algorithms as examples to illustrate optimization processes or end goals. There are already plenty of books on game design algorithms, and we don't feel the need to be overly redundant.

- This book will *not* teach you about the best practices for writing and maintaining your code. Design patterns, refactoring, and dealing with legacy code are subjects beyond this book's scope.

Optimization Lifecycle

Optimization is a cycle that you repeat until your game is fast enough. Let's go into some detail about how the optimization process works. There are many different ways to optimize, but the basic concepts we cover here will serve you

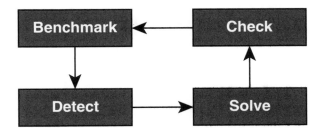

Figure 1.1
All optimization starts with a benchmark. Once a benchmark is found, it is possible to profile, identify the performance problem, and solve it. Finally, we return to our benchmark to see if we have improved performance.

well until you develop your own style. The steps are benchmark (see Figure 1.1), detect, solve, check, and repeat.

1: Benchmark

Let's talk about benchmarks. When you are optimizing, it is essential that you be able to measure your gains. Having a good benchmark makes optimization easier, because you will get immediate feedback on the effect of your changes.

For a game, a benchmark is a point of reference in your game that serves as a standard for comparison against future implementations.

A good benchmark will have a few important qualities. First, it will be consistent across runs. Running the benchmark twice without changing your code should give you the same results. Second, it will be quick. It shouldn't take more than a minute or so to run the benchmark; otherwise, you'll spend more time waiting on the test than working on the fix! Third, it should be representative of an actual game situation, so that you don't waste time optimizing for scenarios that will never arise. Finally, it will be responsive to changes. It should be obvious when you've fixed the performance problem.

The History of Benchmarks

Originally, benchmarks were flat areas carved by surveyors into stones at the survey site, a process called *benching*. These marks allowed the surveyors to place their instruments reliably at the same spot, so they could make repeated measurements with a high degree of accuracy.

For instance, you might decide your frame rate is too low in certain situations. Before you start the process of optimization, you would identify a specific scene in your game that exhibited the performance problems and modify the game so you could easily get to that scene and measure the frame rate. Ideally, the whole process would be automated so you could run the benchmark and get an identical run with consistent behavior. This would make it easy to get accurate measurements.

The important thing about benchmarks is that they let you make relative comparisons—before and after you make a change. System performance benchmarks like 3D Mark are excellent for analyzing the performance of a computer system, but won't tell you anything about your code.

Anytime you start to optimize something, make sure that you can measure your success.

2: Detection

The next step is to gather and analyze data to help identify where you need to optimize. With every change you make, you are hoping for the biggest possible performance increase with the least amount of effort. In other words, you are looking for the biggest return on your time investments. Proper detection doesn't absolutely guarantee the highest ROI, but it does ensure that what you are attempting to optimize is actually a problem. Information, like a flashlight, lets you avoid stumbling around in the dark.

Consider a mechanic tuning a car. Something is wrong with it. The mechanic is trying to fix it as best she can. Sometimes, she can just reach into the engine, make an adjustment, and everything runs better.

More often, fixing the problem is a complex process. She has different tools—a stethoscope, a dynamometer, the on-board computer, her own senses—that can help her. Often, she has to make a guess about where the problem might be and do further work to narrow things down. Eventually, she'll gather enough clues to identify the problem.

In optimization, you always start at the big picture and work your way down to the fine grain problem. The first big division is typically finding out whether the CPU or the GPU is slowing you down more; sometimes the CPU and GPU are equally balanced. There are a wide variety of tools that can help, such as profilers and system monitors. We'll go into the details of detection in Chapter 5, "Holistic Video Game Optimization."

For our frame rate optimization example, we'll start by using a system monitor to see if we are maxing out the CPU or the GPU. If the GPU were underutilized, we might use a profiler to measure the CPU time spent updating each object in the scene. Since the game normally runs fine, it's likely that a single problem is eating most of the time, so that is where we know to optimize.

Don't be confused by the word "single." Since the atomic level of software is the micro-operation, software performance problems are almost always a conglomerate of many subparts. The distinction of "singular" depends on your perspective. For example, a fine grain problem is a CPU stalling CPUID assembly call. A coarse grain problem is an unbalanced graphics pipeline. We use different perspectives to find the biggest "single" problem.

Start at the big picture and work your way down toward a detailed understanding of where specific performance problems are located.

3: Solve

After you've gathered enough information to identify the factor limiting your performance, then you can change something to try to improve the performance. You might toggle a flag, rewrite an algorithm, or change the data you are loading.

Coming back to our example, we notice that there's a loop that's not updating correctly, and as a result, it is running far too often. We expect that fixing it will win us back a lot of wasted CPU cycles, so we go ahead and make the change.

Even the most experienced optimizer will often have to guess at the best solution. The best practice is always to try several options before settling on a solution.

4: Check

Once you have made a change, always measure to see if it really did give a performance win. Typically, you will run your benchmark again and observe the change. A common trap for novice optimizers is changing code blindly based on an assumption (for instance, "inlined functions are faster") without evaluating the effectiveness of the tactic.

In our example, we might find that the loop was indeed not executing right, but the actual slowdown was a bad memory access pattern. If we hadn't measured, we would not have found the deeper issue.

Measuring has another benefit, too. It develops your intuition, giving you data that will help you optimize more effectively next time you encounter a problem. This corrective action will help you optimize even in the strangest situations—on weird hardware, sharing time with odd processes, or even on future architectures.

5: Repeat

In a river, when you remove a rock, the water flows in a new way, down the new path of least resistance. Computer programs are the same.

Removing a bottleneck or a hotspot causes cascades and ripples across the entire performance picture. In other words, every change affects the flow of the program. Your old measurements, and therefore your analysis, may no longer be valid.

After a successful frame rate increase, it is time to begin the process again. You may need to create a new benchmark, but you can always repeat the detection process and begin your search for the new, slowest part of your game.

Like the back of the shampoo bottle says: lather, rinse, and repeat.

Hotspots and Bottlenecks

When you optimize, you are looking for hotspots and bottlenecks.

Lean manufacturing, a manufacturing ideology developed primarily by Toyota (described by Jeffrey Liker in "The Toyota Way") focuses on eliminating waste in assembly lines. There are three types of waste the system focuses on: muda (non–value-added work), mura (unevenness), and muri (overburdening). By removing waste, the system creates efficiency, increases savings, and improves quality. Auto manufactures use these waste descriptions to evaluate their assembly lines.

When you optimize systems made of multiple concurrent elements, you are dealing with a digital assembly line. Data flows from CPU to GPU, and memory accesses are fulfilled while you process. When everything flows smoothly, the system is harmonious. But if one piece must work too hard and others have to wait, there is discord.

Hotspots

When you look at an object like a car motor with an IR camera, you'll see that most of the engine is relatively cool. But a few areas—like the pistons—are hot.

Really hot. So hot that they affect the functioning of the rest of the car. So hot that auto manufacturers have to install fans and cooling fins and coolant systems to keep the car functioning properly.

Hotspots in the context of optimization are places in the code that consume more than their fair share of execution time, memory bandwidth, or function calls. Typically, a hotspot is small in code footprint, but big in performance impact. The Pareto Principle states that, generally, a small fraction of code (in terms of lines) is responsible for the majority of resource usage. You may also know it as the 80–20 rule.

When optimizing, you want to find the "hottest" parts of your program and change them so they run cooler. Other parts of the code then become the new "hottest" part, and you can optimize them in turn.

Bottlenecks

Imagine two machines running in parallel in an assembly line. Each spits out a different kind of widget. Combining the two widgets makes the final product.

Suppose that one machine creates 100 widgets an hour and the other creates only 50. You will only be able to produce 50 products an hour. In other words, the slow machine is the limiting factor or bottleneck in the system. If you wanted to speed up total production rate, the only way to do it would be to get the 50-widget machine to make more widgets per hour.

Any system with multiple elements, such as a computer with multiple cores and a GPU, along with deep pipelines with multiple subunits in those processors, has a bottleneck somewhere, and as optimizers the goal is to minimize its impact on performance.

Trade-Offs

There are three important trade-offs to consider when you are optimizing: performance versus space, accuracy versus speed, and maintainability versus complexity (see Figure 1.2). Let's review all of them.

The first and most important is *performance versus storage*. It's often possible to trade calculation time against memory usage. One example is *memoization*, a term coined by Donald Michie in 1968 to describe a technique where you cache recently calculated results to avoid recomputing values. Memoization replaces

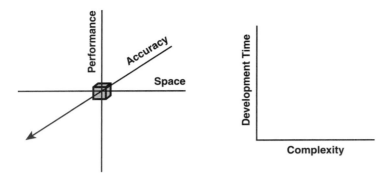

Figure 1.2
Here are three trade-offs to consider when you are optimizing.

expensive calculations with a quick memory read. You use more memory, but save CPU. Another example of trading memory for performance is using a kD-tree to accelerate collision queries, instead of looping over every triangle in a mesh. The tree adds to the memory footprint, but saves you so much extra computation that it is well worth it in most cases.

The second trade-off is *accuracy versus speed*. Sometimes, you can reduce precision in order to increase performance. For an example of this trade-off, you can look to the vertex shader 1.1 instructions `log` and `logp`. Both perform a log_2 operation. The difference is that `log` performs the operation using 10 instruction slots and `logp` performs the operation using one slot. The performance cost represents a trade-off in accuracy; the `logp` function is less precise, but in most situations it doesn't matter for visualization.

Accuracy versus speed plays a role in the data you use to render, too. You can also use lower polygon meshes, as they consume less screen space. A lower detail model isn't as accurate as the highest resolution LOD, but it consumes fewer resources. You can also reduce texture resolution.

Finally, you can apply the accuracy/speed trade-off to gameplay. Distant enemies might require less frequent AI updates. Effects that are purely visual, such as debris from an explosion, might require lower precision physics simulation than gameplay-critical physics driving a player-controlled vehicle.

The final trade-off is *development time versus complexity*. Frequently, there are changes that will yield a speedup but impact the clarity or maintainability of code. Adding a complex image-based caching system to your renderer might speed things up, but getting it to work properly in all cases might be a nightmare—never mind the added complexity in the code base. As you optimize, these trade-offs give you several important angles from which to attack the problem. The most elegant solutions will give you exactly what you want without having to make any trade-offs. But when performance is your goal, understanding your arsenal is the key to winning the war.

Levels of Optimization

There are many approaches to cleaning a hard drive. Some people choose to search for the biggest files and delete the unneeded ones. This is smart because it's likely that most of the capacity of a full drive is spent on a small number of large files. Does that mean that you shouldn't look at the folder that holds a million 1-kilobyte files?

Of course not, but there's another consideration. Maybe you partitioned your hard drive, and you weren't utilizing as much of it as you thought.

When searching for opportunities to improve performance, the answer to what you optimize may lie in the "level" of optimization. We've found it useful to categorize optimizations into three levels: system, application, and micro (see Figure 1.3).

System Level

The system level of optimization focuses on the resources of your machine and their use in your game—the global, holistic performance picture. At the system level, you are looking at broad elements of the computer, and you are concerned with three things: utilization, balancing, and efficiency.

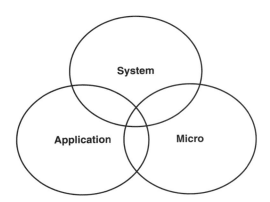

Figure 1.3
These three levels describe the process of optimization. Each level has definable characteristics; however, solutions may involve changes to one or more levels.

- **Utilization** describes how much of a resource's time is spent doing productive work. Your word processor, for instance, might use 50 percent of your CPU time, but it's unlikely to use any GPU time at all. When a resource is not utilized, it is *idle*.

- **Balancing** is when you move work from a resource that is overutilized to one that is idle. For instance, as GPUs grew in power, games had to switch from carefully considering whether each triangle would be visible to sending large batches of geometry. GPUs became so fast that now it's often cheaper to let the GPU determine visibility by drawing geometry than it is to cull individual triangles.

- **Efficiency** is another consideration. Each part of the computer excels at a specific task. Part of system level optimization is making sure that each task is done with the right resources. Runtime data structures should be kept in RAM, not on mass storage. Massively parallel operations like rendering should be done on the GPU, not the CPU. Something that takes the CPU 50 percent of frame time might only take the GPU 1 percent.

It is easy to write a program that will use 100 percent of a system's resources, but it's unlikely that this will translate into a compelling game. You have to put your money on the screen. If resources aren't being spent on making a better game, then they are wasted. The purpose of a game is to be fun and sell lots of units, not maximize CPU usage.

The ideal scenario is a system that is completely balanced, fully utilized, and highly efficient.

Algorithmic Level

Algorithmic level optimizations are the choices you make in the algorithms and data structures that make up your application. The Zen of optimization is in making use of the best algorithms in an elegant manner, maximizing performance and maintainability.

Algorithmic level optimizations focus on removing work using better and typically more complex algorithms.

One of the best ways to analyze a program at the algorithmic level is to use a tool that will show you the call hierarchy of your code. A call hierarchy will trace what lines of code call others, building a tree rooted at the main loop of your program. Additionally, it will tell you how much time was spent in each part of the code, as well as how many times it was run. By looking at this information, you can quickly identify subroutines that are taking the most time and target them for optimization.

For example, after analyzing your game, you may find that one function is being called 500,000 times, amounting to a total of 15 percent of execution time. You realize that the time per call is quite low. Instead of trying to optimize the function (which would probably be hard), you look at the code that calls the offending function, and realize that with a few small changes, it would only need to call it 500 times. After making the change, the offending function is now way down the list at less than one percentage point.

Remember, algorithmic level optimizations are crucial. Good algorithmic level optimizations can trump the best micro-level or be more robust than system level changes. Removing work is an optimization that will benefit all hardware.

Micro-Level

The stereotypical optimization work happens at the micro-level. Pouring over assembly listings, checking instruction timings and pipeline stages, using obscure hardware features to gain small wins—they're all right here. Micro-optimizations are line-by-line optimizations, and they are the ones that most often cause long arguments on mailing lists. Concepts such as branch prediction, loop unrolling, instruction throughput, and latency are all considerations when optimizing code line by line.

Compilers are considerably better at performing micro-optimizations today than they were 15 years ago. The term *optimizing compiler* is rarely used now because it is standard for compilers to perform many advanced optimizations automatically.

Micro-optimizations can give big wins for inner loops, which are small sections of code that are run many, many times. Suppose that you ran a routine every frame that sets each pixel on the screen to a color. The line of code inside the loop accounts for 99 percent of execution time, and as a result, finding a way to speed that one line up could yield a big boost in performance.

There are still some areas where micro-optimizations are the default choice. If you find that a shader is a bottleneck (dealt with in more detail in Chapter 10, "Shaders"), you will almost immediately start with micro-optimization. Because shader programs will be run many times per frame, shaving just a few operations from your shaders can yield significant performance gains.

These performance gains come at a price, though. Micro-optimizations can be hard to maintain, because they often rely on obscure knowledge and specific compiler or hardware behavior. It isn't uncommon to have a game still under development that will run flawlessly on one machine and crash on another. The critical difference may be drivers, hardware, or both.

Micro-optimizations are more reliable on fixed platform such as consoles. Be careful if you are working on the micro-level for a PC game because taking advantage of the latest greatest feature might result in a game that only runs on the latest greatest hardware.

Optimization Pitfalls

You can spend an infinite amount of time tuning, tweaking, and profiling your application. There is never a true ending, a point at which code can't be improved any further. But there are points of diminishing returns, and there are also paths that will take you in unproductive directions. In the following sections, we will identify several pitfalls that lead optimizers astray.

Assumptions

Although it's redundant for us to state this pitfall, it occurs so often, and is so fundamental that it is worth it for us to single out this topic here. You should not make assumptions about what is slow. Instead, you should measure and analyze. Doing so will promote your assumptions to educated decisions. You should, however, understand the underlying assumptions of your hardware and APIs. For example, a GPU and its drivers assume that you will send data with large submissions. The DirectX API assumes that you will not lock a static vertex buffer more than once.

Premature Optimization

Don't sweat the majority of details until you have to.

You've probably heard the saying "Premature optimization is the root of all evil." It's frequently attributed to Professor Donald Knuth, from his 1974 paper "Structured Programming Using Goto Statements."

When an esteemed professor from Stanford declares the root of all evil, people listen. The problem is, however, that they failed to hear and repeat the entire message. The full quote reads, "We should forget about small efficiencies, say 97% of the time: premature optimization is the root of all evil."

In other words, don't worry about optimizing anything until you know it is a big performance sink. Of course, there are those three percent cases where you should not forget small efficiencies. The difficulty is in knowing which three percent, and that's why detection is so essential.

Many people believe you cannot optimize code until you have written it. This is not the case. You can solve 90 percent of your optimization issues by designing flexible, maintainable code. A well-designed object hierarchy, even with the overhead of a language like C# or Java, can be much faster than pure assembly code that is poorly written. If your code is flexible and maintainable, you will be able to manipulate it after detecting the problem.

Optimizing on Only One Machine

When you optimize, you should focus on the worst-case scenario—both in terms of benchmarks and in terms of target hardware. Most developers do their work on only one or two machines. This can lead to a false performance picture. The bottlenecks on a system with a high-end GPU, lots of RAM, and a generous CPU are going to be different than a system with no GPU, minimal RAM, and a basic CPU.

In interactive applications like games, the worst-case performance is generally a bigger issue than the average. Users notice and are distracted by intermittent dramatic slowdowns, while consistent performance, even if it is on the mediocre side, is quickly accepted. We go into more detail on this in Chapter 8, "From CPU to GPU."

Therefore, you should make sure to identify and test on your worst-case system. This will give you a true skewed-to-pessimistic performance picture, keeping you honest when the final deadline looms, and you have to deliver acceptable performance on old, misconfigured hardware.

Test on as much hardware as you can, and especially on the worst you can find.

Optimizing Debug Builds

This mistake is simple to avoid, but easy to fall into. If you aren't going to ship a debug build, don't do your performance profiling on one. Debug builds often run much more slowly, and slower in different ways, than your release build. The compiler, once optimizations are turned on, can change the performance picture significantly.

Make sure that you are testing your release builds. Any good optimization tool will work with them. You can turn on debug symbols and vary your optimization level to trade speed for ease in debugging.

Debug builds do have one benefit: They typically expose performance problems sooner. If you want a pessimistic view of your application's CPU performance, then run in debug mode.

Bad Benchmarks

Sometimes, a bad benchmark will lead you to believe that you have made your game faster, even if you haven't. This often occurs when you aren't disciplined and inadvertently change a variable between runs of a benchmark.

Suppose that a developer identifies a scene that exhibits an abnormally low frame rate. They do their first benchmark in full-screen mode. They analyze the data and make some changes. When they run the benchmark again, though, they run in windowed mode at a different resolution, resulting in a gain in a frame rate, independent of their code changes. Because they changed multiple variables, they can't make a valid comparison between the two runs, and they can't tell if their optimization brought any benefit.

It is very important to control the environment during your benchmark. In order to avoid this pitfall, the only thing that should change from benchmark to benchmark is the code you are optimizing. The best practice here is to fully automate the benchmark so that it runs without user input—that way you can get maximum consistency.

Concurrency

Game development has involved concurrency almost since its inception. Consoles like the NES and Atari 2600 featured multiple chips that cooperated in order to run the game. The arcade space frequently had similar setups. Almost all arcade systems since 1980 featured more than one active CPU, frequently one for gameplay, another for graphics, and a third for sound. Today's consoles (other than handhelds) all feature at least two cores, and frequently many more, in addition to the GPU and other specialized resources.

However, in the PC, concurrency has been absent or hidden until more recently. Graphics drivers deal with the details of talking asynchronously to the video hardware. Most computers had only a single CPU core. Now, multiple cores are mainstream, and CPU design is complex enough that even within a single core, parallelism is present.

Let's talk about instruction level parallelism. In order to delay the need for coarser grained parallelism, chipmakers introduced longer pipelines and out-of-order execution that enabled the chips to perform many instructions in parallel. Without realizing it, your code is performing some level of parallelism, even when you are writing single-threaded code. Instruction level parallelism usually occurs without our knowledge; a compiler will seek to take advantage of this parallelism whenever possible.

Another option for concurrency is the SIMD instruction sets available on many CPUs—MMX, SSE, AltiVec. SIMD—single instruction, multiple data—instructions can operate on more than one piece of data at once. A typical example is an instruction that can add one vector of four floats to another vector of four floats. Older GPUs used SIMD instruction sets almost exclusively, as they were optimized for working on batches of homogenous data. Today, GPUs handle scalar data quite efficiently using a SIMT, or single-instruction multiple-thread approach.

These kinds of parallelism, for all their wins, are invisible from an architectural level.

Multithreading, however, can have major effects on architecture. Driven by physical barriers inherent in building ever smaller, faster cores, chipmakers now add more cores to their chips to increase speed instead of increasing clock frequency. Now, it's difficult to buy a CPU with only one core. By changing an application to run in multiple threads, big increases in speed can be had. But this requires a major change in the application's architecture, to separate it into multiple, independent units.

Middleware

Many of our bottlenecks and hotspots reside in code that we didn't write (see Figure 1.4). Years ago, it wasn't uncommon to write your game with little help from outside APIs. In fact, for a long time, there were no other options and no novel hardware to access requiring an API. Now, however, it is common to use

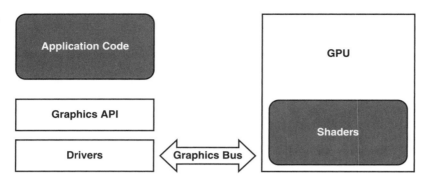

Figure 1.4
Out of the entire graphics pipeline, we only have source code for the application and shaders.

many different APIs and many different pieces of hardware. With many APIs, there is no publicly available source code. This is especially true of graphics APIs. The innards of DirectX, OpenGL, and graphics drivers are not available for review in most situations. In the past, you could optimize all of your game using assembly because you had access to the entire pipeline. Now, you benefit and depend on the APIs and hardware that keep you from optimizing with assembly. The software and hardware you use, not the software and hardware you write, controls a large percentage of your game's execution time. If you didn't write the code, or don't have the source, then optimizing using hand-coded assembly is not possible.

Big O Notation

From theoretical and practical perspectives, big O notation is a key concept. By knowing how quickly the execution time for an algorithm grows as you increase workload, you can determine quickly if an algorithm is feasible, given your dataset and performance requirements.

However, big O ignores the constant factor. You know that an $O(n^2)$ algorithm will generally decrease in speed geometrically as you increase its workload. But if the constant factor is microseconds, even a workload of thousands of items might give acceptable performance. An $O(n)$ algorithm with a high constant factor of a millisecond per item might never be acceptable.

Additionally, because of the context, the increase may not be consistent with the theoretical model. For instance, an $O(n^2)$ sort algorithm might be much faster than the $O(n \log n)$ sort if it can take better advantage of the cache or pre-fetcher.

Big O is a good guide, but you have to make real-world measurements to get the full picture.

Conclusion

In writing this book, we have tried to be mindful of the fact that optimization involves balancing details and trade-offs from a dozen different, daily-changing sources. Just in the past 20 years, we have seen parallelism go through several incarnations, seen CPU calculation speed go from slower than memory access speed to faster, and the speed of all these pieces grow by several orders of magnitude. The landscape for optimization is always evolving, yet the basic principles tend to stay the same.

We hope to pass on those principles to you. Carefully measure, wisely prioritize, cleverly optimize, and you will find success.

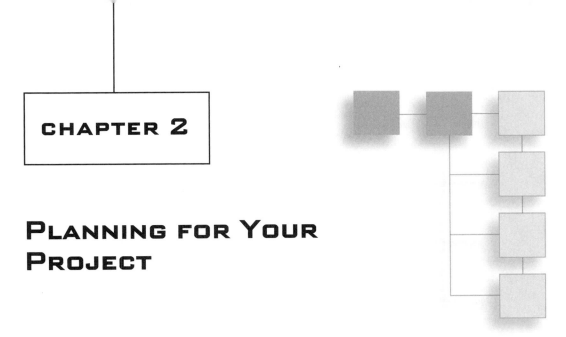

CHAPTER 2

PLANNING FOR YOUR PROJECT

Anyone working on a game will tell you that managing the project lifecycle is quite a task. Basic project management involves several phases: requirement gathering, project estimation, implementation, acceptance testing, and retirement. During these phases, things go wrong, technologies progress, ideas change, and so does the market. All phases result in adjustments and complexity, and it is imperative to have the right team to manage the effort. How does optimization fit into this process?

Unfortunately, optimization is often reactive or an afterthought, although surprisingly, optimizing reactively does work since hundreds of developers ship games this way. That doesn't mean, however, that being reactive is the easiest or best path to achieve the performance goals that deliver the experience you designed for your end-user. Usually, reactive optimization leads to the removal or reduction of features to accommodate for an underwhelming frame rate.

The goal of this chapter is to help you learn how to be proactive instead of reactive. We will focus on how to manage optimization through the project lifecycle.

Managing a project's performance starts before implementation and only ends when the last version ships. Typically, optimization doesn't require a single, large amount of dedicated time. You can save a lot of time by applying consistent, regular efforts and using practices, such as a performance budget, to help guide you.

When we suggest that optimization should be a continual process, don't be afraid. We realize that there are many optimization rat holes that can lead to little return. You don't need to work on every optimization opportunity—just the ones that will make your game run well enough to ship. We'll cover techniques for estimating the return on investment of different potential optimizations.

Lastly, in order for you to gauge your performance issues, you must understand what problems you are trying to solve. In the final section, we will discuss slowness and what it means to your project—there is more than one dimension to game performance underachievement.

Project Lifecycle

Different optimization strategies are appropriate at different times. Consider the following parts of the project lifecycle:

- **Requirement Gather/Estimation**: The project is in design phase and little or no code has been written yet. At this time, the performance targets are being identified and the broad behaviors of the game are being planned. The performance issues are largely oriented around developing the performance budget and determining the broad architecture based on the game's needs.

- **Implementation—Early Phase**: At the start of implementation, major technology decisions are still being made. The codebase is smaller, and there's lots of time left on the project. Furthermore, because there's very little art or gameplay logic and the levels aren't fleshed out, if they exist at all, performance is more than sufficient. You will want to do stress tests at this time in order to get an idea of where performance problems will crop up and what strategies will best cope with them. You may want to re-architect some subsystems now, before more code gets layered on top of them.

- **Implementation—Mid Phase**: As time goes on, more art is added and more gameplay, too. Inevitably, as each aspect of the game is implemented and the artists make bigger and better levels, characters, and effects, performance will typically creep down to the absolute minimum acceptable level. Make it easy for your programmers to tell when there are performance problems, and do your best to educate them so that things don't come to a crisis point (even though they often do).

- **Implementation/Acceptance Testing**: By the end of the project, pro-grammers will be scraping for every millisecond, and important pieces of the game may have to be cut or scaled back in order to ship with an acceptable level of performance. This is the time for last-minute hacks and tweaks to get the most out of your code.

From High Level to Low Level

During the early phases of *Quake1*'s development, John Carmack and Michael Abrash were trying to come up with a very fast software renderer. Rather than trying to come up with a highly optimized triangle draw function or a very efficient 3D math library, they prototyped many high-level approaches in plain, unoptimized C. This allowed them to focus on the relative merits of different rendering architectures. Only after they found an architecture with sufficient performance did they spend the effort to optimize it (www.bluesnews.com/abrash/chap64.shtml, third paragraph in overdraw section).

Architectural changes are a bad idea late in a project. Sometimes it is unavoidable to have to make an emergency fix late in a project, but that is just what it sounds like—an emergency. You want to do these sorts of high-level changes early on. Similar to building a skyscraper, it's a lot cheaper to develop the foundation earlier than it is once the building's frame is built.

Later in the project, architectural changes will be quite a lot harder. As the time left on the project becomes limited, it is more likely that you will have to result to micro-optimization hacks and tweaks, although sufficient proactive efforts will reduce this reactive practice.

When it's a month to final release and you just need that extra 10% performance, you should be in a good place. At least you should know very well what the performance needs for the game are. Furthermore, most of the art and gameplay development is (or should be) slowing down, which means that you're working on a more solid base for measuring and making decisions. At the end of development, the code and developers become more sensitive to change. There should not be much more maintenance in order to ship at this point. You do not want to make big changes at the end of your game; otherwise, you will undermine the efforts already put forth by the quality assurance team.

These are some typical examples of how game development progresses. Some aspects are good, and some are bad. Making this progress as smooth as possible means being proactive and agile.

Project Lifecycle and Levels of Optimization

Figure 2.1 describes where the levels of optimization fit into the project schedule. It is best to focus on system level optimizations early since it is very difficult to implement many system level optimizations later in the game. Algorithmic level optimizations are available throughout the majority of the product's lifecycle. To reduce cascading bugs, you should focus on micro optimizations before a code freeze.

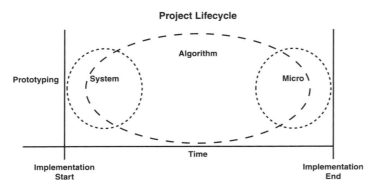

Figure 2.1
As you move from the beginning to the end of your project (left to right on the X axis), different kinds of optimization work make sense.

The Performance Budget

Every project has performance considerations. For example, when using Microsoft Word, a high frame rate may not be a major consideration. But users will want Microsoft Word to be responsive when they type, so it can't suffer latency issues when the program is working with a big document.

Setting Specifications

When you start developing a game from an early stage, you will have an idea of the kind of hardware you want your game to be able to run on and of the broad kinds of activities your game will need to be doing. For example, a chess game will need to be able to display 64 squares and their contents and run some intensive AI routines. A first-person shooter will need to display compelling, immersive environments with minimum latency, while running all the logic for the things that live in that world (that is, AI and physics).

To begin your budget, you must determine two high-level specifications: performance goals and hardware specs. For instance, the target might be 30fps on a low-end system with a certain video card and CPU, and 60fps on a high-end system with a better video card and faster CPU. With these two pieces of information, you can begin to develop a performance budget.

You can, and probably should, be quite detailed in your description of the hardware. You can include GPU specifics like the version and count, or CPU information such as core count and gigahertz. You will also likely have two specifications—one for the high end and one for the low. It is a great idea to build a machine (or a few machines) that is representative of your high- and low-end specifications. Developers can use these machines to test and validate their implementations.

Setting Performance Goals

When developing a performance budget, consider the display of your system. Displays typically update at a rate between 60 and 120Hz. Rendering additional frames will not give you any benefit because the user won't see them. You may choose to use extra time to sample input more frequently, do higher quality physics calculations, or otherwise increase the fidelity of the game, but be careful not to chase frame rate for the sake of frame rate. You can do better if you are focused on specifics.

The other end of the display path is the human perceptual system. A frame rate of 100fps is enough to give the illusion of perfectly smooth movement, even when rotating the camera rapidly. The difference between 60Hz and 30Hz is easily detectable to most serious game players. Of course, if you are not building a twitch game, then the requirements will be less stringent.

There's no need to set performance goals above the level of human perception or hardware capabilities. Setting lower goals, such as 25 frames per second, is reasonable when trying to develop games on the bleeding-edge of computation. Hardware tends to get faster, and 25fps on today's high-end hardware might be 30fps on the hardware that is available on your launch date.

Developing Line Items

After developing the specifications, it's time to turn the budget into a plan that is usable by the entire team. You can do this the same way that accountants disseminate their budgets—by using line items. A line item is a subelement of the total budget.

A budget of 30fps on a high-end system may have the line items shown in Table 2.1.

The "Frames Per Second vs. Time Per Frame" sidebar goes into more detail, but you will want to do your performance budgeting in terms of milliseconds per frame. Because it is simple to calculate, regardless of the system's total frame rate, this approach makes it easy to enforce an easy-to-measure time budget for each subsystem. For example, you may allocate rendering 10ms per frame, physics 5ms, sound 2ms, and gameplay 17ms. The conversion from fps to ms is easy—simply take 1,000ms and divide by the desired fps.

$$30fps = 1000ms/30 = 33 \text{ and } 1/3ms$$

Table 2.1 High-End Performance Budget Line Items @ 30fps

Subsystem	CPU	DRAM	GPU	VMEM	Mass Storage
Rendering	10ms	20MB	10ms	50MB	10MB
Physics	5ms	10MB	0ms	0MB	10MB
Sound	1ms	10MB	0ms	0MB	100MB
Gameplay	17ms	10MB	0ms	0MB	1MB
Misc.	1ms	10MB	0ms	0MB	10MB
Total	34ms	60MB	10ms	50MB	131MB

Repeat this budget for the low-end specifications. Developers can implement fallbacks that use lower fidelity processes to stay within budget.

Developing line items is useful and gives developers and managers a target to aim for before writing a single line of code, which saves experienced developers a lot of time. But it can be a useful guiding tool for a producer or project manager as well. The allocation of hardware resources should reflect the game design goals. A single player chess game with a small budget for AI is likely not consistent with the desired end-user experience.

Your budget doesn't need to represent every single line item. Leaving a buffer is a good idea, to handle feature creep and to compensate for misconfigured computers full of system-draining processes, viruses, or bit-torrents. In the previous example, we created a category called "misc" to allow for the unexpected. The more you allocate for the future, the more flexibility you will have.

Frames Per Second vs. Time Per Frame

The way you express performance can skew your performance picture. FPS is a useful and obvious measurement, but it can lead you astray. Ultimately, a high frame rate is about only spending so much time on each frame.

Budgeting with frames per second is hard, because frames don't break down easily into logical subunits. If you have a target frame rate of 60fps and five subsystems, then each of those subsystems has to run at 300fps. At extremely high frame rates (or very low milliseconds), you should be careful since timing is less accurate and OS time slicing plays a bigger role.

It makes a lot more sense to do budgeting in terms of time per frame. Writing code to detect if you are spending more than 3.3ms on physics per frame is much simpler than trying to infer a frame rate. In addition, it also makes it obvious if there are other factors affecting fps. For example, if all five subsystems are taking 1ms each, but frame rate is not up to par, you know the issue is elsewhere.

The performance budget, much like a financial budget, is typically not perfect. It is a benchmark for measurement and guidance. Don't get trapped into thinking that everyone will always make the budget and don't expect the budget to be flawless the first time you develop it. Use the budget to determine problems and to forecast and manage change. Computer systems are complex, and the performance budget is a representation of what the actual results will be. Don't let this process overwhelm you.

Going overboard with scope and granularity is a surefire way to develop a specification that will create too much process overhead and reduce efficiency. Use the appropriate level of detail for the job. For example, if there is too much detail, then the budget will be overly burdensome, and you will be constantly updating it to reflect changes in subsystems. If you use too little detail, then you have not provided enough guidance and multiple developers may overdraw resources from the same line item (for example, three developers use 24ms (8×3) from a budget of 10ms).

Developing a performance budget is difficult. The experience and practice of developing and enforcing budgets will refine your judgment and provide you with the expertise you need to fully utilize the budget as a tool.

For example, consider the details regarding the budgeting of memory. There are several considerations you must understand when developing the memory budget. First, low DRAM usage means there is less chance of memory being swapped to mass storage. Second, a smaller footprint effectively increases the usefulness of the cache. If your game uses 100MB and there is a 2MB cache, then $1/50^{th}$ of application memory is likely to be in the cache at any given time. (This is a gross simplification, of course.) But if you use 1GB with the same cache size, only $1/500^{th}$ will be loaded, guaranteeing more cache misses. Finally, a smaller footprint reduces the memory bandwidth the application will consume, and less time waiting on the front-side bus due to bandwidth strain leads to better performance.

A performance budget can range anywhere from a few notes jotted down on a scrap of paper to a formal project specification document. But it is a key touchstone for any project—without it, you're flying blind.

Developing for a Line Item

You will never fully know what your performance picture will be like before you write your program, but you can take steps to manage performance. We talked about making a performance budget, which is a good way to keep things in order in a global sense.

When you are implementing a subsystem or module, use these tips to formulate the relative cost a line item has on your overall performance landscape.

- **First, look at the theoretical performance.** Think about the workload your code will be dealing with. If you will have large numbers of items, steer clear of $O(n^2)$ algorithms. Will your code bias toward inserts, removals, or searches? There are a lot of great algorithms out there, each tailored to different situations. Learn them, love them, use them.

- **Second, look at the hardware.** Is there a hardware feature or resource you can take advantage of? You have to prioritize resource utilization, but if you know you have lots of memory and not a lot of CPU time to spend, you might want to store data rather than calculate it. Or there might be a specialized instruction that does exactly what you want. Or maybe the work can be done more efficiently on the GPU. If your subsystem implementation doesn't fit inside the envelope of the line item, try a different approach or negotiate resources with the owner of the performance budget.

- **Third, reduce the workload.** The fastest code is the code that is never run. The cheapest triangles are the ones that are never drawn. The fastest disk reads are the ones that never happen. Instead of trying to make rendering routines really fast, it might be more effective to add culling so that you don't waste time on objects that can't be seen. The same concept applies in nonrendering contexts, such as a database organizing data in a tree so it can discard large chunks with very few computations.

- **Finally, just implement it.** Get a basic version up and running as quickly as you can. This will give you the data you need to make intelligent optimizations. From there, you can rewrite until you get where you need to be performance-wise, safe in the knowledge that you're making forward progress, not just building castles in the air. By prototyping or rapid development, you are helping to refute or support the budget you've been given.

Typical Project Trajectory

After you've identified your performance budget, you will have some parameters to help you know when to start optimizing and when you are done. But that's not the only factor you should be using to look at your application's performance. The chart in Figure 2.2 shows the typical trajectory for a small game; for a large game it's often similar but repeated for every major milestone. Projects tend to follow a trajectory in terms of performance. They start out with a minimal amount of test art. Most effects and gameplay are still under development. There are some glitches, typically due to a desire to keep things simple—for instance, the sorting of translucent objects may not be 100% right.

As the project goes on, artists and designers add more and more art, effects, and gameplay. Since these team members generally aren't as technically proficient as the core programmers, performance problems often arise. For instance, a level

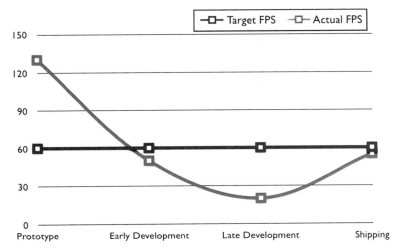

Figure 2.2
Performance over a project lifecycle, shown in actual FPS vs. target FPS.

designer might abuse the physics system to set up a puzzle, resulting in far more CPU usage than is needed to achieve the desired effect. Artists might use over-detailed textures and exceed the VRAM budget. A gameplay scripter might not be aware of the fastest way to do something, and might end up emulating it very expensively in script.

The result of this is that the game's performance will drop dramatically as the project moves forward. At some point, typically near a major deadline, it will become obvious that something has to be done to get back within the perfor-mance budget. The programmers will go on an optimizing spree, beating down the biggest hotspots and widening the narrowest bottlenecks. In addition, some issues that were glossed over at the beginning, like translucent object sorting, will have become stressed and lead to highly objectionable artifacts, requiring a more expensive solution to keep things looking good enough.

Despite the best efforts of programmers, performance will tend toward the minimum acceptable level, and by the time the game ships, the game will struggle to fit inside the performance budget. Stay vigilant and do your best to use the performance budget as a measuring stick for managing this tendency.

When the project is still small, consider building small test cases to see what the future might hold for you. If you are expecting to deliver 50 objects in a scene, don't wait until the artists have all 50 objects done. Implement your system for one average object and replicate it 50 times. You don't need the final art to get a vague idea of your implementation.

Run weekly reviews or develop unit tests that measure performance of subsystems against the current performance budget. Discuss budget projections and deficiencies at daily or weekly meetings. Being aware of the typical project trajectory is a skill you will develop over time and adjust for automatically.

Maximizing Return on Investment

Optimization is always contextual. Just like you might not want to bring up your collection of stuffed animals at a biker convention, some kinds of optimizations only make sense at specific times.

In general, as optimizers, we want to do small amounts of work for huge performance gains. An ideal optimization would be quickly changing one line of code to get a tenfold performance increase. But, all too often, developers change hundreds of lines of code for a one-percent gain.

You can maximize your return on investment (ROI) by removing performance-related bugs. These consist of obvious erroneous code that can cause bad performance; for instance, a loop that runs twice as often as it needs to, or incorrect usage of an API that disables hardware acceleration. API tools usually provide a means for extracting error and warning messages in debug output streams, such as the DirectX Output Debug, or error retrieval code, such as OpenGL's GetLastError(). Optimizing without removing bugs may undermine your efforts and point you toward the wrong optimizations. Some bugs are nonissues, while others can lead to significant performance changes.

You can also maximize ROI by measuring. Don't make assumptions. The tools and processes may sometimes be complex or underdocumented, but the aim of this book is to provide that process by exposing some of the tools and methods we use. Chapter 5, "Holistic Video Game Optimization," focuses on a process that maximizes ROI across the entire system.

After you measure, you can use the Levels of Optimization, outlined in Chapter 1, "The Basics of Optimization." The levels of optimization guide you away from performing smaller-grained (micro) optimizations that may change, or even disappear, when you perform coarser-grained (system, algorithmic) optimizations.

When considering an optimization, you can also affect ROI by choosing the wrong type of changes. These include maintainable and unreliable changes.

- **Maintainable changes** are those that do not cause cascading changes in the future. These changes will often be fundamental design issues that affect a system's performance. For instance, in most situations a game geared toward software rendering (like *Quake 1*) will not run as fast as a game designed around a programmable GPU (like *Quake 4*). If you can assume the presence of a GPU, there are design decisions you can make that will give major speedups in rendering.

  These situations are medium risk, meaning there is the potential that things will break, and fixing these issues can involve large changes to the codebase. However, once the change is done, the system remains flexible and easy to maintain. The optimization is maintainable.

- There are also **unreliable changes**. Also called "hacks" or "tweaks," this is what many people think of when they think of optimization. It includes taking advantage of weird, complex, or esoteric behaviors in hardware or software to get maximum performance. Examples of these types of optimizations include inlining all the math in your physics library, rewriting inner loops in SIMD, or manually processing and ordering game assets for faster loading. They may increase performance now, but may not be reliable from hardware to hardware. The downside to these changes is that they are risky and tend to produce brittle, hard-to-maintain code. Usually, this brittleness can be localized (for example, by replacing a slow routine in a math library with an optimized one), but sometimes they end up making whole modules very difficult to work with (like optimizing a texture-processing library with SIMD or hand-inlining code). This can introduce bugs while at the same time making them hard to fix.

In general, you should fix bugs whenever you find them, implement maintainable changes as much as possible, and only consider unreliable changes when necessary, followed by a lot of testing.

Visualizing Performance

The best way to keep a project on track for performance is by making it easy to tell if its performance is meeting your goal. Cryptic debug messages and internal counters might work well enough for programmers, but having a clear visualization of the performance picture makes it easier for the programmers and possible for everyone else to understand what's going on.

For instance, the Source game engine from Valve has a visualization called the *netgraph* that visualizes network traffic of local players, other players, entities, sounds, and other resource consumers. Even in a single-player game, the net-graph shows useful information, and if you leave it running, it becomes very intuitive when the game is running well and when it is not.

Quake 4 has a simpler performance visualization geared more toward rendering. Even for an artist without a heavy technical background, it's easy to determine where time is going and what the possible causes might be. In addition, there is enough detailed information so that if a programmer gets a screenshot of a problem area with the HUD up, he can easily debug the performance problem.

Performance visualization will help make your team more effective at keeping within the performance budget. If you make them intuitive, simple, and easy to access, and train everyone on the basics of reading them, then you'll find that many performance issues will never hit crisis mode.

Alternatively, you can implement easy-to-use shortcuts for using third-party tools. OGRE, for example, has an option for running the application in NVIDIA's PerfHUD.

Understanding Slowness

Slowness is an issue of perception, and many factors affect our perception of performance. Effective optimizers will spend their time on slowdowns that don't meet a user's expectation and ignore issues that are not really problems.

In the right circumstances, humans are sensitive to delays on the order of mil-liseconds. In other circumstances, huge delays are accepted without comment. For instance, although users can discern the difference between a 100ms delay and an immediate (<10ms) response, double-clicking to open a file has resulted in about a one-second delay on computers ranging from the most recent models to a Mac Plus from the '80s (http://hubpages.com/hub/_86_Mac_Plus_Vs_07_ AMD_DualCore_You_Wont_Believe_Who_Wins).

For games and other interactive applications, the baseline for user perception is the feedback loop, which is the path from user input to a displayed response to that input. Frame rate is important because the minimum delay from input to response is one frame, but it isn't the only consideration.

High Frame Rate

A high frame rate is the most ubiquitous standard of performance. Most hardware reviews include benchmarks reporting frame rates from popular games. Low frame rates can render a game unplayable.

From a perceptual standpoint, persistence of vision requires a certain minimum frame rate to convince the eye that things are moving smoothly. And even once you've achieved that minimum threshold, the illusion is made stronger with higher frame rates. To completely fool the eye, an update rate of around 100Hz is needed; until that point, motion of objects in the scene is convincing but rotation of the whole scene is not.

A high frame rate also benefits the responsiveness of a game. Consider if you're running at 24Hz and you sample input at the beginning of the frame. Worst case, it might take nearly two frames before the game shows any reaction to user input. For example, if a button is pressed right after the input sampling at the start of one frame, the input won't be registered until the start of the next frame and won't be shown until the end of that next frame. And that's assuming the input causes a big response immediately. If it's something like pressing the left key to cause a car to start steering left, it might be a couple more frames before the effect in the game world is large enough to notice. In the best-case scenario (where the game responds immediately to input once it's detected), you'd have an input lag of 84ms from button press to effect in the game. Compare that to a game at 60fps, where the same scenario would only result in a latency of 32ms.

From a performance perspective, a low frame rate indicates that you have a bad average case. Every frame is taking a long time to process.

The Value of Consistency

Consistency of frame rate, although measured less in benchmarks, is more important than the frame rate being too high. The human eye can adjust to a low but consistent frame rate. However, it is very good at detecting changes in rate, and varying frame rates stand out like a sore thumb.

First, here is an example of how inconsistent updates can stand out. Imagine a bouncing ball animating on a computer screen. In each frame, the ball moves up or down a small amount. When it reaches the top or bottom of its arc, it might squash or stretch to exaggerate motion. A new frame is displayed quite frequently, say 30 times a second.

Now, the human eye is very good at tracking moving objects. When someone throws a ball at you, you can glance at it, instantly determine how it's moving, and place your hand in its path to catch it. The eye tracks that animating ball with the same intensity. And if a frame is dropped, it can spot it immediately. To the eye, the ball appears to stop momentarily and then continues on its way—a *hitch*.

Hitching is the most common scenario with irregular performance. Frequently, it is due to some infrequent process kicking off, like a garbage collector activating, or an asset loading from disk to meet some unexpected need, or even the OS taking time unexpectedly to deal with something unrelated.

There are also a ton of potential causes that are less legitimate, like badly written, intermittently run code inadvertently taking a thousand times longer than it should. Sometimes, hitching can be addressed by limiting how much processing is done in a frame—for instance, only doing one A* path calculation per frame, or only paging in so many resources in a single frame.

Less abrupt, but still problematic, varying frame rate is also common. Most games exhibit this; if you stick the camera right up against a blank wall, the frame rate shoots up. Generally, varying frame rate isn't a big issue, but if any gameplay elements are frame rate-dependent instead of based on elapsed time, it can result in weird and disorienting effects, where the game world appears to run faster or slower.

While this is a performance issue, optimization won't solve it. No matter what, a small amount of content will always draw faster than a large amount of content. To hide this issue, be sure that all your update logic is based on elapsed time, not elapsed frames. Subtle issues can crop up when the game runs faster or slower than expected, and time-based updates help prevent them.

From an optimization perspective, inconsistent frame rates indicate that you have intermittently slow performance. This scenario is a lot harder to analyze than an overall slow game, because profiling tools tend to average data over many frames, wiping out spikes caused by a brief interval of slow performance. You may have to add special detection logic to monitor performance every frame and only display the captured information if the frame is over a certain performance threshold.

There are some other factors to consider when it comes to "how slow is too slow." Most displays only update at 60–80Hz. Rendering frames beyond that rate likely won't give any increase in perceived speed. (You may want to run your game update code more frequently than that, however, as more updates lead to smoother input processing and can also reduce instabilities in your game simulation.)

Conclusion

In this chapter, you learned that you could do more than just react to your performance problems: You can plan and adjust accordingly.

You can manage optimization by understanding the project lifecycle and playing close attention to the ROI of different optimizations to ensure the most efficient use of your time. Optimization is a job that can continue indefinitely so being efficient is a necessity. You use tools like performance budgets to predict and achieve this goal. By visualizing your performance information, you let everyone help determine where the game is slow and why.

Finally, we discussed slowness. The problem is bigger than simply having a slow "average" case. Hitches and input latency are also problems that optimization gurus must solve.

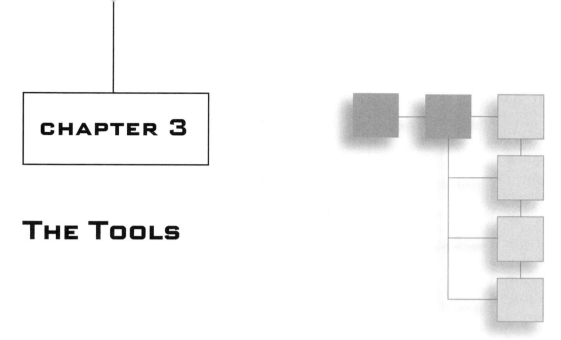

CHAPTER 3

THE TOOLS

All the techniques in the world of optimization are useless if you cannot see the results of your actions. Imagine trying to make fine jewelry without a magnifying glass, or build a complex piece of electronics without a logic probe. Bach can compose brilliant music without hearing what he is playing, but the rest of us have to be able to tell what we are doing.

Feedback loops are crucial to any process of improvement. In many natural endeavors, the feedback is automatic. If you don't walk correctly, you will fall over and hurt yourself. If you don't stay on the road, you will crash. Corrective action is obvious.

In the world of performance, what's going on is anything but obvious. Without the right tools, *everything* is invisible except frame rate (and even that can be hard to measure accurately without an FPS counter). Many game projects have millions of lines of code—never mind the operating system and other assets. Trying to take corrective action is like stumbling around a dark room—painful and a waste of time.

Tools help you measure. They enable you to see the performance picture clearly, and when you can see what's going on, the right choice often becomes obvious. In this chapter, we will categorize tools and discuss the basics of using them. Being able to measure effectively is a key optimization skill.

Intrusiveness

The act of measuring performance takes resources from other running programs like the game you are trying to measure. Depending on the kind of measurements you are gathering, it might only take a little bit. But for really in-depth, reliable data, the performance cost is often high. A profiling tool that reduces performance while running is *intrusive*. Those that add little overhead to the application are considered *nonintrusive* tools.

There is another aspect of intrusiveness. Some tools actually change the program they are measuring. For instance, they might add a little code at the beginning and end of each function that records that the function was run and how long it took. It's useful information, but the overhead can be high. Some tools, like the open source project, Valgrind[1], run the entire application in a virtual machine to get very detailed performance information.

There are a couple broad categories of intrusiveness that tools belong to. The least intrusive category contains sampling tools. These tools sample at regular intervals to try to build a picture of what is going on. For instance, a sampling profiler will stop the program being profiled every so many instructions or intervals in order to see what code is executing. By doing this for a relatively long period (a few million cycles), you can build up a pretty accurate picture of where time is being spent in the program.

The next level of intrusiveness occurs in tools that intercept access from your program to some external resource. For instance, PIX intercepts every DirectX call so it can track and measure graphics activity. Network sniffers intercept network traffic so you can see if you're using the Net efficiently.

The most intrusive level contains tools that actually modify the program to get their information, a process called *instrumentation*. The GNU tool chain's profiler, gprof, can give detailed performance information but requires that you pass special flags when you compile your program. VTune can instrument your program for similar purposes but requires you to generate a relocation section, a setting found in Visual Studio in the properties under Linker > Advanced > Fixed Base Address.

There are many different scenarios that require performance measurements. Most mature systems will provide you with good profiling tools, but sometimes you may need to write your own. If you are writing a custom profiler (something we don't recommend), you should be aware of the overhead you are introducing into your application. Make sure that the cost of measuring performance doesn't overwhelm what you're trying to measure and that the accuracy of your measurements is reliable for analysis.

Types of Tools

All tools fall into just a few categories. In the following sections, we'll describe each of those types and how it works. Keep in mind that a single tool might fall into multiple categories. For instance, Intel's VTune[2] has both a profiler and a system monitor tool.

Profilers

Profilers are the most common tools we think of when we think of optimization tools. A profiler gathers information about resource usage, typically the CPU, during a profiling session. For instance, your profiler might tell you that 50% of your execution time was spent in one function, and the other 50% was spent in another. Profilers can also track other statistics, such as cache misses or memory allocations.

Some profilers are very general and only give a high level of information; other profilers gather very specific data and present many views of the data collected during a run. In whichever way you choose to view the data, a profiler will collect information about time spent and events that occurred. The following are some common terms that you might encounter while using a profiler:

- **Total time:** The amount of time that was spent running a given function, and all the functions it calls. For instance, your main function will show up as 100% total time, because all time spent executing your program results from functions called inside main().

- **Self time:** The amount of time that was spent in a given function, not counting the functions it calls. In the main() example, the self time for main() will probably be very low, like 0.01%, because it immediately transfers control to other code. A routine that contains the inner loop for your collision code might show up as 15% or even higher.

- **Calls:** The number of times that the application called the function during the profiling session.

- **Total wait time:** The time spent in a function while the OS suspends a thread.

System Monitors

System monitors collect global information about your computer. For instance, one might show that your CPU is, overall, about 80% utilized. System monitors also measure the amount of a given resource that you are using (i.e., 235 megabytes of RAM).

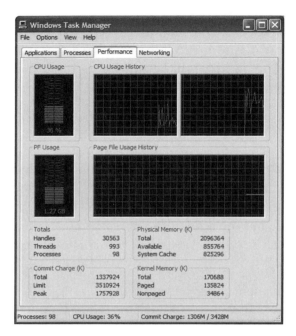

Figure 3.1
The Windows Task Manager lets you easily see how your hardware resources are being used.

Windows XP gives you two system monitors out of the box. The Windows Task Manager is the first one (see Figure 3.1) By clicking the Performance tab, you can view information about the stage of the current hardware. The second is an administrative tool called *Performance* (see Figure 3.2). This tool is a bit more in-depth, and lets you choose what statistics you want to monitor.

System monitors are also available for the GPU. Knowing how efficiently the GPU is used is critical when profiling. The first step, after creating a benchmark, is to determine if the GPU is running near full utilization or not. NVIDIA's PerfHUD, AMD's GPU PerfStudio, and Intel's VTune all have systems that will monitor hardware resources and return information on usage.

System Adjusters

System adjusters are a less obvious type of tool. An adjuster alters the behavior of the system to help find performance problems. For instance, on the GPU such a tool might let you disable rasterization so you can see if your scenes are fill-rate-bound. Or a system adjuster might vary the clock speed of your CPU so you can see if you are compute-bound. System adjusters typically require adjusting during runtime of the game.

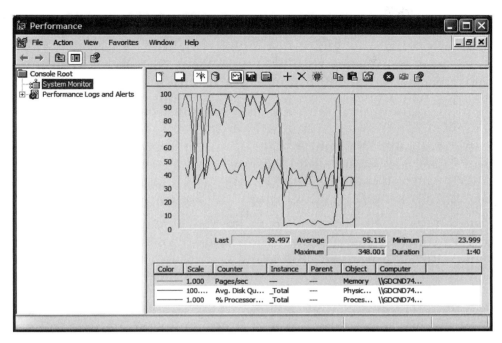

Figure 3.2
The Windows XP Performance monitor lets you quickly access the usage of hardware resources.

Detecting Bottlenecks by Varying CPU Speed

> When running a video game, you can adjust the CPU frequency lower and see no difference in frame rate. That means the biggest bottleneck is not the CPU. Subsequent optimizations on the CPU may result in zero gains in performance. Your application's limitation is the GPU, bus, or possibly memory.

Timers 101

When it comes to profiling, if you aren't counting something, you're timing it—and often both. Of course, the accuracy of your measurements is going to depend on the accuracy of your timer.

The typical CPU has a clock speed in the multiple gigahertz. That clock is fast and very accurate—it has to be for the CPU to work. It's unfortunate that it can be hard to get accurate timing data from inside your application.

There are three main flaws you will run into. First, look out for timers that do not have enough accuracy. Many system-level timers display precise values to the microsecond or nanosecond, but they are only accurate to the nearest millisecond. It's easy enough to spot this. Simply vary the workload being timed and see if the timer's results only change in granular intervals. When you are doing measurements, consider the amount of error that might be introduced. If your code takes between 0.9 and 1.1 ms to execute, a timer with 1ms resolution will introduce 100% error!

Second, look out for timers that are shared. As an example, reading the CPU's timestamp code can give weird results because it is a shared resource. It might get reset or altered by another process. If the CPU changes power modes, the amount of time represented by the timestamp will change. Additionally, it is core-specific, so it's shared by all the processes on a core, but your process might be bounced from core to core, reading completely unrelated values from different cores' timestamp registers.

Finally, look out for timers that are costly. This is more important when you are doing hierarchical timing or other calculations where the duration of your `GetTimer()` call has an impact. You may have the option to trade between accuracy and the expense of getting the time, which can throw off other timing. And the bookkeeping of storing the results from the timer can introduce significant overhead as well.

The best bet here is to keep your timing relatively granular: The bigger the chunk of execution you are looking at, the more likely your numbers are to be accurate. Trying to time your timing routines is painful. It's better to pursue other strategies, such as only making relative comparisons rather than confronting the issue head on.

Code Instrumentation

The second half of this chapter will discuss the many tools you can use to measure your program. They are powerful and varied, but you should be aware of the basic tools you can implement yourself. They will serve you well when you are in an environment that doesn't support fancy tools, or if you ever doubt the results from the tools.

Simple Timing

This is the most primitive of all measurement techniques. Start a timer when your program starts and stop it when it is done. You can do this with a stopwatch or a wall clock if you have to—for instance, to time how long it takes to render a thousand frames, a common benchmarking technique.

Of course, automated timing is more accurate. On UNIX, there is a command to time the duration of execution of a command. It's called time.

The next step after timing global execution is to time a specific subsection of your program. For instance, you might track how long you spend specifically in your render routine or how long a physics update takes. You can report it directly or average it over many frames to get a more accurate number. You may want to track several subsystems simultaneously and present their results all at once.

Hierarchical Profiling

Eventually, you will want to track time hierarchically. For example, with a given operation, how much time was spent on suboperations? For a common operation, like sorting an array, how much time was spent over the life of the program? And what high-level operations caused the most array sorting?

Implementing a hierarchical profiler is fairly straightforward, and gives you a lot of insight into how your program's execution time is spent. Because you delineate the timed sections yourself, you can have it report data that is more meaningful than raw function names. And because it is integrated, it's always available, as opposed to booting up a tool.

Counters

It can also be useful to track how often certain events happen. For instance, you might want to track hits and misses for an internal cache. The number of draw calls or state changes in a frame might also be of interest. It's very easy to set up a few global variables, increment them at strategic times, and display their values every so often.

You can also do more complex behaviors, like averaging over multiple frames, calculating histograms, or other analysis.

Reports

Reporting the results of your data gathering is just as important as the data gathering itself. Data is only useful insofar as it gives you something to act on.

With the performance test harness, a tool that we used in writing this book, we exported data to XML in a format that Excel could process, and also used Google Charts to produce plots of the data. These are low-impact ways that visualize data more clearly. Other options include sorting and filtering dumped data by simple rules inside your own code.

Tool Spotlight

The following section highlights some of the tools that we commonly use. This list is not exhaustive. Choices are evolving constantly, and new features are making optimization easier.

Intel VTune

VTune is a powerful CPU analysis tool. In stating that VTune is a CPU analysis tool, it is important to recognize that it will tell you very little about your GPU performance. (Intel does provide GPA, which is a graphics-focused performance tool.) In fact, it will only tell you about Intel processors since it is accessing proprietary hardware counters built directly into the hardware. VTune will expose different counters on different processors, so expect the availability of counters to vary from processor to processor, especially if you are profiling older processors.

VTune has multiple data collectors, two of which, the counter monitor and sampling, are nonintrusive. The call graph is an intrusive view that allows you to view function call relationships. We'll discuss each type in detail in the following sections.

Counter Monitor

The counter monitor is a tool that shows information about the system level (see Figure 3.3) and the micro level. Once you have selected the counters that you want to track, the counter monitor will display tickers showing the counters' values over time.

For example, you can use the counter monitor to figure out your CPU utilization. If your CPU utilization is not 100%, then you are not using your CPU to its fullest potential. A CPU utilization of less than 100% is an almost certain sign that your game engine is GPU bound.

You can also use the counter monitor to discover how you are using memory or how threading is behaving.

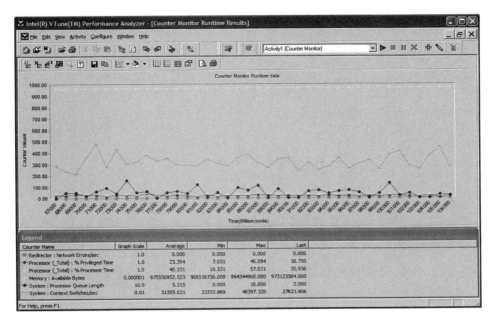

Figure 3.3
Intel offers a system monitor data collector for measuring resources at the system level.

When beginning your optimization on the CPU, you should run the counter monitor first to give an overall system view of how your application is executing.

Sampling

Sampling is a useful tool for viewing system, application, and micro level optimizations. Sampling gives system information by showing all the modules and threads currently running (see Figure 3.4). It returns application information by giving class and function views.

Sampling uses a nonintrusive approach to gathering and reporting data. According to Intel, the overhead of sampling is around 1%[3].

Sampling measures events and time at defined intervals. For time, this interval default is 1ms; for events, VTune uses a specified number of processor events. When the interval occurs, VTune increments a counter for the specified line of code. Over time, enough data aggregates to show hotspots and bottlenecks (see Figures 3.5 and 3.6).

Occasionally, you may find yourself looking at a function that doesn't run very often. Line-by-line data for functions that don't run often may not be that useful for forming a hypothesis about performance.

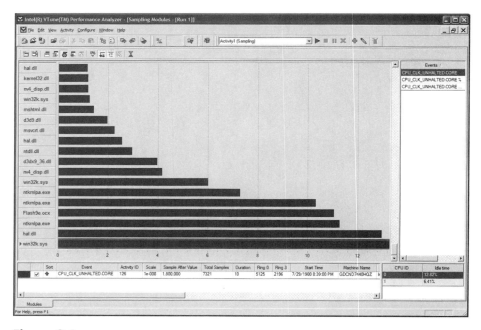

Figure 3.4
VTune's profiling view for module data.

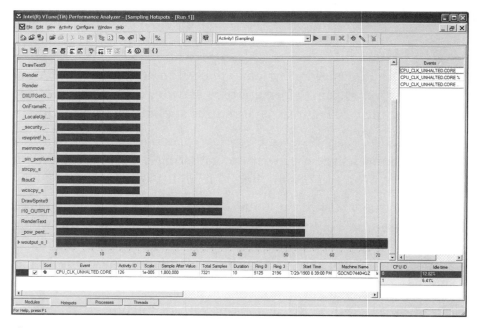

Figure 3.5
VTune's profiling view for hotspots.

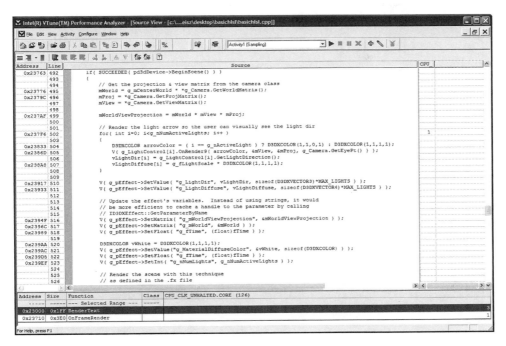

Figure 3.6
VTune's profiling view for source code.

There just simply isn't enough information to determine if a particular line of code is slower than another since VTune wasn't able to collect enough information for a reasonable comparison.

From C++ to Assembly

Remember, code doesn't execute as a high-level language. To really pick apart line-by-line measurements, choose a disassembly or mixed view. Optimized assembly code doesn't map one-to-one to high-level language statements. Trickiest of all, many of the optimizations a compiler does include reordering and combining instructions to execute more efficiently. So for a given line of C code there might be one, none, or many scattered blocks of assembly instructions that correspond to it in the final executable.

Call Graph

The call graph is an excellent tool for application level optimization. You are required to compile your application by generating relocation information in order to allow VTune to gather parent/child relationships. Each function is represented as a node (see Figure 3.7). For each node, you can view the total time, self time, number of calls, and other valuable information.

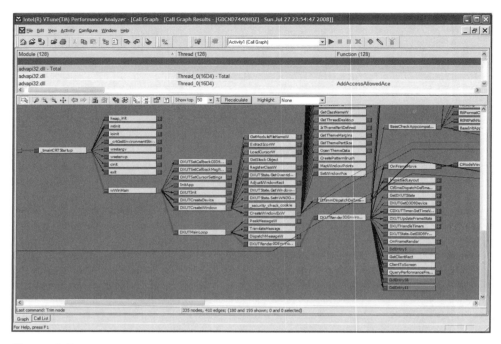

Figure 3.7
The call graph shows each function as a node. The call graph will show how many times a function is called and the path in which the calls were made. The red line (visible on your monitor) represents the critical path.

The call graph will also tell what your longest path from the root of your application thread to the slowest function is. This path is what is referred to as the critical path. Enhancing the performance of the critical path is almost always a way to guarantee a performance increase on your CPU.

The call graph will not give any information about what line of code is performing slowly; therefore, it is not the best tool for micro-optimizations.

Microsoft PIX for Windows

PIX is a tool that is distributed for free with Microsoft's DirectX API (see Figure 3.8). It logs all DirectX activity from a given program, noting active resources, as well as the timing of events. With the right settings, it can fully log every texture and vertex buffer, allowing you to replay and analyze a sequence of rendering activity from inside PIX.

PIX by itself is useful for giving information about the way you are using the API. It is extendable by allowing plug-ins. Both AMD Graphics and NVIDIA have

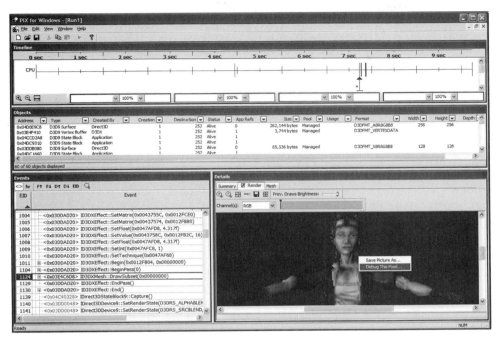

Figure 3.8
PIX showing a screen capture. You can debug a shader by right-clicking a pixel in the rendered image.

plug-ins for PIX. In addition, you can make calls to special DirectX functions in order to give PIX more information about your program.

PIX also supports shader debugging. In early versions of DirectX 9, shader debugging was done from inside Visual Studio; however, it was very difficult to tell which pixel's shaders you were debugging. Later versions of DX9 shifted from Visual Studio to PIX, which has the convenient ability to let you click a pixel and view information about how the rendering passes constructed the final pixel color.

As of the November 2008 update, PIX provides draw call timings. This can give clues both to your program's performance (for instance, big gaps on the PIX timeline usually indicate times when your program is doing other tasks), as well as what parts of DX9 are causing slowness (when an action like a lock or unlock results in a long delay). You can either view the measured time for this call, or run a simulated timing multiple times while in the event view after your program finishes running.

NVIDIA PerfHUD

If you are using an NVIDIA card, then PerfHUD will be a valuable tool. PerfHUD will not only report information about the GPU, such as percentage of idle time, but it will also allow you to manipulate the graphics pipeline without changing application code. It gives a high-level view of your application's behavior, which makes it easy to see your GPU performance picture at a glance (see Figure 3.9).

One of PerfHUD's most useful features is the frame profiler (see Figure 3.10). This mode runs an experiment and returns profiling information about all draw calls in a chosen frame. If you are GPU limited, PerfHUD will help you determine the limiting bottleneck of your application by simply following a process and pressing some keys.

PerfHUD also gives you the capability to modify shaders during runtime (see Figure 3.11) for a quick and easy way to view the differences in your shader as you

Figure 3.9
The performance dashboard mode of PerfHUD 6.0. The performance dashboard provides a high level overview of the GPU's activity.

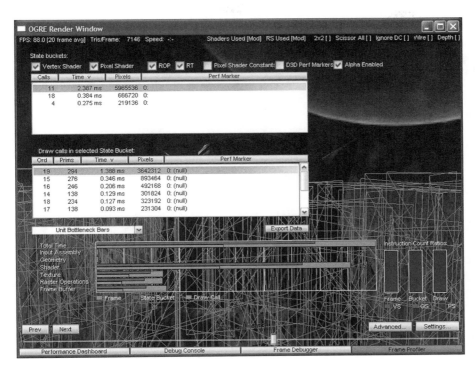

Figure 3.10
The frame profiler mode of PerfHUD 6.0. The frame profiler sorts, filters, and displays draw calls and state buckets for analysis.

change the code. When optimizing shaders, it is very valuable to switch back and forth quickly between the original and optimized shaders to determine if your code changes affected the visuals of your game.

PerfHUD is available for free. In order to use it, you will need to download a special instrumented driver that exposes these capabilities to the application. Downloading the driver is not necessary if you are using Windows Vista. If you can afford to have a dedicated machine for profiling, and it has an NVIDIA card, then installing these drivers is well worth the rewards you will get from using PerfHUD.

As of this writing, PerfHUD does not support OpenGL. However, NVIDIA's instrumented drivers do. In the NVIDIA Developer Control Panel, you can access GLExpert, which supplies various reports. You can have it report to your debugger, to `stdout`, or to your program via a callback.

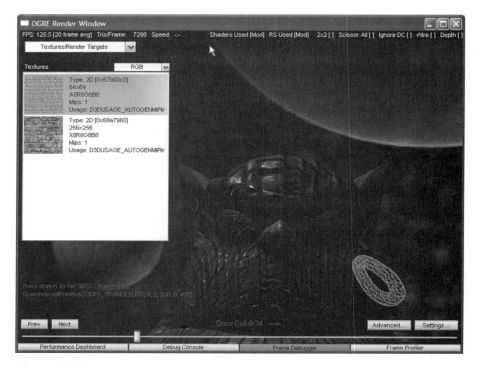

Figure 3.11
The frame debugger mode of PerfHUD 6.0. The frame debugger provides several utilities for modifying shaders, textures, and the ability to scrub through a given frame's worth of draw calls.

NVIDIA FX Composer

NVIDIA's FX Composer is for both artists and programmers looking for a tool that will help manage shader development (see Figure 3.12). Its useful interface is full of drag-and-drop capabilities and is also intuitive and well organized.

The FX Composer goes beyond facilitating flashy effects; it also provides a GUI interface for NVIDIA's ShaderPerf 2. Using this interface, you can execute shaders in a test environment that returns profiling information about estimated performance of a given shader on virtual NVIDIA GPUs.

Another useful feature of ShaderPerf 2 is a command-line interface. This will aid in regression testing and other forms of automation to determine if a small change has made a big difference in one or more of the NVIDIA cards.

DirectX Debug Runtime

You may not think of the DirectX Debug Runtime as a performance tool, but you should. The DirectX Debug Runtime is activated in the DirectX Control

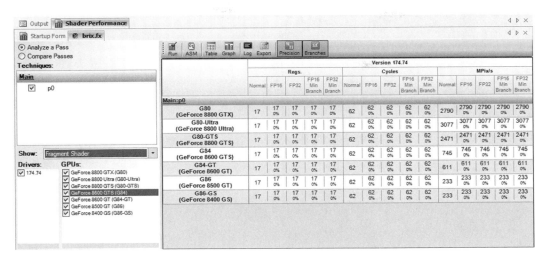

Figure 3.12
A cropped image of the NVIDIA FX Composer. This window is part of the GUI interface for NVIDIA's ShaderPerf 2.

Panel, in the DirectX SDK, not the Windows control panel (see Figure 3.13). It points out errors that may be hurting performance or causing incorrect behavior. You can view the runtime information in the output window of Visual Studio. Showing little or no warnings or errors under DirectX debug mode means you aren't forcing DirectX to fix your mistakes, keeping the path clear for fast and bug-free execution.

We *highly* recommend getting your application running clean under DirectX debug mode. Dealing with all of its output seriously is a great preventative maintenance activity. In some cases, you may decide to simply tolerate some warnings, but if you can remove the bulk of them, you have much better odds of having your application work correctly and fast everywhere.

Look out for the Debug Runtime!

Don't forget to switch DirectX back from Debug to Retail after fixing any errors and before doing extensive profiling. The debug version of DirectX is considerably slower than the retail version because of the extra validation it performs. This is invaluable when you are trying to get your program functioning properly, but if you are doing profiling, it can really hurt you. DirectX Debug mode can also break well-known applications (some versions of 3D Studio MAX as well as many commercial games), because they do not operate cleanly and trigger validation errors, so if you run into problems with them be sure to switch back to Retail mode.

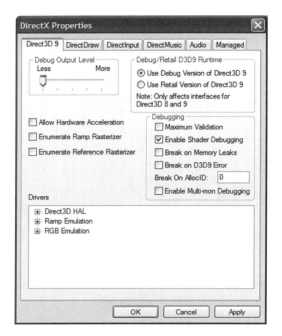

Figure 3.13
DirectX developer control panel. Notice the toggle for Debug/Retail mode in the upper right.

gprof

If you are using the GCC toolchain, there is a profiling tool called gprof already available to you. By passing -pg to GCC, it will compile your program with hooks that will dump performance information to a disk file. You can run the resulting binary through gprof to get flat or hierarchical information about how time was spent.

AMD CodeAnalyst

AMD CodeAnalyst is a useful, general purpose, high-level CPU profiler. It is most similar to VTune, but focuses on AMD chips. It provides a similar feature set, including sampling-based profiling and detection of performance events (such as cache misses).

AMD GPU PerfStudio

AMD's answer to NVIDIA's PerfHUD is GPU PerfStudio. A good tool for determining the overall usage of your pipeline, GPU PerfStudio is somewhat lacking in the ability to determine draw call performance on the GPU. Don't get too caught up in which tool someone thinks is better, though, because in the end, you should try to use all tools to test every piece of hardware you can get your hands on.

Using the following strategy in GPU PerfStudio yields successful results. First, use the Analyzer window to run, gather, and report a table of information about the performance bottlenecks in your graphics pipeline. This will give you the general lay of the land. If the suggestions provide your solution, then you are on your way to the next bottleneck. If they don't, try altering state overrides that modify your graphics pipeline from the back to the front.

GPU PerfStudio supports not only DirectX 9 and 10, but also OpenGL; however, the documentation warns that OpenGL debugging is intrusive. To reduce the intrusiveness, you can disable the Real Time Update checkbox and still perform state changes.

Conclusion

There are many tools to help you find performance problems, and more are being developed every day. (For example, NVIDIA's Nexus is a promising tool that is currently in beta at the time of this printing.) There are libraries you can include in your program and tools that interface with the performance monitoring capabilities built into the hardware you are running.

Whenever you start developing on a new platform, take some time to find the best tools for measuring performance. Learn how to use them so you can save yourself the effort of shooting in the dark. There's nothing worse than being led astray by incorrect measurements!

Don't be afraid to roll your own measuring tools, either. You need to be careful to make sure you are getting accurate results, but with a little time and effort you can have a robust, useful set of tools built right into your application—tools that will run everywhere your app does.

Sources Cited

[1] *Valgrind.* (n.d.) Retrieved October 26, 2009 from Valgrind: http://valgrind.org.

[2] Intel. (n.d.) *Intel® VTune™ Performance Analyzer 9.1.* Retrieved October 26, 2009 from Intel Software Network: http://software.intel.com/en-us/intel-vtune.

[3] Intel. (n.d.) *Intel Software Network.* Retrieved February 26, 2009 from www.Intel.com: http://www.intel.com/cd/software/products/asmo-na/eng/vtune/220022.htm.

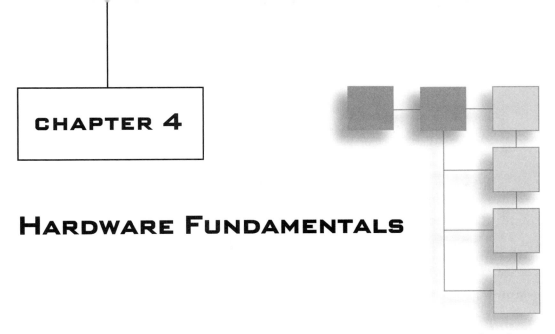

CHAPTER 4

HARDWARE FUNDAMENTALS

The best optimizers know their medium. You have many great hardware resources at your disposal and to get the best performance, you need to understand not only what exists, but a little bit about how it works. That's what this chapter is for. We won't be diving into code examples here; rather, we'll cover them in future chapters. This is the final chapter covering the fundamentals you need to begin optimizing your game. In the next chapter, we will be diving head-first into the high-level, holistic process of optimizing a game and knowing the lay of the land will be essential.

Memory

If instructions are time, memory is space. Every bit that a computer operates on passes through its memory. Your average desktop computer has a wide variety of storage elements, tailored for every imaginable scenario (see Figure 4.1).

Performance-minded programmers optimize memory in a way that reduces latency, increases bandwidth, and decreases capacity. Latency is the time it takes for a request to get to the resource and back. Bandwidth is the rate that data can be transferred. And capacity is the number of bytes that can be stored.

Memory systems with multi-tiered caches and blocks of memory are called *cache lines*, and they have architectures that assume you share these same goals. If you take advantage of the architecture, performance increases will be significant; if you don't, you will be working against the hardware designed to help you.

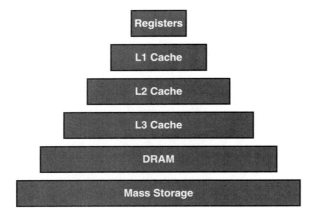

Figure 4.1
The memory hierarchy hides and reduces latency by using tiers of memory that fetch data parallel to execution.

Chapter 6, "CPU Bound: Memory," is where you will find the details on memory optimization, but first, you must understand the fundamentals of the hardware.

Registers and Caches

Let's start at the heart of the CPU. The easiest memory to access—and in simpler CPUs the only memory on the chip—are the registers. Registers are low latency, high bandwidth, and very low capacity. Register numbers vary from processor to processor but counts range from around 45 on IA-32 architecture to over 400 on the Itanium.[1,2] Certain instructions, which we'll cover in Chapter 7, "CPU Bound: Compute," have their own extra-wide registers to accommodate instructions that operate on multiple data values concurrently. Some registers are also used to store status information, such as error codes and math flags.

Registers are accessed directly by the CPU and do not require any additional loading. They act as a fast scratchpad for the current calculations. Anything the CPU wants to manipulate will end up getting loaded into the registers, which is a shame because fetching data from off-chip sources is slow. Writing, too, can be a performance hog. Since memory read/write patterns are often localized to the same area of memory, most CPUs have several levels of cache on board. The cache is fast, but costly because it is typically built directly on the chip. Therefore, there is a limited amount available, typically several megabytes spread across several caches. For example, the Core 2 Duo has up to 6MB of L2 cache shared between cores and 32Kb L1 data and instruction caches per core.[3] High-end Xeon processors support up to 16MB of shared L3 caches.[4]

The cache acts as an intermediary between the CPU and all off-board memory devices. Whenever you request some memory, the memory system checks the cache first. Then it sends a request out over the bus.

Memory Mapping

Wait—devices? Doesn't the CPU only talk to DRAM? Actually, through memory mapping, the memory system is able to communicate to a variety of devices, like video cards, hard drives, and clock chips. Each device is assigned a memory range, and IO with it is as easy as reading and writing to the right memory address. To add to the complexity, in certain cases, the CPU isn't the only hardware reading and writing.

Memory mapping is also used for multitasking. Each process is assigned its own memory space to reduce the possibility of one process corrupting another. They're still all in the same physical RAM, but the CPU has virtualization hardware that enforces the mapping. The OS can see everything as it truly is.

Dynamic Random Access Memory

Also known as *system memory* or *core memory*, Dynamic Random Access Memory (DRAM) is the main storage place for volatile data. Whenever something is loaded from disk, it ends up here. System memory has good bandwidth, lots of storage, but much higher latency than registers or caches.

Farthest from the CPU are the mass storage devices: hard drives, CD-ROMs, Blu-Ray, and solid state drives (SSDs). These devices have immense amounts of storage, but very high latency and lower bandwidth. The best way to deal with disk IO is to do it in another thread and process it at completion. A disk request involves waiting for thousands or even millions of cycles.

Direct Memory Access

Direct Memory Access (DMA) is another example of how concurrency can solve latency of memory access. DMAs occur when memory moves from an external memory source, such as video memory or a memory buffer of an external camera, into system memory without involving the CPU. DMAs help the system be less reliant on the CPU for memory operations by freeing the CPU from memory copies that occur between peripherals and system memory. As a video game optimizer who is not working on embedded systems, you won't use DMAs directly.

Typically, DMAs occur at the driver level. Understanding the fundamental concepts of DMAs will guide you in understanding some of the nuances in communication between the CPU and GPU.

Virtual Memory

One more wrinkle to mention: virtual memory.

Virtual memory lets applications use more memory than is physically available by paging memory that hasn't been used recently from RAM to disk. Even with multiple gigabytes of RAM, having dozens of complex programs open can exceed RAM capacity. The upshot is that the computer doesn't crash even in taxing situations. The downside is that any memory access might take tens to thousands of milliseconds to page back into physical memory. In terms of performance, the best practice with virtual memory is to avoid paging in your game. Make sure that your program's *working set*, the set of pages associated with a given process, fits into physical memory, and cross your fingers that users don't run too many other programs concurrently.

GPU and Memory

GPUs have hundreds of megabytes of storage onboard VRAM. This gives them a significant performance advantage, because they don't have to contend with the rest of the system for bandwidth. It also means they have their own perspective on memory.

There are two aspects to consider here. First, consider transfers from your application to the GPU over the PCIe bus—things like textures, vertex buffers, and even rendering commands. Second, overflow data that doesn't fit in VRAM will be stored in system memory by the video driver and streamed over when needed. The region of system memory used for this is called *nonlocal VRAM*. This is similar in spirit to virtual memory with the exception that nonlocal memory is pinned memory, meaning it uses pages marked as nonpageable.

Alignment and Fetching

As the preceding section might have tipped you off, good optimizers have an intimate relationship with memory. Knowing how and when to fetch data for highest efficiency is one of the keys to good performance. Let's talk about how memory is fetched and why alignment matters.

When memory is fetched from DRAM, the desired address is transferred over the address bus to the memory. The bus transfers a fixed-size chunk of memory back across the data bus. For instance, a 32-bit wide bus will return 32 bits of memory. Additionally, the bus can only return memory at multiples of that size. So if the bus returns four bytes of memory at a time, it can only return the first four, or the second four, or the third four bytes, but not the second through fifth bytes.

The alignment of the address is defined by the address itself. An address that is a multiple of four is 4-byte aligned. An address that is a multiple of eight is 4- and 8-byte aligned. Figure 4.2 shows a value that is 4-, 8-, 16-, and 32-byte aligned.

Alignment keeps the bus simple and fast, which is good, but it requires that transfers be aligned for best performance. Reading a single byte won't cause problems at any offset, but if you need to fetch a 32-bit int that's stored starting at byte 2, you're in trouble (see Figure 4.3). You should avoid unaligned reads and writes whenever possible. Your compilers, through padding, will often align data to natural boundaries.

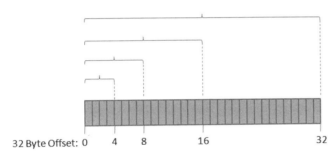

Figure 4.2
Data alignment.

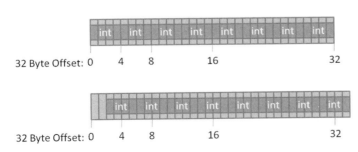

Figure 4.3
The top array is an aligned array of integers, while the second is unaligned. Subsequent reads to the unaligned data may cause a hardware exception.

Different processors deal with unaligned reads in different ways. Most throw a hardware exception; in this case, the OS might catch it, issue two reads, assemble the result, and resume execution. This is the typical case in Windows, but with Itanium architecture, Windows expects the exception to be handled in the application. If the exception isn't handled, the application may crash or hang.[5] The compiler may be able to detect the problem and generate multiple load instructions, or the CPU itself might silently issue multiple reads behind the scenes.

Regardless of the behavior of the system, misaligned reads will waste memory bandwidth and require more time to complete. We will cover this topic in more detail in Chapter 6, "CPU-Bound: Memory."

Stay Focused!

Don't get too caught up trying to optimize for memory alignment as a first step in optimization. For now, we want you to be aware of the nuances that lie within the memory systems. Chapters 5 and 6 will give you the context to know when to split hairs on memory alignment issues and the returns you can expect.

Remember, you should always start with a benchmark, then profile, and then optimize. Don't proceed with optimization work unless you have data to guide you.

Caching

Caches are a fundamental building block for high-performance computing. CPUs have several caches on board of varying size and speed. These caches are referred to as level 1, level 2, level 3, etc., with higher numeric values indicating increasing size and latency.

At the highest level, caches (see Figure 4.4) can save a round trip across the memory bus when a fetch occurs. If the working set for an algorithm fits entirely in a cache, only the first load will require substantial overhead. This initial load of memory to cache is known as a *compulsory cache miss*, but there are more benefits than this.

Caches are in the business of cramming gigabytes of memory into a few kilobytes of storage. Every new request pushes old data out of the cache. Not only must the cache have storage for each byte, but it also must have information about where that byte came from.

Well, not every byte. Caching bytes individually is very expensive and quite unnecessary. Usually when data is needed from one place, the next read will

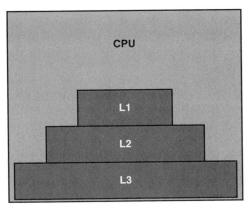

Figure 4.4
Modern CPUs contain on-die caches instead of relying solely on external memory chips. In fact, the majority of today's CPU die is cache (the flat rectangular areas shown).

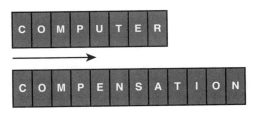

Figure 4.5
A string compare reads one byte at a time in sequential order.

happen nearby. Imagine a string comparison routine—it reads one byte at a time in sequential order from the two strings it is comparing (see Figure 4.5).

It turns out that it is much simpler and more effective to cache multiple bytes at a time. A cache stores data in sets called *cache lines*. Typically, cache lines are a small power of two in size—16, 32, 64, or 128 bytes in size.

The side effect of this is that reading a single byte causes a full cache line to be fetched and stored. In the case of the string comparison routine, this actually works in your favor, as only every 16th byte results in a cache line fetch. In fact, because the hardware will try to predict your read patterns, you might be better off than that—it might recognize the linear read pattern and fetch the next cache line before you need it.

You could also add a software prefetch intrinsic to hint to the hardware what data will be needed. Pre-fetching isn't always necessary or a performance gain, but in the right circumstances it can make a big difference. See Chapter 6 for examples of using software pre-fetching.

Because data is brought in a cache line at a time, respecting cache alignment can make a big difference. A good trick is to identify data that will be used at similar times and group it. For instance, suppose cache lines are 16 bytes long and you're implementing a linked list. By making sure that the previous and next pointers are adjacent in memory and 16-byte aligned, you can make traversal of the list more efficient.

SIMD (Single Instruction Multiple Data) instructions, such as SSE instructions, have similar concerns since they work on large amounts of data. Alignment is crucial. A deeper discussion of SIMD instructions is available in Chapter 7, "CPU Bound: Compute."

CPU

Understanding the basics of a CPU will help you gain insight into performing micro-optimizations in your application code. For many of our examples, we will focus on older processors, such as the P4 or Pentium M, because while they may seem old, they provide the foundation for many of our processors today. Although no processor is the same, understanding the basics of one processor will help guide you in the discussion of optimization for the CPU.

Lifecycle of an Instruction

A revolution occurred in processing and many of us missed it. Most of us were looking at chip frequency to tell us about how many instructions we could perform, while chip makers and electronic engineers were looking for ways to do more instructions at the same time.

Doing more than one instruction at the same time, within the same thread, is what hard-core developers and electrical engineers define as *instruction level parallelism*. This concept is the fundamental reason for chip performance increase over the past couple of decades. Now, multi-core technologies are the trend that chip makers are banking on to take us through the next decade or more of performance increases.

Performing instructions in parallel does help us increase performance; however, this performance increase also increases the complexity of the lifecycle of an instruction. In the following sections, we will analyze this process by breaking the pipeline of the P4 into three stages: Load/Fetch/Decode, Execution, and Retirement.

Load/Fetch/Decode

The main task of the first stage is to fetch instructions from memory, decode them into micro-ops, and predict branches. The front-end stage runs in order, which means that the stage processes its data in the same order that it is written by the compiler.

Fetching and decoding instructions can be a slow process and for modern processors, fetching and decoding performance is extremely important. As long as the front-end stage is able to keep the execution stage busy, performance is maximized. But it can easily become a bottleneck that slows down everything else.

In order to increase performance, the front-end stage usually contains a cache known as the *trace cache* or *instruction cache* (commonly referred to as the *i-cache*). Instead of decoding an operation twice, the front-end stage will first check its cache to see if it has recently decoded the operation.

Something interesting occurs at this stage. Programmers are familiar with if-else statements. An if-else statement is one type of conditional branch. When the front-end stage encounters a conditional branch, it guesses what the answer will be and sends those encoded micro-ops to the execution stage. Why does the processor perform this guess? What happens if it guesses incorrectly? We will answer that question in a few more paragraphs.

But first, let's talk a bit more about the guess. Luckily, the guess is not random. Branch Target Buffers (BTB) keep track of which way branches flow for more accurate guessing.

Execution

The execution stage is where all the magic happens for the modern processors. Unlike the front-end stage, the execution stage runs out of order. That means that this stage can process its operations in a different order than the order determined by the compiler.

The execution stage achieves its performance by operating in parallel. That's right, even a single core processor can execute multiple instructions at the same time. The execution stage contains an instruction pool where micro-ops buffer in order to perform parallel execution. A dispatch unit selects micro-ops from the instruction pool so that the execution unit can perform as many operations as possible.

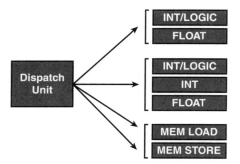

Figure 4.6
The dispatch unit delegates work to the execution units, which in turn, perform instructions in parallel.

Getting overly specific about the execution unit would probably not be useful to the average game optimization guru, so let's look at the "forest" view. The P4 execution core contains seven execution units. Three of the units support integer operations, two support floating-point operations, and two support memory operations. Of the two memory operations, one is for loading, and one is for storing.

The dispatch unit (see Figure 4.6) acts like we do when trying to optimize our applications. If it were to schedule only one unit at a time, our utilization of the execution units would only be 14%. Like an application developer, the dispatch unit will do its best to keep utilization near 100%. Since the dispatch unit is choosing the micro-ops from a pool that is out-of-order, it is more likely to achieve this goal.

By writing programs with this architecture in mind, you can ensure that the instruction pool is able to accommodate the dispatch unit. Your compiler, if at least recently modern, will be aware of this architecture and will do a very good job of compiling code that will execute with a high degree of instruction parallelism. There may be the odd occasion where you can outperform your compiler and achieve better instruction level parallelism, but this is the exception, not the rule.

Retirement

The back-end stage retires micro-operations from the instruction pool, updates the machine state, updates the BTBs, and throws exceptions. The back-end stage executes in order, returning the flow operation processing to the order originally defined by the compiler that created the application.

The back-end stage is where you notify the pipeline of anything that didn't go as expected. If the front-end stage incorrectly guessed the result of a branch, the back-end stage notifies the front-end of the mistake and the processing of the correct branch begins. The back-end stage updates the BTBs to reflect the new statistics for future branch predictions.

An exception is the result of an error that prevents further execution. For instance, dividing by zero is an impossible task, and trying it will result in a hardware exception. Application code can similarly trigger software exceptions.

Running Out of Order

Modern processors process data out of order to achieve better parallelism. Good compilers and really smart programmers can order their code for the best utilization of the processor's capabilities. Doing so requires that you understand why out-of-order execution can work and what will break it.

Data Dependencies

Data dependencies are the biggest enemy of instruction level parallelism. Typically, the CPU's execution stage will process instructions out of order. However, there are many cases where out-of-order operation is impossible, and data dependency is often the cause. Let's start with a simple example:

```
1. A = 10;
2. B = 20;
3. A + B = X;
```

Lines 1 and 2 can run in any order without changing the value of X. In fact, lines 1 and 2 can execute at the same time without changing the value of X. However, running line 3 is impossible until lines 1 and 2 have completed. Adding two variables is impossible until you know what their values are.

Now consider the next example:

Code A:

```
1. Sum += Array[0];
2. Sum += Array[1];
```

```
3. Sum += Array[2];

4. Sum += Array[3];

5. return Sum;
```

The value for Sum will be the same for any order of lines 1, 2, 3, and 4; however, data dependencies still exist. A data dependency can occur if the compiler were to place the variable Sum in only one register, because you cannot store more than one value to a given register at the same time.

Now consider a similar example with no data dependency.

Code B:

```
1. Sum0 = Array[0];

2. Sum1 = Array[1];

3. Sum2 = Array[2];

4. Sum3 = Array[3];

5. return Sum0+Sum1+Sum2+Sum3;
```

This demonstration creates only one data dependency, which occurs at line 5. Lines 1, 2, 3, and 4 are now completely parallelizable.

You Can Trust Your Compiler! (Mostly)

Even though what you have learned is true, it is *probably* okay to write your code similar to the code in Code A. Why? Because your compiler should optimize the assembly to execute as written in Code B. Checking the assembly output is the only way to know for sure how your compiler is interpreting your higher-level language code. The only way to know that the code is faster, however, is to measure it.

When a cache miss occurs, you usually create a data dependency while you wait for the memory load to occur. This is the most deadly of all data dependencies and the culprit for many inefficient CPU-bound applications. We will cover cache misses in greater detail in Chapter 7.

Understanding data dependencies is key to understanding how branching, which is the topic in the next section, can hurt your performance.

Branching and Branch Prediction

A branch occurs when instruction flow changes. You can split branch predictions into two groups: conditional and unconditional. Unconditional branches, such as the call assembly instruction, change flow but aren't going to affect instruction level parallelism since these branches only have one possible location for the instruction pointer to be set to. Conditional branches may cause a disruption in flow since a data dependency exists on the condition.

The most recognizable form of a conditional branch occurs in the if-else statement. Depending on the condition, the code will execute either the "if" section of code or the "else." When a modern processor encounters a branch, it will guess the condition before processing the actual result. As stated in the "Load/Fetch Decode" section, this guess is known as a *branch prediction;* when a condition is guessed incorrectly, a branch prediction miss occurs.

It may sound unreasonable for a processor to be guessing, but let's examine what would happen if the guess didn't occur.

```
1. int i=x;
2. int j=y;
3. if ( j < i )
    {
4.       x=x*x;
5.       y=y*y;
    }
   else
    {
6.       x=y*y;
7.       y=x*x;
    }
```

In this example, lines 1 and 2 contain no data dependencies. Line 3 is dependent on lines 1 and 2. What about the code inside the branches? The data dependency created by the conditional requires the CPU to wait for the load/fetch, execution, and retirement states to complete the condition before knowing which branch to take. It's cheaper to guess, especially since branch prediction is often accurate.

Since the CPU has to go one way or the other, it can either attempt to execute lines 4 and 5 or lines 6 and 7 at the same time, or it can guess. For example, let's assume that the processor chose to execute lines 4 and 5. If the condition were to resolve to true, nothing is lost and the cost of the branch would be nearly zero in respect to performance. If the processor chose lines 4 and 5, and the condition were false, a branch prediction miss would occur.

If a branch prediction miss occurs, the processor won't change its path until the condition reaches the retirement stage. At this time, the retirement stage will notify the load/fetch decode stage, which will restart processing using the correct path.

Although branch prediction misses sound slow, their impact on your performance is usually not that bad unless you are in a very time-consuming section of code. There are typically so many other opportunities for slow performance that, usually, branch prediction misses don't make our high priority list for opportunities to increase performance in a game. The takeaway is this: When writing code, don't feel too guilty about writing a branch that has a highly predictable condition.

Having a branch prediction miss is nearly the same as the performance of not using branch prediction at all, so for chip makers, including branch predictions is a no-brainer.

Let's spend some time discussing the guess. Branch prediction can be quite accurate in many cases. This is due to a piece of hardware called the *Branch Target Buffer* (BTB). This buffer, which acts somewhat like a memory cache, stores recent and often-used branches. Along with the branch, the processor stores a statistic about the history of that branch.

Some branches, such as a `while` loop, will be very easy to predict. If the `while` loop is iterating 100 times, chances are that the processor will decide to stay in the loop (assume the condition is true). The processor may assume that the loop will run 101 times since the prior 100 branches resolved to true. When the processor guesses incorrectly, it will correct its mistake and continue with the code as if the 101st loop never occurred.

Other branches, such as one based on an unpredictable condition, cause more branch misses.

We will cover methods for optimizing branch predictions in Chapter 7.

Simultaneous Multi-Threading

Simultaneous multi-threading, branded by Intel as *hyper-threading technology*, enables simultaneous thread execution without having multiple cores or processors. A process is a collection of one or more threads scheduled to take turns with other processes' threads by the operating system to allow seamlessly operating multi-tasking environments. Simultaneous multi-threading duplicates the load/fetch decode and retirement stages, but utilizes a shared execution stage. Doing so increases performance in several ways.

First, simultaneous multi-threading increases performance by allowing a thread to utilize the execution units if the other thread is waiting on a data dependency. This occurs when one thread is waiting for memory due to a cache miss. This ability exists for other data dependencies, but since the cache miss data dependency is the most costly, the benefits are greater.

Second, having two threads executing is likely to increase a processor's execution unit utilization. If one thread is looping through floating-point operations, like you would see in a particle system, it is possible that the other thread is utilizing the other units, such as those dedicated for integer arithmetic. While the two threads run, an overall improvement in execution utilization occurs.

Multi-Core

Instruction level parallelism largely affects the compiler designer and assembly developer, but the C++ developer can write code without being overly burdened by the details of the process. This is not the case for scalable, efficient, multi-threaded code.

With a multi-core processor, there are multiple load/fetch decode, execution, and retirement stages on one die. With most current designs, each core possesses its own L1 cache, but shares an L2 and, if available, L3 cache with other cores.

Multi-core programming is tricky, because it involves synchronizing states between independent entities. Understanding the nuances of memory is very important when learning how to perform efficient and accurate multi-threaded programming. We'll explore the world of optimal multi-threaded code in Chapter 13, "Concurrency."

GPU: From API to Pixel

The graphics processing unit (GPU) is the key to efficient rendering of second and third scenes. Although software rendering is more capable than you would expect, it's generally smarter to offload your graphics work to a secondary piece of hardware where it can run in parallel, either a dedicated graphics card or an embedded graphics chip.

Understanding how the rendering processing works is essential to making it faster. The next few sections discuss how rendering works, tracing from the API calls in your application to the changes to individual pixels on the screen.

Application Calls API

The first step to any rendering is the application—your application—calling the API. The specifics of this tend to change from version to version, platform to platform, and API to API. Graphics APIs come in two varieties: immediate mode and retained mode.

Immediate mode APIs expect the application to maintain information about the world's state and issue drawing commands as needed. Both DirectX and OpenGL are immediate mode APIs, and this style is used on most consoles as well. In an immediate mode API, you can draw a spinning sphere by preparing a buffer of vertices and then setting some render state and issuing a draw command. Regardless of how things work behind the scenes, the API acts as if any command you issue is processed immediately.

Retained mode APIs maintain world state for you and provide you with the means to update the world state as needed. You can draw a spinning sphere by creating the sphere once and letting the API keep track of it. In every frame, you can update the world database by changing the transform for the sphere. Libraries such as OpenGL++, Performer, OGRE, and OpenSceneGraph provide this sort of functionality. The API never lets you draw directly—everything is stored in the scenegraph and subsequently drawn by the API for you.

Every graphics application has some properties of retained mode, since it has to track the position and state of objects from frame to frame. In addition, getting good performance from a retained API is often a matter of figuring out how to manipulate it so that it makes the right immediate mode API calls. For these reasons, we will not focus on the use of retained mode APIs; if you know how to do general optimization and are familiar with the immediate mode APIs, it's straightforward to get retained mode libraries to do what you want.

Because the API interfaces with drivers and ultimately the GPU, calling the API can have a much higher cost than calling equivalent code in your own application. For instance, locking a buffer (holding, for instance, vertices or texture data) to update it or read from it may cause a flush of the GPU's deep pipeline. In addition, in Windows XP, the driver runs in the kernel, so some API calls may require a context switch, which can make those calls several orders of magnitude more expensive than a simple function call.

Don't despair. Despite all this, almost any graphics card from the last five years is capable of rendering complex scenes at an acceptable frame rate. Be aware, though, there are a few cards that are consistent thorns in developers' sides. In general, graphics cards will fall into two categories: those with competent capabilities and drivers that might require some degradation of screen resolution, shader complexity, or texture resolution, but basically will run your game just fine; and those with poorly written drivers and incomplete capabilities that are hard-pressed to run any application well, least of all your game. If you are targeting low-end systems, you may want to consider licensing a software-rendering library like Pixomatic or SwiftShader. Software renderers may not run as fast as even low-end GPUs,[6] but they run consistently, which makes for a reliable fallback.

There is one more wrinkle between your application and the graphics card. This is the command buffer. The drivers try to keep the application and the GPU as isolated as possible, to maximize the potential for both to be busy at the same time. As commands are generated by calling the API, they're put into a queue and passed to the GPU as it finishes work. In the best case, this means that the GPU can have several frames' worth of rendering queued and ready for processing, while the CPU is busy with other things. Once the command buffer is full, API calls will block until the GPU catches up. Similarly, certain requests (as mentioned earlier) may require the command buffer to empty out before they can be serviced. These are easy to spot because you'll see graphics calls causing inexplicable spikes in your profiler.

Geometry

Once data gets to the GPU, the first thing that is done is geometry processing—the vertex and index data you pass via the API. There are several stages that this data goes through before it is drawn onscreen in a process called *rasterization*. (See Figure 4.7 for the overall flow.)

First, vertices are assembled. Graphics APIs often let you combine several discrete sets of data into a single set to be drawn. For instance, texture coordinates might be stored separately from position and normal. Or instance-specific data might

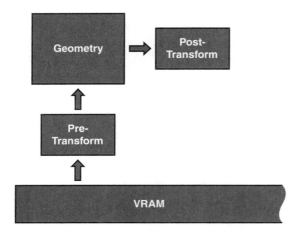

Figure 4.7
The geometry stage is accompanied by the pre- and post-transform caches. The pre-transform cache increases the performance of vertex fetching. The post-transform cache reduces the overall number of processed vertices by storing the results of recently transformed vertices.

combine at different frequencies for better efficiency. This data is fetched out of VRAM and stored in a small pre-transform cache.

Second, vertex processing is performed. Typically, this involves running each assembled vertex through a vertex shader. New attributes (like a lighting term) might be calculated, or existing attributes (like position in a skinning algorithm) might be updated. On lower-end, fixed-function cards, there may be only a limited set of possibilities available. At the end of this, everything is transformed into screen space. The results of this transformation are cached in the post-transform cache. To use the post-transform cache, you must use index buffers since the index is the key to the post-transform cache lookup.

Finally, a geometry shader may be executed. Geometry shaders can generate or destroy geometry, unlike vertex shaders, which can only emit a single vertex for each vertex provided. This gives an opportunity to offload further calculation to the GPU, much like vertex shaders did. For instance, stencil shadows can be done entirely GPU side without introducing extra overhead.

Rasterization

After vertices are transformed, primitives, like lines or triangles, are generated. They are passed to the rasterization stage for final rendering. This stage starts by linearly interpolating the values at the extremes of the primitive so that for every

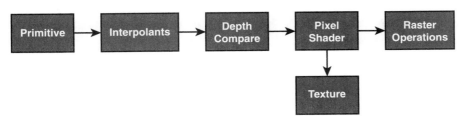

Figure 4.8
Here is a process flow that starts with the primitive and ends with raster operations that blend and resolve the pixel into screen space.

pixel onscreen, it knows the position, texture coordinates, and other values. Figure 4.8 shows the process in detail.

This linear interpolation, incidentally, dictates which calculations can be done in the vertex shader and which must be done in the pixel shader. Values that only vary linearly across the face of a polygon, like position or normal or texture coordinate, can be done in the vertex shader. Values that vary in a nonlinear fashion, like normals affected by a bumpmap or surface color, have to be done in the pixel shader. Of course, that's for correct rendering. For performance reasons, you may find it useful to push a calculation out into the vertex shader, even though it doesn't vary linearly.

Interpolated values being known, rasterization proceeds. After rasterization, the depth of the resulting fragment is compared against the values stored in the depth buffer. This is known as z-testing. If the test succeeds, then the fragment continues to the pixel shader; if not, the hardware rejects the fragment and the pixel shader won't receive the invisible fragment.

Now that you know the texel is visible (didn't fail the test), you have to calculate what color the fragment is. This is done by evaluating the pixel shader, which is passed to the interpolants calculated previously. It may sample from one or more textures, access shader constants, or perform various mathematical operations, or a combination of all three. Ultimately, the result of the pixel shader is an RGBA color. (Fixed function cards operate similarly, but on a more simplistic level; approximately, they can do everything a SM 1.x pixel shader can do.)

Finally, the color output returned from the shader resolves to the render target (a texture, or the framebuffer) using a fixed function set of operations known as *raster operations*. This can be done in several ways; the simplest and fastest is to overwrite the previous value. However, all cards support blending, which allows the colors generated by the shader to be combined with existing values in the framebuffer in various ways.

For instance, the alpha component might be used to blend between the existing and new values, in order to simulate transparency. The two colors might be added, multiplied, or subtracted. This capability is limited to just a few possibilities by the API (i.e., it is currently not programmable), but with some cleverness a wide variety of graphic effects can be achieved. It's also possible to implement your own blending operations by using render targets, although this introduces overhead as you have to "ping-pong" from one texture to another.

An important consideration involves the various types of anti-aliasing that most cards implement. Earlier in this chapter, we talked exclusively about pixels. However, for better image quality, one, zero, or more executions of the pixel shader may be required for each visible pixel. To clarify this, many people refer to the pixel shader as a *fragment shader* and the result of each execution as a *fragment*. Multiple fragments are combined to get the final color of each pixel.

GPU Performance Terms

There are a few important numbers to be aware of when we talk about performance for rendering. These apply to CPU implementations and GPU implementations equally. We'll be going into much greater detail about their meaning and implications in later chapters.

The first term is *overdraw*, which refers to how many times a pixel is drawn to each frame. The overdraw for a frame is the average of all the pixels. For instance, a scene of a city might have a high overdraw of 10 or 12 due to many buildings overlapping one another. On the other hand, with proper culling, overdraw could be reduced to only 3 or 4. In addition, because rejecting pixels at the depth stage is so cheap, drawing buildings from front to back can also reduce overdraw. Figure 4.9 shows a visualization of overdraw from PerfHUD.

The second term is *fill-rate*. Fill-rate refers to the rate at which pixels can be drawn. For instance, a card's box might indicate that that card can draw textured and lit geometry at 400 megapixels/sec. From this fact, you can determine that if you want to maintain 60Hz, you can only draw 400,000,000 pixels/sec divided by 60 frames/sec equals 6,666,666 pixels/frame. Knowing your target resolution is 1,920 × 1,080 or 2,073,600 pixels means you can only shade each pixel onscreen

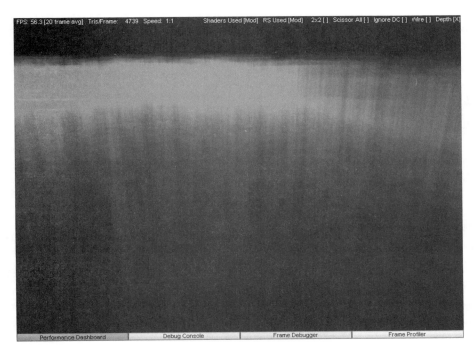

FPS: 56.3 [20 frame avg] Tris/Frame: 4739 Speed: 1:1   Shaders Used [Mod] RS Used [Mod]   2x2 [ ] Scissor All [ ] Ignore DC [ ] Wire [ ] Depth [X]

Performance Dashboard   Debug Console   Frame Debugger   Frame Profiler

Figure 4.9
PerfHUD visualizes overdraw for quick detection of high overdraw areas. Areas of high overdraw are bright red (shown in grayscale here), while areas of low overdraw are black.

about three times. This implies that your overdraw had better not be higher than three, assuming your pixel shader is not a bottleneck.

The third term is *texture bandwidth*, sometimes also called *texture fill*. This number indicates the cost of sampling from textures. Many cards are very, very fast at drawing unlit, untextured polygons. But because they are limited in their texture bandwidth, by the time you throw a pixel shader that samples from three or four pixel shaders on those same polygons, you might have reduced your fill rate by a factor of ten.

The texture cache is an important element here. Typically, sampling a texel that's already in the cache is free. So reading from a small look-up texture can have a very low cost, as it will remain resident in the cache at all times, while reading from a very large texture can have a consistently high cost because data is constantly being fetched from outside of the cache. Additionally, with enough texture sampling in a shader, you can hit a performance cliff when the texture cache starts thrashing.

Mipmaps and texture filtering, two elements that affect texture performance, are subtopics in Chapter 9, "The GPU."

GPU Programmability

Before graphics cards, if you wanted to add a new rendering feature to your game, you simply rewrote part of your software renderer. Since the CPU wasn't designed for handling large streams of data in parallel, the way graphics pipelines are today, the ability to write these algorithms was very defined by the limits of CPU performance rather than the developer's ability to write intense effects.

The first mainstream 3D graphics card was the 3dfx VooDoo 1, which achieved popularity circa 1997; this class of hardware only supported hardware-accelerated pixel operations. This generation of hardware, along with closely following counterparts developed by Matrox, NVIDIA, and ATI, were dedicated rasterizers. They didn't have any of the hardware-accelerated vertex or pixel processing found in today's cards. While they were much faster than a pure CPU solution, they were limited.

This changed with the advent of the programmable pipeline. First, vertex shaders opened the door for creating unique programs for geometry processing. Next, pixel shaders allowed for procedural per-pixel effects. Mainstream adoption of pixel and vertex shaders occurred with the joint introduction of DirectX 8.0, Shader model 1.0, and NVIDIA's GeForce 3. Most recently, geometry shaders gave developers the ability to add and remove triangles and access triangle adjacency information in hardware.

In the past, graphics cards implemented a fixed-function hardware pipeline and a programmable pipeline. Today, the fixed-function pipeline exists purely as emulation and is not supported by every API. Fixed-function commands are compiled into shaders dynamically by the drivers during submission to the graphics card.

The history of the programmable pipeline, like many of our techniques, is an evolution of sciences developed in the nonreal-time domain. Most people link shader development to the program Renderman, which introduced the concept of trees of shading instructions described in a 1984 SIGGRAPH publication by Robert L. Cook entitled "Shade Trees." This publication defines many of today's popular rendering techniques, such as normal mapping and displacement maps. It is likely that shader technology will continue to converge with Renderman technology.

Shader Hardware

Shader support is definable by two attributes: language support and hardware support. There are many different versions of shader languages and many different levels of hardware support. The shader model, a standard driven by Microsoft, defines expected levels of support for functionality of a language and hardware. Oftentimes, we define the graphics card by which level of API it supports. For example, it's not uncommon to define a particular card as a DirectX 9 or DirectX 10 card. While this is beneficial from a consumer perspective, developers need a more accurate description.

Others, still, choose to describe the card using a shader model. A shader model gives driver developers a standard to comply with. It's not uncommon to hear someone describe a card as a shader model 2.0, 3.0, or 4.0 card.

Shader models and languages will tell you a lot about the card; however, the only way to truly know what a card supports is to ask it. When using OpenGL, the `glXQueryExtensionsString` function call will tell you what extensions exist; with DirectX, you can use the `GetDeviceCaps` call to return the device capabilities or use the new model, which uses the concept of "feature levels" to describe what functionality is available.

Shader Languages

There are several options available for writing shaders. DirectX 8 uses a DirectX shader assembly language and DirectX 10 supports the High Level Shader Language (HLSL). DirectX 9 versions support either HLSL or DirectX shader assembly. OpenGL's HLSL equivalent is GLSL. Lastly, NVIDIA provided a high-level language that supported both OpenGL and DirectX with CG, its answer to HLSL.

The final result of all these options is compilation to a proprietary, opaque, vendor, and possibly hardware-specific microcode. This conversion occurs in the drivers and is handled similarly in DirectX 10 HLSL, GLSL, and CG.

Shader Models

Shader model standards are considerably more specific than their usage as a description for graphics hardware. The model extends to specifics for a vertex shader, pixel shader, or geometry shader. For example, shader model 1.0 includes vertex shader 1.1 and the now depreciated pixel shaders 1.1, 1.2, 1.3, and 1.4.

Shader model 2.0–2.X and DirectX 9 can be exceptionally confusing when taking a historical view. DirectX 9, which introduced shader model 2.0–2.X, broke the pattern of the point releases in DirectX 8.0 and 8.1. The initial DirectX 9 release followed letter numbers a, b, and c, before moving to bimonthly updates. Shader model 2.0 corresponds with the release of DirectX 9, as does 2.a to 9.a and 2.b to 9.b. DirectX 9.c corresponds with shader model 3.0. In case you wondered, shader model 2.b is actually a subset of shader model 2.a. Wow, that's a lot of versions.

Shader models (excluding 2.a and 2.b) add functionality to the earlier version. New shader models add a combination of new instructions, added precision, dimension (meaning supporting a vector as opposed to a scalar), and registers (general, temporary, or specific memory locations).

Shader model 2.0(x) introduced the concept of flow control. Introduced in this model are the concepts of Booleans, if-else, loops, and subroutine calls. The 2.0(x) shader implements these flow-of-control statements with limitations, including maximum number of loops, maximum number of nesting depths, and subroutine call depths.

Shader model 3.0 introduced two important concepts: the ability to control input register frequencies and texture fetch from the vertex shader. The former enables hardware instancing, which uses one index buffer, vertex buffer, and a buffer holding information per instance, to render multiple instances of a mesh with varying instance data. The latter enables the vertex shader to access data from textures for techniques, such as displacement mapping.

Shader model 4.0 is described in the DirectX documentation as a significantly different paradigm from its predecessor models. Shader model 4.0 introduces the geometry shader, which can generate 3D primitives procedurally during run-time. Also, shader model 4.0 unifies all three shader types with a single common feature set.

Shaders and Stream Processing

Constraining a problem often makes it possible to solve it faster or more reliably. GPUs are fast because they are geared toward solving a highly constrained problem. Simply put, a GPU is similar to a rail yard of trains, and the CPU is similar to a fleet of trucks. Both are good at their respective jobs but in different ways. Understanding how the graphics card processes streams of data will help you understand the basics of how shaders execute.

A GPU supports instruction level parallelism in a very different way than the CPU. A CPU will use control hardware to increase parallelism; the GPU requires users to format data into large (the larger the better) streams of data where considerably less control hardware is required. The CPU, not including the memory architecture, requires very little organization of data and does its best to organize instructions in a way that utilizes the execution units. The GPU will not reorganize instructions or data (except in a few limited cases). Instead, states are maintained for each stream. Changing this state for the GPU is expensive, since overhead exists in starting or stopping a stream to free the hardware for a new stream and a new state.

Let's examine how the CPU and GPU would handle a small stream of pixel operations.

Consider the following CPU code:

```
Vec4 color(1.0,1.0,1.0,0.0);
Vec4 texel(0.5,0.2,0.3,0.6,0.0);
for( int i=0; i<numPixels; i++ )          //line 0
{
    temp.x = PixelIn[i].x* color.r;    //line 1
    temp.y = PixelIn[i].y* color.g;    //line 2
    temp.z = PixelIn[i].z* color.b;    //line 3
    temp.w = PixelIn[i].w* color.a;    //line 4

    PixelOut[i].x = temp.x*texel.r;    //line 6
    PixelOut[i].y = temp.y*texel.r;    //line 7
    PixelOut[i].z = temp.z*texel.r;    //line 8
    PixelOut[i].w = temp.w*texel.r;    //line 9
}
```

The CPU would perform a branch on line zero, but since the branch prediction hardware supports prediction, this line would result in an accurate prediction. Lines 1 through 9 would operate as parallel as possible; however, with only a small fraction of the hardware being dedicated to any single data type (say two execution units for floating point math), full parallelization of all these lines is not possible. Automatic hardware pre-fetching would ensure that memory is available so that the loop isn't stalled while waiting for memory from the cache system and system memory.

Now let's consider how you would program the GPU to handle this same process. It is difficult to map the way pixel processing works on the GPU to pseudocode; so instead, we will generalize using an image.

The GPU has several advantages when processing streams of data. GPU hardware does an amazing job of processing streams of data where many threads of the same program (i.e., a shader) can execute concurrently on its many cores. Streams of data are easy to split into chunks that the drivers can distribute across the GPU's cores. Because the inputs to each chunk of work are well defined (chunks are usually vertices or pixels), it's very easy to limit the memory that each chunk must read or write. Compare this to a general purpose CPU, which cannot make as many assumptions and must perform costly commits to keep all its various caches in sync.

Data in stream form is ideal for concurrent processing. Each piece can be processed separately. A set of a thousand vertices can be processed all at once, if you have enough cores. The only synchronization needed is at completion. Compare this to a typical program on your CPU, where only a few instructions can be in flight at once.

The GPU has several disadvantages that make it bad for processing nonstreaming data.

This again, is attributable to the GPU's architecture. GPUs have many more cores than CPUs, but there is less hardware dedicated to prediction and caches. Prediction helps with flow-of-control operations that are standard fare in any nontrivial application. The GPU makes an assumption about how data is submitted for processing. In some cases (image processing), this can be a big win; in other cases (AI and gameplay), it is a loss.

Changing rendering states takes considerable overhead. The GPU design excels when state changes are minimized and uninterrupted; when efficiently processed, streams are maximized. From a graphics programmer's perspective, this translates into changing states and calling a draw call such as DirectX's `DrawIndexedPrimitive`.

The difference between GPU and CPU is especially pronounced when you consider that many CPU algorithms cannot be efficiently mapped to the GPU. If they are too synchronous, it is unlikely that they will move over well. Heavy branching is also another factor. GPUs are getting better all the time, but predictive execution takes a lot of silicon. It's more efficient for the GPU to go with lots of cores and a massively parallel algorithm in most cases.

Additional Shader Considerations

Understanding the basics of shader execution opens the door for some additional considerations with respect to shaders. These additional considerations are not exhaustive, but are important in later optimization discussions.

- **Constant Registers**: Constant registers are blocks of memory that can be set from the application and read from the shader. Setting constants is one of the many render states that describes what you are rendering. The number of constants vary from card to card, but the shader model specifies a minimum number of constants. Here are those amounts:

  VS 1.1 = minimum of 96
  VS 2.0 = minimum of 256
  VS 2.x = minimum of 256
  VS 3.0 = minimum of 256
  PS 2.0 = minimum of 32
  PS 2.x = minimum of 32
  PS 3.0 = minimum of 224
  Shader model 4.0 = no limits on pixel or shader limits

- **Swizzling**: Swizzling is a very powerful utility that allows you to reorganize the elements of a vector. For example, let's assume a four-dimensional vector named `vec` is set with the values 1.0, 2.0, 3.0, and 4.0. Using swizzling to reference this array in the order it is stored in memory, you would type `vec.xyzw`. To reference this array in backward order, you could write `vec.wzyx`. Let's look at some other uses of swizzling shown in Table 4.1.

- **Masking**: Masking looks very similar to swizzling, but its use is quite different. Masking controls which variables are used (or not used) in an assignment statement. For example:

  Assume a vector named `vec` is set with the values 1.0, 2.0, 3.0, and 4.0.

  And assume it uses the following syntax:

  `vec.xyzw = float4(0.0, 0.0, 0.0, 0.0);`

Table 4.1 Swizzle Syntax

Operation	Example Syntax
Reference a scalar value of a vector	`vec.x, vec.y, vec.z, vec.w`
Reference a vector of 2 from a vector	`vec.xy, vec.xz, vec.zw, etc.`
Convert the scalar of a vector into a vector	`vec.xxxx, vec.xx, vec.zzzz, etc.`
Different shader models support different levels of swizzling.	

Table 4.2 Masking

Operation	Example Syntax
Write a scalar value from a vector	`vec.x = float4(0.0,0.0,0.0,0.0);`
Write a vector of 2 from a vector	`vec.xy = float4(0.0,0.0,0.0,0.0);`
Write one component to multiple components	`vec.xyzw = 1.0;`

Different shader models support different levels of masking.

The new values of `vec` would be 0.0, 0.0, 0.0, and 0.0.

Using the following syntax:

`vec.xy = float4(0.0,0.0,0.0,0.0);`

The new values of vec would be 0.0, 0.0, 3.0, and 4.0. By specifying only x and y in the destination variable, we successfully exclude z and w from the write. Let's look at some other uses of masking shown in Table 4.2.

■ **Flow Control**: Understanding the basics of how stream processing works will reveal one of its flaws: flow control. A branch on a CPU, when considering branch prediction, is quite complex. A GPU branch is considerably more complex.

The GPU does not handle every branch with the same method. In fact, differences exist from GPU to GPU, making the performance ramifications from GPU to GPU even more volatile.

Some graphics cards do not support branching natively. In those cases, emulation can occur. Predication, which uses per-channel comparative conditions and masking, is available as part of the 2.0 shader model. Using predication, both the branches execute. Only the branch that satisfies the condition is saved to the final register (see `setp_comp` shader assembly instructions). In doing this, the total time of the branch is equal to the sum of both branches, plus the added overhead of the comparison.

Conclusion

A big part of optimization focuses on your hardware and the assumptions that the chip makers have. You can alter your program to require less processing power, but there's no assembly instruction that simply makes the chip run faster.

In this chapter, we discussed memory, the CPU, and the GPU. Memory uses multi-tiered caches and batching (cache lines) to hide the latency of memory fetching. Furthermore, memory alignment, which defines boundaries of certain memory operations, such as loading, is a fundamental part of your hardware. An awareness of alignment can play a crucial role in certain algorithms.

The CPU, which measures performance in frequency, is a very complex processor. While frequency is important, you must also understand topics such as instruction level parallelism, data dependencies, and branch prediction.

The GPU uses a different approach from the CPU by focusing on more cores, less cache, and an architecture that requires data to be in a format suitable for concurrent execution of many GPU cores.

We also discussed the variations of GPU functionality. This evolution of GPU hardware capabilities is mind-boggling, and we are probably only at the tip of the iceberg.

While we did discuss some of the finer details of these components, as a programmer optimizing a game, it's probably still unclear where you should apply this knowledge. The next chapter will lay the battle plans for optimizing a game from the top down.

Works Cited

[1] Intel. (2008, November) *Intel® 64 and IA-32 Architectures Software Developer's Manual*. Retrieved March 11, 2009 from Intel.com: http://download.intel.com/design/processor/manuals/253665.pdf.

[2] Intel. (2006, January) *Intel® Itanium® Architecture Software Developer's Manual*. Retrieved March 11, 2009 from Intel.com: http://download.intel.com/design/Itanium/manuals/24531705.pdf.

[3] Zhislina, V. (n.d.) *On the Road to Concurency Core Architecture*. Retrieved January 12, 2010, from Intel.com: http://software.intel.com/file/9907.

[4] Intel. (n.d.) *Intel® Xeon® Processor 7000 Sequence*. Retrieved March 11, 2009 from Intel.com: www.intel.com/products/processor/xeon7000/index.htm?iid=servproc+body_xeon7400subtitle.

[5] Gatlin, K. S. (2006, March) *Windows Data Alignment on IPF, x86, and x64*. Retrieved March 11, 2009 from MSDN: http://msdn.microsoft.com/en-us/library/aa290049.aspx#ia64alignment_topic4.

[6] Glaister, A. (2008, November) *Windows Advanced Rasterization Platform (WARP) In-Depth Guide*. Retrieved March 11, 2009 from MSDN: http://msdn.microsoft.com/en-us/library/dd285359.aspx.

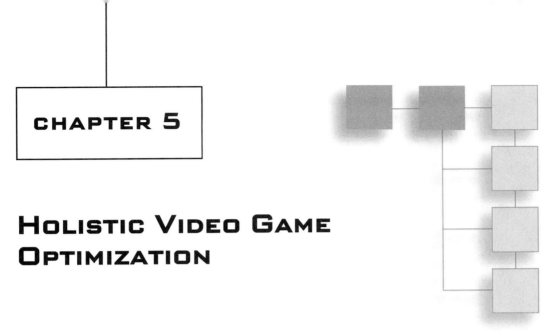

CHAPTER 5

HOLISTIC VIDEO GAME OPTIMIZATION

It's time to start answering the question, "How do we optimize a game?" The last four chapters set up the battlefield, but now it's time for WAR!

No games conference is without several talks on optimization. But most presentations and papers discuss how to optimize for individual vendor's products—perhaps how to write fast code for the latest PlayStation, or the newest NVIDIA/ATI card, or DirectX or OpenGL. However, there's not much on systematic approaches for optimizing games; most information focus on how to increase performance once you have found the problem.

In this chapter, we introduce a holistic approach to video game optimization. We describe a high-level process for determining which resource you need to optimize next to get the best ROI on your optimization efforts.

For more detailed information on detecting and addressing specific bottlenecks, you should refer to Chapters 6 through 16. Chapters 6 and 7 present optimizations for CPU bound applications, while Chapters 8 through 10 focus on GPU optimizations. The remaining chapters cover other specific optimization topics.

This process will build heavily upon "detection" from Chapter 1. In that chapter, we focused on a high-level view of detecting performance problems; now it is time to dig deeper and expose the detection process in greater depth.

Holistic—The Optimal Approach

Throughout the first four chapters of this book, we mentioned latency and parallelism frequently. Latency is unavoidable, but with careful use of parallelism, it can be hidden. If the latency of some operation is fixed, then doing more in parallel finishes the entire job faster. The trend of parallelism across all granularities from the instruction level up through threads and even into the design of hardware itself is likely to continue.

Parallelism and a Holistic Approach

In a serial system, optimizations will usually achieve a throughput increase. Consider the following example of a serial system.

A dealer hands a deck of cards to one person and asks her to sort the deck into red and black cards. Let's assume the task takes two minutes. If we were to optimize the process by 25%, the task would take one minute and thirty seconds.

Now, let's look at the same task and use two people to parallelize the operation:

A dealer hands a deck of cards to two people and asks them to sort the deck by red and black cards (see Figure 5.1). Let's assume that person A sorts the deck in one minute and person B sorts the deck in one minutes and thirty seconds. The duration of the task is equal to the slowest person's part; therefore, the overall time is one minute and thirty seconds. If we were to optimize person A, the fast person, by 25%, the total task will still take one minute and thirty seconds. Optimizing the wrong person will cause no overall performance increase.

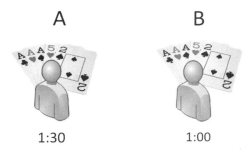

A   B

1:30   1:00

Figure 5.1
Optimizing for parallel situations differs from that of serial ones. CPUs and GPUs reach their peak performance when parallelism is maximized.

What's the point of these examples? Think of each person as independent parts of a computer. Let's say that person A represents the CPU and person B represents the GPU. Targeting the wrong person/subsystem for optimization means we'll see no overall performance increase.

If we optimize person B, the entire task would finish faster. If we optimized person B so he completed the task in 33% less time, the new overall finish time would be one minute. Unfortunately, if we optimized person B by more than 33%, then we wouldn't see more of a performance increase. Why? Because once we try to go below one minute of total runtime, person A becomes the bottleneck.

Optimizing a parallel situation is very different than optimizing a serial one. Computers are built from subsystems such as CPUs, GPUs, memory, networking, and mass storage operating in parallel. Optimizing requires that you look at the entire picture to ensure that you are optimizing the bottleneck. This will give you the biggest ROI on your work. Focusing on the part of the system that isn't a bottleneck won't change your overall performance picture.

From Example to Real World

Our example comparing person A and B to a CPU and a GPU is a little bit oversimplified. In theory, the CPU and GPU can be totally independent. But, in practice, the CPU and GPU communicate multiple times during the course of a single frame. We will address this in detail in Chapters 8, 9, and 10, where we discuss optimizing the GPU.

Sometimes, you'll luck out and see an increase in performance even when you don't optimize the bottleneck. This often means that the optimization has affected a dependency of the resource that *is* a bottleneck. For example, if you find that your game's bottleneck is the GPU, then it's possible to increase overall performance by optimizing CPU code if it enables the GPU to be more efficient.

An alternative is that you've misidentified the bottleneck. Serendipity is good, but not an efficient way to work. You should strive to be intentional in your actions, and to do that you have to understand the big picture.

The Power Is in the System

The biggest performance gains occur at the system level. Let's get some perspective by examining Proebsting's Law, by Microsoft researcher Todd Proebsting. Proebsting noticed that all the efforts to optimize with compilers in the past 36 years pale in comparison to the performance increases due to hardware advancements.[1]

Proebsting ran benchmarks with and without optimizations and measured the performance difference. Comparing these numbers showed the contribution of optimizing compilers to overall performance. He found a ratio of around 400%, and noted that people have been working on these compilers for around 40 years.

In other words, compiler optimizations double computing power every 18 years.

Proebsting's conclusions are simple and important. CPU horsepower increases at roughly 60% per year, while compiler optimizations increase performance by 4% per year. His conclusion is that we could better spend our time researching programmer productivity instead of compiler optimizations. In other words, it's better to figure out how to make programmers more productive through things like better libraries, languages, and IDEs/tools, rather than developing better auto-optimizing techniques.

This back-of-the-napkin analysis shows that the real source of performance gains lies in properly leveraging hardware, not in micro- and occasionally algorithmic-level optimizations. In other words, the biggest performance gains are at the system level.

When you optimize on the system level, you are ensuring that you are using everything that is available to you. If you are only using 20% of the GPU, should you optimize that 20% of use down to 10%, or should you determine why you aren't using the other 80%? Without a system-level view of your optimizations, you will be unable to balance work effectively. In this example, you could move work from the CPU to the GPU in order to achieve better GPU utilization.

As a game developer, you will want to identify your hardware target as soon as possible and do your performance measurements against that target. You want to run into performance walls early, so test on the lamest hardware you can find. If your app can run there, it can run anywhere. Otherwise, you won't know if you are using your available resources effectively. If you develop your game using a sports car, and everyone else runs the game on an economy car, the performance picture will be very different.

The Process

In Chapter 1, we discussed the six steps for optimization: benchmark, measure, detect, solve, check, and repeat. In this section, we are going to go into a little more detail, and we'll talk about how to apply this process to the software

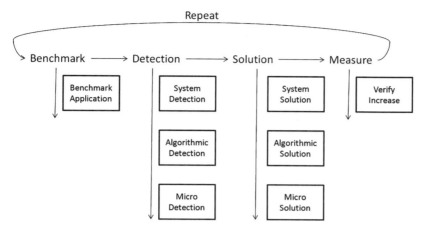

Figure 5.2
Diving deeper into the optimization lifecycle from Chapter 1, you'll learn that the detection and solution benefit from an understanding of the levels of optimization.

components of your game. Figure 5.2 shows these six broad steps along with some important substeps.

Start by benchmarking—coming up with a repeatable situation you can measure. Next comes detection, so look for the biggest optimization opportunity/return on investment using your profiling tools. The detection process works from system level, to the algorithmic level, down to the micro level. Each level will have a bottleneck you can focus on as you move down to ever more specific areas. Nearly all performance problems fit this pattern.

As you enter the solution phase, consider a game with a CPU animation bottleneck caused by having too many bones, leading to too many matrix multiplications. You can decompose the performance problem into three levels, each more specific than the last:

- **System**: CPU is the limiting resource.

- **Algorithmic**: Too many matrices interacting with too many vertices.

- **Micro**: Too much addition, multiplication, and memory fetching (the elements of a matrix multiply).

After you understand the "DNA" of the bottleneck, it becomes much simpler to identify a solution. Of course, there are many solutions to a given bottleneck. To figure out which will be most appropriate, you need to look to the levels of optimization for guidance. Except now you'll use the order of system, algorithmic, and micro as guidance for your priorities when solving, as opposed to using them to order your profiling activities.

In general terms, it is most desirable to implement the appropriate system level optimization, followed by algorithmic, and then micro. (See "The Levels and the Process" in this chapter for more on this subject.) While this can lead to big performance gains, it isn't always possible to tear apart your whole game's codebase at the drop of a hat.

Coming back to the animation example, you can develop solutions at different levels:

- **System**: Move animation to the underutilized GPU.

- **Algorithmic**: Don't perform matrix multiplications for matrices with very small influence over a vertex.

- **Micro**: Convert addition and multiplication to use SSE instructions. Make the fetches more cache friendly.

Whatever solution you implement, you need to measure performance to verify that it improved things. And if performance still isn't where it needs to be, you will need to repeat the process to find something new to optimize.

The Levels and the Process

The notion of seeking solutions from large to small scale is largely common sense. Performing optimizations in order of system, algorithmic, and micro also makes sense from a theoretical perspective. However, in practice, you may find yourself using a different order, and that's okay.

Why should you work in this order?

The biggest reason is that working from system, to algorithm, to micro helps to map your program to the hardware. The system level tells you how you are utilizing the hardware, the algorithmic level removes work completely, and the micro level speeds up work you haven't been able to offload (system) or remove (algorithmic).

Why wouldn't you work in this order?

Going from high to low can be inefficient in coder hours. System optimizations are likely to cause rewrites of entire subsystems. For example, if you move your animation system from the CPU to the GPU, you will throw away a lot of your CPU code. Imagine optimizing the CPU code and then deciding to move it to the GPU later. What a waste of time and code!

The same relationship tends to exist between algorithmic and micro. You wouldn't want to micro-optimize eight lines of code for a week only to ditch the algorithm and start over. You must balance the cost of rewrites and maintenance against the potential performance benefits.

You won't always work in the recommended order, but you should at least glance at the other levels before diving into implementation. If you perform due diligence, you'll often find low hanging fruit that keep the process flowing in the natural progression: system, algorithmic, and then micro.

You can take the process defined in Figure 5.2 and map it to performance-sensitive components of hardware and software to give a holistic roadmap for optimizing games. We will use the flow chart shown in Figure 5.3, which includes these elements, as the basis for the remainder of this chapter (and in many ways the remainder of the book).

The process flow begins at the benchmark and moves its way through a decision tree. You measure and analyze, moving through different levels and looking at different parts of the system. The left side of the diagram focuses on CPU-related issues, while the right side focuses on the GPU, which requires different tactics.

Each leaf node in the chart is a hotspot or a bottleneck. Once you arrive at a leaf, you have a strong understanding of what is causing your performance problem. At this point in the process, you have the opportunity to implement a system,

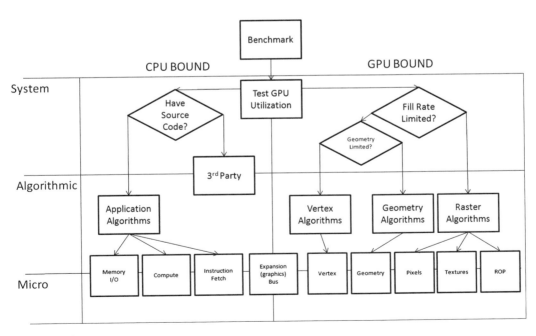

Figure 5.3
By adding the hardware and software dimensions to Figure 5.2, we arrive with a process flow that aids in detecting performance bottlenecks.

algorithmic, or micro-solution to your system, algorithmic, or micro-bottleneck. It is important to note that the leaf notes tend to straddle levels. For example, the leaf node "compute" is detectable on the algorithmic or micro-level, depending on the performance problem.

There are some special cases not covered by this chart since they are outside of the scope of a typical game. A game that is streaming terrain could conceivably be limited by the performance of the hard drive, which is not an area that is called out in the chart. You always want to keep your eyes open for new performance wins. Of course, slow hard drive accesses would show up as a disk read call in your application code that took a long time to complete, and following the chart would quickly lead you to the problem. We discuss these problems further in Chapter 12, "Mass Storage."

The flow chart is likely to lead you to the next biggest bottleneck, but solving that bottleneck doesn't guarantee a big frame rate increase. This can be frustrating, but not unexpected. Think of a bottleneck as a key that unlocks the door to the next bottleneck.

Sometimes, moving from the current bottleneck to the next rewards you with a huge performance increase, but sometimes it doesn't. It depends entirely on the next bottleneck's characteristics. Either way, you will have to deal with all the bottlenecks keeping you outside of acceptable performance.

Finally, when you successfully solve a problem, start the process again at the top of the flow chart. There's always the "next slowest thing" that you can look at fixing.

The Benchmark

The very first step when you sit down to optimize is to determine the benchmark you will be using. A benchmark, described more in Chapter 1, is what you will use to measure your performance gains as you go through the multiple iterations required to complete an optimization and move on to the next bottleneck. As stated earlier, consistency, simplicity, and relevancy are key to a good benchmark.

It can be difficult to know which benchmark to choose, even after satisfying the basic requirements that differentiate a good benchmark from a bad one. Moving from the large and the general (system level) to the local and specific (micro) applies to your benchmarks as well as your optimizations.

The flowchart repeats after every solution, potentially requiring a new benchmark. Initial benchmarks should be well rounded. In other words, use balanced scenes that work all the major parts of your game's codebase. By optimizing based on this kind of benchmark, you can "raise the tide" of the whole game's performance.

After these general benchmarks are running acceptably, you can move on to isolating and targeting specific problem areas, such as dense particle systems, complex scenes, or intense firefights. If you are already satisfied with overall performance, then you can overlook this step and move on to the areas of your game that require localized and scenario-specific optimizations.

Stress tests are smart when you are early in a project and don't have representative scenes. Depending on the kind of game you're building, you will be able to make some rough estimates about the likely stress points. For instance, a massively multiplayer online (MMO) game might benefit from stress tests that place dozens of characters in the same small space, whereas a first-person shooter (FPS) might benefit from stress tests that simulate firing dozens of weapons simultaneously.

But be careful—you don't want to spend lots of development time profiling scenarios that will never happen in the real game. Performance never scales forever, and optimizing an extreme case won't always help performance in the final shipping game. In fact, focusing too much on specific subsystems can simply lead to other areas being bottlenecks.

GPU Utilization

Let's divide the performance picture into two parts: the CPU and the GPU. You can do this by measuring utilization of each. Except for perfectly balanced applications, one will always be waiting on the other—and the one that's holding up the show is the one you'll want to optimize.

GPU utilization is dependent on the CPU, but the opposite isn't true in most cases. This is due to the producer (CPU) and consumer (GPU) relationship of the two processors. When GPU utilization is low, you know that the CPU isn't giving it enough work. When CPU utilization is low, you can't really determine much about the GPU since it doesn't submit work to the CPU. Of course, the CPU might be waiting on results from the GPU, in which case things are simpler. When a CPU is waiting on the GPU, you are probably using the API in ways that weren't intended for performance. We'll cover these topics in greater detail in Chapter 8, "From CPU to GPU." In general, a slow CPU will be slow for non-GPU reasons. But let's explore a few situations that can cause the CPU to wait on the GPU.

If your GPU utilization is very high, then the command buffer is probably very full, creating a nice deep buffer that works well with the GPU's deep and numerous pipelines. This deep pipeline can introduce a latency of several frames between when the CPU issues the command and when the results show up onscreen. Additionally, if the CPU runs too far ahead, the driver may block until the GPU catches up (usually the threshold for this is around three frames). On DirectX, this blocking occurs in the Present call and misleads developers to believe that the Present call is slow.

Another performance-draining situation can occur when you are waiting for data from the GPU. Anytime you access data from the video card, you introduce the possibility of the driver stalling the CPU until the GPU can service the data. In addition, the GPU may have to stop doing some work while the CPU is working with the data. These two processors perform best when they are operating asynchronously, but requesting data from the GPU and waiting for it to return is a serial operation. If you have a lot of work in the pipeline, the GPU usually has to clear all of that work out before the two can synchronize to service the lock.

Let's consider a situation that involves the CPU waiting on the GPU—locking the Z-buffer. Before the advent of occlusion queries, developers would lock the Z-buffer and access its data to detect occlusion. When the CPU locks the buffer, it stalls to wait for the data return. On first thought, a developer may believe that the performance bottleneck of this process is the bandwidth of the graphics bus; however, that is only one piece of the equation.

Two other factors involve the command buffer. If the command buffer is very full, then the CPU sits idle while the command buffer is emptying by the consuming GPU. The other factor is the deep pipeline of the GPU. It is true that the GPU is massively parallel, but those moments of parallel execution exist within a sequential, assembly line-like set of stages. In order for the GPU to return the latest Z-buffer information, this assembly line must be completely flushed.

The Decision

Determining CPU/GPU utilization will point you toward optimizing for the CPU or the GPU. Once you've decided, you'll find that each requires different techniques. The key is in understanding where the equilibrium, meaning equally CPU and GPU bound, exists.

To replicate the process of determining your card's equilibrium, you can do the following.

Create a GPU bound application (probably 99% GPU utilization) and add CPU work until the frame rate changes. When you begin increasing CPU work, the frame rate will not change. This is because your application is completely GPU bound. Eventually, the CPU will begin to affect your frame rate. When this begins to happen, you have reached the point at which you are equally CPU and GPU bound. This typically occurs between 80 and 90% GPU utilization, but this number may vary from card-to-card, between the tools you use, or from application-to-application.

The main takeaway is this: If your game is very GPU bound, don't optimize for the CPU; if your game is very CPU bound, don't spend your time optimizing the GPU until you solve the CPU problem. If it's not clear (>90% is GPU bound <50% is probably CPU bound), do some CPU-based tests, such as adding strenuous CPU work and looking for a decrease in frame rate. Similarly, you can also add work on the GPU side and see if that decreases performance. It is always smart to identify the bottleneck before optimizing!

A Quick and Dirty CPU Bottleneck Test

If your application isn't clearly GPU or CPU bound, try adding some dummy work. This is a function that is called every frame, which performs a variable workload. Set it up so that you can scale the workload with a key press.

Once you're in the game, start the loop with a low workload and increase the workload while keeping an eye on frame rate. If you increase the CPU load and your frame rate doesn't change, you are GPU bound. Watch out because your compiler might identify your dummy work as unnecessary and remove it. Adding the result of your work to a global variable will often stop this compiler optimization.

The Tools

Determining GPU utilization may sound easy, but it's not always as easy as it seems. Your operating system won't tell you how hard your GPU is working because it doesn't necessarily know. The graphics API may be able to help a bit, but in the end, they will just be asking the drivers. If you want reliable access to GPU utilization numbers, then you need to go straight to the source. This means using proprietary tools. If you are using an AMD card, then ATI's PIX plug-in will assist you. If you are using an NVIDIA card, then NVIDIA PerfHUD is your tool. Intel provides the Graphics Performance Analyzer.

Many graphics cards have a hardware counter that measures time spent by the GPU idling. If you measure GPU idle time by percentage and subtract that number from 100%, then you will know your GPU utilization. Using NVIDIA's PerfHUD or ATI's tools will get you this number. Unfortunately, without access to hardware counters, there isn't a quick and reliable way to measure this.

CPU Bound: Overview

If you have determined that your application is CPU bound, it's time to break out a profiler. At this stage, you can categorize your application's code into two broad sets: third-party modules with no available source, and modules you can build yourself with available source code. When areas that you have source code for bind an application, you have many options for data collection. However, when you don't have the source code, the best you can hope for are the symbols from your debugger, and if you're lucky, a profiling tool built into the module.

Third-party modules can be almost anything. Their biggest defining characteristic is that you don't have the source code. For game developers, the most common third-party modules that cause problems are the graphics API, the drivers, and the OS.

You can solve all three of these problems in the same way—by using the API better or hoping that an updated version fixes the problem. Determining whether an application is bound by your application, graphics, API, drivers, or OS is easy to do with any profiler. Look for the routines taking the most time! If it's in your code, start looking at that routine. If it's not in your code, usually the tool will give you some clues, such as the DLL or API call that's taking the time; that will let you identify the third-party module that's causing the problem, and possibly even what usage of that module is triggering that problem.

DirectX Debug Runtime

One example of a particularly useful tool for debugging API issues is DirectX's Debug Runtime. We covered the Debug Runtime briefly in Chapter 4 and again in Chapter 9. Many optimizers won't even begin looking for optimization opportunities until accounting for all errors and warnings.

CPU: Source Bound

When your application is CPU bound, and the offending code is inside the application code that you wrote, you are again at a crossroads that will require more measurement and analysis. When a game is CPU source bound, the application is slow due to computation, memory, or instruction fetching.

What to Expect

When you are application bound, you may have the urge to find the tightest loop with the most math and show off your assembly (or algebra) skills by speeding up the calculations it performs, but don't act with too much haste. You may be missing out on a better opportunity. The first step is to measure and be sure you have correctly identified the performance problem. Sometimes it's simpler than you think, once you're sure you've identified the problem.

Always stop and think about the bigger picture: system, algorithmic, and micro. Do you have a system level optimization? Can you move this work from the CPU to the GPU where it may operate up to 50 times faster? Is the algorithm a good fit for multi-threading? Can you develop a better way to LOD or partition the work? If these aren't good options, or your deadlines are looming, it's time to break out the micro-optimizations and get ready to sweat out some performance gains.

For example, in Chapter 4 we discussed that cache misses can cost hundreds of cycles, which is a high cost when a multiply or add operation might only take one or two cycles. If your application has thousands of cache misses and thousands of computations, your time would be better spent reducing the cache misses. For a fuller treatment of memory and performance, see Chapter 6, "CPU Bound: Memory."

Usually, compute bottlenecks are right where you'd expect them—in the physics routines, in AI, in particle systems, or anywhere else where you do a lot of processing. But be careful—don't blind yourself to low-hanging fruit by only assaulting the most difficult parts of the problem. Sometimes, your performance is being eaten by a slow OS call or a bug!

The Tools

From VTune's module view (see Chapter 3, "The Tools" for more information), you can proceed to the next view by selecting your executable name from the list and selecting the hotspot view. The hotspot view shows the function calls listed in order of self-time. By viewing the hotspot view, you are closer, but still don't know enough. You must also perform a cache analysis.

Running the program again and measuring cache misses will get you as close as you can probably expect to get. If the biggest hotspot for overall time is equal to the biggest hotspot for cache misses, then you should consider optimizing the memory for that function. If it doesn't show up on your radar for cache misses, then it's likely time to optimize for compute. For a detailed explanation of this process, see Chapter 6's sidebar titled "Using VTune to Find Cache Misses."

You can also use VTune to determine if you are bound by instruction fetching. A high value for the ratio of CYCLES_L1I_MEM_STALLED/ CPU_CLK_UNHALTED.CORE suggests that the working set of instructions is too large to be cache efficient. It's fairly uncommon for application performance to be bound by instruction fetching. It's possible, though, and typically occurs around loops that contain many conditional jumps and bloated code.

Third-Party Module Bound

If your limitation is a third-party module, then you are in for some pain. Simply put, if you don't have the source code, then your hands are somewhat tied. Without the source code, you'll be limited to seeing what symbols are causing the performance loss or maybe only the offending API call. Even tools like VTune won't always be able to give you fine-grained information.

So how does an optimizer proceed? With care, visual inspection, and a carefully selected bag of tricks.

PIX, when run in the "A single-frame capture of Direct3D whenever F12 is pressed" mode, will show a list of API calls and timings. In the August 2008 release of the DirectX SDK, Microsoft enhanced the API calls to include the timings of API calls, and knowing those numbers will get you much closer to knowing where the driver is spending its time. NVIDIA's PerfHUD allows you to ignore all draw calls, which is helpful in including or excluding draw calls from issues with other DirectX API calls. Of course, we discuss this more in Chapter 8, "From CPU to GPU."

Lacking a tool like PIX, your fallback is to comment out code and see what happens. This approach isn't always the most efficient, but it may be all you have. Carefully comment out code and try to isolate what API calls are causing the biggest change in performance. Work your way down from whole engine components (like the terrain or character renderers) to individual calls or functions.

Lastly, none of these techniques is very useful unless you understand a lot about your API. APIs make a lot of assumptions about how you are going to use them, and often, those assumptions are implicit. For example, making too many `DrawIndexedPrimitive` calls and changing render states, such as shader settings, is the cause of many games with driver and DirectX API performance issues; however, the idea of minimizing the number of draw calls to, let's say ~2,000, isn't listed in the documentation of `DrawIndexedPrimitive`. Without reading the section titled "Performance Optimizations" in the DirectX SDK documentation or this book, you might never know.

Using an API without errors and using an API correctly are two very different things.

GPU Bound

The following section assumes that your application is GPU bound.

Jumping back across the pond, let's take a few steps back up the flow chart and talk about what happens when you are GPU bound. Cards that use a unified shader architecture share their multi-processors for vertex, geometry, and pixel shading work. Let's first cover what it means to be GPU bound for nonunified shader architectures. Typically, shader model 4.0 cards or higher use a unified shader architecture.

Pre-Unified Shader Architecture

Shader model 3.0 card discussions can be split into two major categories: the pixel half and the vertex half. Although both halves contain multiple components, it is sometimes useful to take a quick measurement about which side is causing a bigger effect on your performance.

Luckily, this test is very easy: Set the graphics API's scissor rectangle to be infinitely small and watch the frame rate. If the frame rate increases, you know you are somewhat pixel limited, but if the frame rate increases tremendously, you are very pixel limited. If the frame rate stays the same, then the pixel half of your graphics card is a short straw in the tent of bottlenecks, and you can focus on optimizing other areas.

The Tools

There is another way to test this effect. Using PerfHUD, you can easily set the scissor rect to zero size (something you can do without PerfHUD, but not as easily). This causes the rasterizer to reject every pixel when it comes time to rasterize it. If the application maintains the same frame rate, then you know you are not pixel bound, and the bottleneck lies elsewhere.

Unified Shader Architecture

Shader Model 4.0 is made up of vertex, geometry, and pixel shaders. However, most SM4 cards have a unified architecture, which means that vertex, pixel, and geometry shaders run on the same unified shader core. As a result, on SM4 hardware, it is more meaningful to consider all shader operations as a whole for performance purposes.

The Tools

It's hard to measure how shader cores are being used without gathering information from the hardware. Luckily, tools like PerfHUD exist to get this data. Using the Performance Dashboard, you can measure not only your shader utilization, but also determine what percentage of the cores are being used for what kind of work—vertex, pixel, or geometry.

Kernels

Determining if you are fill limited or geometry limited helps you understand, at a more abstract level, how your entire GPU graphics pipeline is performing. But in order to determine what your performance solution is, you need more detailed information. With enough information, your performance bottleneck will stick out like a sore thumb.

The best way to get this data is to perform a series of tests starting from the back of the pipeline to the front. These tests isolate a graphics pipeline stage and vary the amount of work it has to do. Sometimes, this can mean changing the visual results of the application, but because you're working from back to front, you can be sure of spotting where your time is going. When a test is performed, you evaluate the frame rate and see how it reacts to a change in workload. If, upon changing the workload, you see no significant change in frame rate, then you can reject that stage as a potential bottleneck.

This works because the graphics card behaves like an assembly line. In fact, it operates like many assembly lines with the common goal of generating all the data for a scene (such as diffuse, depth, stencil, and other render targets). From the system level view, if you reduce the work for a given kernel of the pipeline and the overall performance doesn't increase, then you know that kernel is not a bottleneck.

Each stage of the pipeline does a different task, so each stage requires its own unique solutions. We will briefly give an overview of some of the possibilities in this chapter, but the GPU chapters following will go into a lot more detail.

Balancing Within the GPU

If you were to write a simple, single-threaded 3D rasterizer, you would notice that the graphics pipeline is made of many nested loops. The pseudocode for your typical rasterizer looks like this:

```
foreach( draw call )
{
      // triangle creation
      foreach( triangle )
      {
            // pixel creation
            foreach( pixel )
            {
                  // shade & blend into framebuffer
            }
      }
}
```

Looking at this code, it's easy to see that there are more pixels to shade than there are triangles to create in almost any rendering scenario. Because of this, if you look at how the hardware is allocated, you'll find that most of the effort is spent on per-pixel calculations (pixel shaders), somewhat less work is spent on triangle-related calculations (vertex shaders), and not much work at all is spent on draw calls.

At a basic level, if you were to swap this pattern around, you'd quickly run into performance problems. For instance, if you had more triangles or draw calls than pixels, you'd be in a lot of trouble, performance wise, since the effort of setting up for the pixel shading loop would be mostly wasted.

As a side note, different rendering architectures deal with this in different ways. For instance, a tile-based rasterizer will sort the geometry in each tile before doing any pixel work, so it will deal with scenes with high-overdraw differently. If you are developing on an exotic hardware platform (like a game console, or an embedded device, or maybe even a PC from the future), be sure to do your homework so you understand what exactly the GPU and drivers are doing with your commands.

Fragment Occlusion

The graphics pipeline processes graphics primitives to get them into screen space for rasterization. Then the hardware converts triangles into fragments and draws into the framebuffer. Graphics pipelines project from 3D to 2D early in the graphics pipeline. This is a foundational part of their design and gives you several opportunities to discard information that, in the end, will never make it to the screen. There are several "early outs" that reject fragments and pixels.

The first is a coarse-grained rejection. After geometry processing, the rasterization unit converts triangles into fragments. At this stage, the hardware can reject blocks of fragments if it determines that the fragment block will never be visible (i.e., it's behind something opaque). There are several cases, such as when using full screen quads to write depth instead of Clear calls, which will cause you to miss out on this optimization or reduce its effectiveness. AMD refers to this capability as *HiZ* (short for hierarchical-z) and NVIDIA uses the terminology *ZCULL*. For full details on these triggers, check their documentation for the hardware you are using. Chapters 9 and 10 discuss this more fully, too.

The next fragment rejection opportunity happens before running the shader. This process is per pixel and saves your application valuable pixel shader resources. In general, the GPU tries hard to save itself from having to run shaders when it doesn't have to.

By rendering opaque objects from nearest to farthest (from the camera), you ensure that the nearest depth values will be written first, giving more opportunities to reject occluded pixels. Compare this with drawing back to front, which means that every occluded pixel will be fully drawn and then overwritten. Sorting can impose a cost, but if you have a well-designed scene graph (see Chapter 8, "From CPU to GPU"), it should be minimal.

There's a final trick you can use. Would you believe that you can render your scene twice and have it be faster than rendering it once? It's true.

Early Zculling involves performing two passes per frame. On the first pass, color writes are disabled (D3DRS_COLORWRITEENABLE in DirectX) and the scene is rendered. This initializes the Z-buffer with every pixel's depth information without doing the costly diffuse color operations.

On the second pass, turn color writes back on and turn off Z-writes (but don't clear the buffers). This time, you can set the Z-comparison function to equal (D3DCMP_EQUAL in DirectX) since you only need to render pixels that match the already initialized Z-buffer.

This technique makes the hardware's fragment- and pixel-based occlusion very efficient and leads to significant pixel performance increases. Modern hardware has built-in optimizations for this technique that make the first faster than your typical pass that has color writes turned on.

This technique has some trade-offs. You have to issue twice as many draw calls, but you don't have to set up your pixel-shader state more than once. If the overhead from draw calls is low, your vertex overhead is low, and your pixel overhead is high, then doing a depth pre-pass can be a big win. Otherwise, simply drawing back to front may be enough.

Graphics Bus

We have saved the least for last. By least, we mean one of the areas that is least likely to cause you problems if you are using the API correctly (which can be a difficult task). If the graphics bus is your bottleneck, you are either using an antiquated bus, like AGP, or you are doing something incorrectly.

Sometimes, you may do processing on the CPU and upload the results to the GPU. For instance, some procedural geometry techniques may require CPU support. Streaming resources may have to be transferred to the card. A 3D modeling program (or a game that has deformable environments) needs to update its GPU-side assets to reflect user input. Even the state from API calls has to be transferred over and may represent a bottleneck. The OS or another program may be using the bus at the same time as your game. In any case, large amounts of data can overwhelm the bus. In addition, the bus introduces some latency, and draw commands that depend on data from the bus can stall until it catches up.

In other cases, you may stress the bus due to video memory overflow. As mentioned earlier, when you run out of video memory, swapping occurs between video memory and nonlocal video memory. This process is better than the graphics card crashing, but it comes at a high cost.

The process of measuring and analyzing is called *detection*, but when it comes to graphics bus detection, we should probably call it *elimination*. If you determine that a GPU bound application is not limited by any of the GPU kernels, then the only remaining hardware is the bus. This process is simple, unlikely, and somewhat time consuming since it requires a lot of analysis.

Example

Let's put this theory into practice.

A manager, named Ted, gives a developer, Doug, the job of increasing the frame rate of a game until it is above 60fps. It is two months before the second of five milestones and Doug's GPU is top of the line. The engine is roughly 600,000 lines of code, overwhelming the developer with fears of failure. Doug's first inclination is to search relentlessly looking for mistakes or code that looks slow. Then he remembers this chapter.

He recalls the first step: create a benchmark. Where does he start? Doug first decides to look for the slowest frame rate, which happens to occur when moving the camera very close to a particle system waterfall that is off in the distance. He stops and thinks to himself, "This particle system is off in the distance and probably won't affect the overall performance of the game." He decides to change course and picks a more general location in the middle of the map that is representative of an average frame for this game.

"This benchmark will help me increase the performance of my overall game," Doug exclaims. He notes the location of the camera and uses the engine's scripting language to modify the camera's initial position on game start in order to save time during the process.

Next, he uses NVIDIA's PerfHUD to determine GPU utilization (other vendors have tools that can do the same thing). Upon doing this, he finds that the GPU is busy 40% of the time. Using his knowledge base from this chapter, he determines that his program is likely CPU bound. He adds a small section of superfluous CPU code and notices that the frame rate drops, which confirms his suspicion. Now, what?

"It's time to break out a CPU profiler."

Ted checks in on Doug to see how he is doing. "The game is CPU bound, so I'm going to use VTune. I'd bet it's the update loop for the character skinning," says Doug. "Wait a second," says Ted. "How do you know the problem isn't in the driver?" Doug sits back and remembers the levels of optimization. "I guess I need to know what is going on from a system perspective before I can optimize."

Using VTune's module view, Doug finds that the game is spending 40% of its time in the driver, 20% of the time in the hardware abstraction layer, and 20% of the time in the actual executable. "How can that be? Our engine has over 600,000 lines of code." "Trust me," says Ted, "It can happen quite easily. There are over 5,000 objects in this scene, and if we aren't careful, we can cause a lot of work in the driver."

Fast-forwarding one week…

"Ted, I've solved the driver issue. Turns out it was all those objects like you suspected. I've implemented instancing (covered in Chapter 9), and the driver overhead was dramatically reduced. Our fps for the initial benchmark is now 60.3Hz."

"But you aren't done," says Ted. Doug scratches his head. "Did you test this on multiple machines?" "No!" says Doug.

Since Doug's machine has such a high-end GPU and he only tested on that machine, his job isn't over. To optimize for the game's entire audience, chances are he will need to run the game on a lower spec machine. By doing this, he may find that the bottlenecks are very different. His high-end machine may be CPU bound largely because the GPU is relatively fast. On a lower-end GPU, he may find that he needs to optimize the shaders. By optimizing many different machines of low and high specification, he is optimizing on machines that are representative of the user base.

Conclusion

This chapter has laid out the battle plan (the grand strategy) for your attack on bad performance. The process flow (see Figure 5.3) is the key to diagnosing performance problems.

By looking at the performance problem globally and then progressively narrowing down the causes, it is possible to determine quickly and reliably the source of low performance. Once the problem is identified, it can be solved.

Again, you should look to the levels of optimization to provide you with a guide to your solution. Search for system optimization followed by algorithmic and micro-level optimization. Too many times, novice optimizers will try to solve their performance problem without looking at the big picture. Fumbling in the dark rarely works out well, especially when you're on a time crunch.

As we move forward, we will build on this chapter and begin breaking down each leaf node in the optimization process flow chart. In each chapter, we will describe the specifics for detecting and solving performance problems in that domain.

Works Cited

[1] Proebsting, T. (n.d.). *Proebsintg's Law*. Retrieved March 14, 2009, from Research.microsoft.com: http://research.microsoft.com/en-us/um/people/toddpro/papers/law.htm

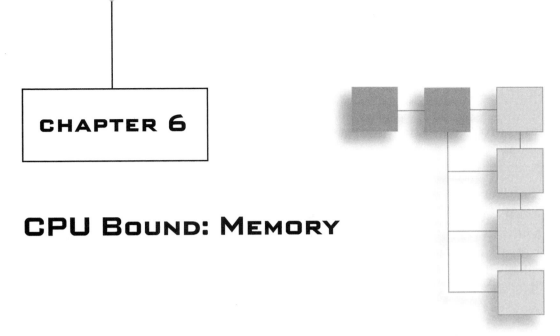

CHAPTER 6

CPU BOUND: MEMORY

Computers operate in time and space. In this metaphor, instructions represent *time* and memory is *space*.

In the real world, factories optimize their space. Parts must flow from one place to another for maximum efficiency. If distances are too great, time becomes a factor. If the space is not laid out well, workers cannot complete their tasks efficiently.

Inside CPUs, transistors switch ever faster. However, the speed of light imposes hard limits. A chip—a single computational unit—cannot be the size of a room. It must fit into a small footprint. Electrons have to transfer charges from one part of the machine to another for work to be done, and while transistors are orders of magnitude faster than they were a few decades ago, electricity travels at the same speed now that it did at the beginning of time.

Similarly, as on-die memory sizes, such as L1 and L2 caches, increase, we are bound by the amount of memory we can access in a fixed time period. Hundreds of instructions can be processed in the time it takes a cache line to be fetched from main memory. Caches help, but they are expensive and limited in size by physical and financial constraints.

Herb Sutter suggests that CPU clock speed increases have outpaced memory speed increases by 150% since the early 80s. Rico Mariani, a software architect at Microsoft, likened the modern processor to driving a sports car in Manhattan (Sutter, 2007). Optimizing the CPU is like driving a car: You can spend your time optimizing the car or removing the stoplights. In this context, stoplights are cache misses, and they affect performance more than you would expect. The faster your CPU, the better your code needs to be about reducing cache misses; otherwise, your sports car is idling at stoplights instead of cruising down straightaways.

Naturally, optimizing memory at a fine level is going to be very hardware-specific. Different memory topologies and processors have different requirements. If you tune an algorithm too far for a specific processor, you might find that you're hitting a performance cliff on another processor. Because of this, we will spend our time focusing on general techniques that give better performance in all cases. As always, we will measure our performance at every step so that we avoid performance pitfalls.

This chapter will also guide you toward a more specific understanding of memory performance. A program is not just "memory" bound; there are always underlying problems, such as bus bandwidth or capacity, and various solutions, such as access patterns or alignments.

The problems discussed in this chapter do not really end with data. Instructions, after all, are represented by data. The CPU has to fetch them from memory just like everything else, and in some situations, this can become a factor in performance.

Detecting Memory Problems

Memory access is invisible in most cases. Unless you are looking at assembly, the means of memory access are pretty much invisible. You might be accessing a register, the stack, the heap, or memory space mapped to a device on the other end of a bus. The data might be cached in L1, L2, or L3 cache. It might be aligned or not.

Memory access is invisible until it becomes a problem. Because of this, it's easy to overlook. If an algorithm is slow, is it because it is using memory in a slow way, or because it is doing a lot of computation? Sometimes, this can lead to counter-intuitive situations. For instance, a binary search is faster from a big O perspective, but it may have bad memory access characteristics because it is jumping around randomly. A linear search may be much faster if it can take advantage of hardware pre-fetching, even though it is doing more work. A lot of the time, the size of the dataset is the tipping point in these trade-offs.

The best tool for finding memory-related performance analysis is an instruction-level sampling profiler like gprof or VTune. If memory is a bottleneck, then you will see a lot of time being spent on seemingly innocuous memory load instructions. Profilers that read hardware counters (like VTune or Code Analyst, which both work on AMD and Intel chips) are also useful because they can tell you which regions of your code are causing lots of memory stalls or cache misses.

If you don't have special tools, hope is not lost (but you may have to do more work). If you have basic timing capabilities, it's easy to guess-and-check to find hotspots in execution. From there, you can do visual inspection (or experimentation if you have a benchmark) to see if it's memory access that's hurting you. For instance, you might temporarily change a loop to do the same amount of work but only over the first item in an array. That removes cache misses as a potential source of performance loss.

First things first—you have to determine if the application is CPU bound. There's no ROI optimizing the CPU when another resource is the bottleneck! We've covered how to do this already in Chapter 5's discussions on CPU-bound applications.

After you've identified the CPU as a bottleneck, the next step is to look for cache misses. CPUs have counters to measure this, so you have to find a tool to access them; otherwise, you will spend your time looking for what you think are cache misses. Learning the patterns that cause cache misses is the main topic of the remainder of this chapter.

Using VTune to Find Cache Misses

VTune sampling provides a useful means for detecting performance issues caused by cache misses on CPU-bound applications. This example uses the Performance Test Harness test: "memory/traverse/randomStatic."

First, open the Advanced Activity Configuration (one way is to right-click the activity) and add the following VTune Event Ratios to the sampling:

    L1 Data Cache Miss Rate

    L2 Data Cache Miss Rate

If the highest function hotspot for time is also the highest hotspot for data cache misses, then it's time to use the tips in this chapter to get the best ROI.

In Figure 6.1, the yellow bar represents the time spent inside of a function. The biggest opportunity for performance increase is the initStatic function; therefore, it's probably a better idea to optimize or remove that function before optimizing for L1 (light red) and L2 (dark blue) cache misses.

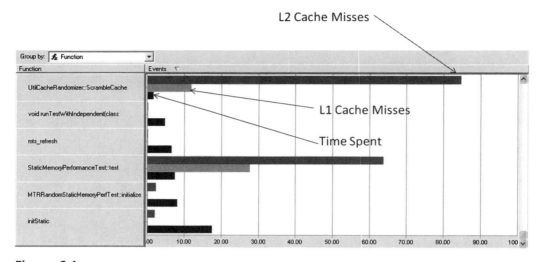

Figure 6.1

Comparing time to cache misses is important when considering the performance impact of cache misses.

> Always consider time when optimizing for memory. `UtilCacheRandomizer::scrambleCache` has more cache misses; however, the net effect on performance is not as bad as the `StaticMemoryPerformanceTest:test` function, which consumes more time.

Solutions

Physical constraints make it difficult for hardware manufacturers to decrease memory latency. Instead of trying to break the speed of light, manufacturers focus on hiding latency by using caches and predictive techniques like pre-fetching.

The best tactics for optimizing memory usage involve leveraging the cache:

- Reducing memory footprints at compile and runtime

- Writing algorithms that reduce memory traversal/fetching

- Increasing cache hits through spatial locality, proper stride, and correct alignment

- Increasing temporal coherence

- Utilizing pre-fetching

- Avoiding worst-case access patterns that break caching

Two of these tactics are simple, and we'll cover them immediately. The others are more involved, and the following sections will address them. Fundamentally, all of them are about using the hardware in the most efficient manner.

Reducing the memory footprint of your application is the same as getting a bigger cache. If you can access 16 bytes per item instead of 64, you are able to fit four times as many items in the same size cache. Consider using bit fields, small data types, and in general, be careful about what you add to your program. It is true that today's machines have a lot of system memory, but caches are still on the order of several megabytes or less.

Reducing memory traversal or fetching relates to the importance of application optimizations. The fastest memory is the memory you don't access; however, the price of L2 cache misses, in the magnitude of hundreds of cycles, is so high in comparison to cache hits, that a developer should be aware of the trade-off between naïve algorithms that traverse memory with few cache misses and algorithms that fetch memory less often and cause many cache misses.

Pre-Fetching

CPUs may perform automatic hardware pre-fetching in an attempt to hide latency by recognizing memory access patterns and getting "ahead" of the executing program's memory needs.

This is generally a win. It allows the hardware to deal with otherwise naïve algorithms. It hides the latency in the system and requires no difficulty to maintain pre-fetching logic from developers or compilers. As always, you should measure to make sure that hardware pre-fetching is helping you. There are scenarios where it can hurt rather than help.

Hardware pre-fetching does not typically help with small arrays. Hardware pre-fetching requires several cache line misses to occur before it begins. Therefore, an array that is only a few cache lines in size, on the order of 128 bytes (Intel Software Network, 2008), will cause useless pre-fetching, which consumes bandwidth unnecessarily.

The alternative to automatic hardware pre-fetching is software pre-fetching, a topic we will discuss later in this chapter. In general, the hardware pre-fetch is preferable to the software pre-fetch, since hardware pre-fetch decouples your code from the pre-fetching implementation. However, you may encounter hardware that does not implement hardware pre-fetch, or you may encounter one of those rare situations where software pre-fetching truly is a win.

Access Patterns and Cache

But choosing the "optimal access pattern" is easier said than done. The only way to find the best patterns and more importantly see how much of a difference there is between different patterns is to test. As part of the performance tests that come with this book, we have implemented several different traversal patterns and compared their performance.

The code shown here in the text is simplified to make its operation very clear. In practice, the compiler will optimize them to nothing. Review the memory/ traverse section of the test suite in order to see the details of our implementation.

We will discuss each pattern and then compare its performance.

The first access pattern we will discuss is a *linear access forward* through an array of integers:

```
for( int i=0;i<numData;i++ )
{
    memArray[i];
}
```

Next, let's consider the same loop, but instead of stepping through code from front to back, let's move back to front. We will call this *linear access backward* through memory.

```
for( int i= numData-1;i>=0;i-- )
{
    memArray[i];
}
```

Next, let's step through memory using regular strides. This sort of traversal occurs when you step through a list of structures and access only one member. We will call this access pattern *periodic access* through memory:

```
struct vertex
{
    float m_Pos[3];
    float m_Norm[3];
    float m_TexCoords[2];
};
for( int i=0;i=numData;i++ )
{
    vertexArray[i].m_Pos;
}
```

Finally, the last access pattern we will discuss is *random access*. This one is important because it typifies most complex data structures. For instance, a linked list, a tree, a trie, or a hash table will all exhibit fairly random access patterns from the perspective of the hardware. The code for random access is:

```
float gSum = 0;//global memory

void Test()
{
    for( int i=0;i=numData;i++ )
    {
        gSum+=vertexArray[RandI()];   //actual code uses a pre-
    }                                 //randomized array instead
                                      //of RandI() due to
                                      //latency

}
```

Now, you can see the results of our tests in Figure 6.2:

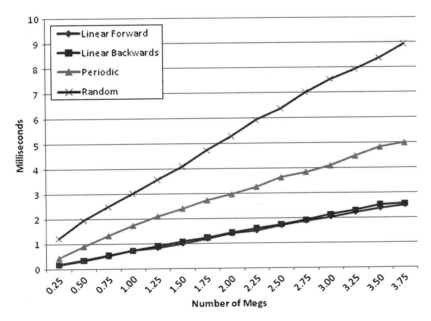

Figure 6.2

Linear forward and linear backward access patterns have nearly identical performance when stepping through 1 to 4 megabytes of global memory. Our workload is performing floating-point addition on the stored 32-bit values.

Let's discuss these results. Notice that the linear access forward and linear access backward times are nearly the same. In fact, it's difficult to tell that there are two lines. The slope is also low relative to the other approaches, which is indicative that hardware pre-fetching is reducing the cost of traversing the memory.

Now look at the random access line. The slope is much worse than the linear lines—pre-fetching, if it is occurring, has less benefit. The difference is large at every dataset size. Finally, the periodic access falls between the linear and random patterns. Depending on the stride size, different results will occur. As we increase stride size, we see the performance move closer to that depicted with the random line (and in some unique cases, periodic access can have worse performance than random—more on this later in the section, "Fix Critical Stride Issues").

Allocating memory in big chunks for linear traversal can be more difficult, but as the previous chart shows, the returns are significant. Graphics APIs do a good job of forcing you to give them memory in big buffers through objects like vertex buffers.

However, you will not always be working with linear arrays of data. It may not be possible to design for linear access in every situation. Allocating and freeing may become too costly if you maintain a linear array. Or the data may need to be traversed in a specific order. You have to weigh the trade-offs when you implement or choose data structures.

There are solutions that lie between fixed allocation and a dynamic allocation; using the strategy of a dynamic array provides more flexibility with cache advantages of linear memory. Instead of allocating and deallocating objects one at a time, use blocks to batch the overhead effectively. When adding objects to a dynamic array, allocate large blocks by a "bucket size." This bucket size can change dynamically as well. Many implementations of dynamic arrays grow the bucket size as the array count grows. A bucket size of 5 may be appropriate for an array that will never grow over 50. An array that is the size of 1,000 would probably benefit from a bucket size of 100.

For bulk data processing, the chart shows the benefits of linear access. However, there are some trade-offs at work that you should be aware of. In some cases, linear access isn't always best.

The more common case is when nonlinear traversal lets you reduce your working set significantly—the random access times are below the linear access times when the working set is about an eighth of the size. A tree structure can easily give you this kind of reduction. You will want to measure before deciding on one option over another.

The other situation is less obvious. If you have a lot of computation to do on each item, then you can "hide" the cost of out of order accesses via pre-fetching. Of course, this requires you to think through your access pattern carefully, and you will need to be able to calculate the pre-fetch location before the previous computation ends. For more info on pre-fetching, see "SSE Loads and Pre-Fetches" near the end of this chapter.

While the CPU is crunching away at the work of each memory location, the memory system can be fetching data in anticipation of its use. When you access memory linearly forward or linearly backward, the hardware pre-fetching is at its best and the cache is used most efficiently.

Randomness

Is random access always slower? It depends on the scale. Cache lines act to even out small-scale randomness. For instance, if you have a small `struct` and access its members out of order, you may not notice a difference in performance. If the `struct` fits in a cache line and is aligned, then the order won't matter at all because accessing one member has the same cost as any other. As the scale of randomness varies, for instance with larger `struct`s, then the effects are more pronounced.

How Random Is Random?

We have implemented a test to explore randomness confined to a stride size. This source for this test is available in the Performance Test Harness: "memory/traverse/linearLT512byteRandomStatic." The results are shown in Figure 6.3.

Each data point represents traversal through four megabytes, with the stride of random access getting larger at every point. This performance test is similar to stepping through an array of structures and accessing each current structure's member in a random order.

Streams

So far, we have only discussed automatic hardware pre-fetching's impact on accessing a single stream of memory. Most CPUs can actually support multiple streams. The number of effective streams is difficult to generalize. It depends on

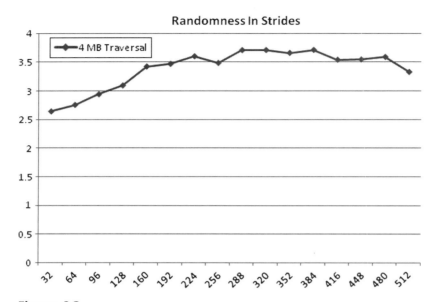

Figure 6.3

Randomness in fine granularity (from 0 to 512 bytes granularity) yields the best performance when randomness strides are very small.

the number of active processes, the specific chip, operating system behavior, and so forth.

The Intel documentation suggests that the number of concurrent streams in Intel processors differs from processor to processor but is in the range from 8 to 16 (Intel, 2008). The best practice is to measure it—which we've done—and design your application to rely on a minimum of memory access. Figure 6.4 shows our results.

So what is the conclusion? In the quad-core 3Ghz Intel Xeon used in the test, hardware pre-fetching will suffice when you have fewer than eight memory arrays streaming per processor. The more streams you use, after eight, the worse your performance will be. (Again, this number can and will differ from processor to processor, so you will want to do your own tests on your target hardware.)

An important side note: We chose arrays slightly smaller than 4MB for several reasons. One, it is slightly smaller than an OS memory page. This is important because many hardware pre-fetch implementations do not allow more than a single stream per page (Intel, 2008). Unfortunately, iterating at a stride of exactly 4K causes problems with the cache on our test systems. This issue is discussed more in the "Fix Critical Stride Issues" section of this chapter.

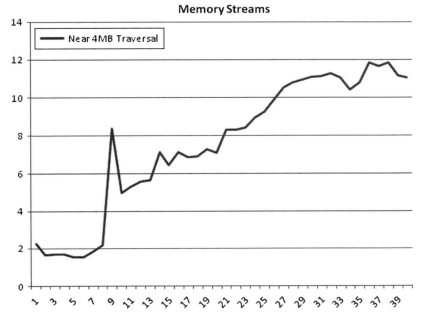

Figure 6.4

The number of arrays we are reading concurrently changes our performance. On this Intel Xeon, there is a significant penalty reading above eight streams. We traversed slightly less than 4MB, because parsing exactly 4MB causes a different cache penalty. The source for this chart is available in the perf Test Harness test "memory/stream/memorystream."

AOS vs. SOA

Layout of memory is crucial, and one way to maximize linear access through memory is to choose the appropriate data structure. There are two major possibilities for laying out memory.

Typically, we create array of structures (AOS). They take the following form:

```
struct aos
{
    float m_Float1;
    float m_Float2;
    float m_Float3;
    float m_Float4;
};

aos myArray[256];
```

AOS is used in a lot of scenarios. Most APIs organize their data this way. OpenGL is notable in supporting both AOS and SOA.

The other, somewhat less popular format, is a structure of arrays (SOA):

```
struct soa
{
     float m_Float1[256];
     float m_Float2[256];
     float m_Float3[256];
     float m_Float4[256];
};

soa myArray;
```

The difference is subtle. They both hold the same amount of data, and they are functionally equivalent. Why choose one structure over the other?

In Figure 6.5, you can see the effect of each structure in memory. Interleaved memory, like the AOS, would be appropriate if you were planning to iterate through every member and every iteration. But what if you were only going to iterate through one member at a time?

By using the array of structures and iterating through only one member, you are much closer to periodic access. If you use the structure of arrays and iterate through one member, your access pattern is more similar to linear than periodic.

Understanding the difference between AOS and SOA is helpful when writing multi-threaded code as well. We will discuss this in Chapter 13, "Concurrency."

Solution: Strip Mining

When using an AOS, you can still make some accommodations for better cache usage. When you strip mine, you split iteration of single members (periodic

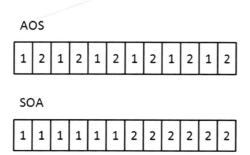

Figure 6.5

The position of members for an array of structures as opposed to a structure of arrays.

access) into cache-friendly chunks. This technique increases both temporal coherence and spatial locality.

Consider the following code:

```
for( int i=0;i<numStructs:i++ )
{
    m_Vertex[i].pos = processPos(&m_Vertex[i].pos);
}
for( int i=0;i<numStructs:i++ )
{
    m_Vertex[i].normal = processNormal(&m_Vertex[i].normal);
}
```

As the first loop iterates, the automatic hardware pre-fetch will fetch data in anticipation of its use; if the loop is large enough, later parts of the loop may evict values fetched earlier. If the evictions occur, the second loop will not benefit from the first loop's use of the cache.

A solution is to perform both loops together using blocks of access and performing memory loads on both members. This is called *strip mining*.

```
for( int j=0;j<numStructs;j+=blocksize)
{
    for( int i=j;i< blocksize;i++ )
    {
        m_Vertex[i].pos = processPos(&m_Vertex[i].pos);
    }
    for( int i=j;i<blocksize;i++ )
    {
        m_Vertex[i].normal = processNormal(&m_Vertex[i].normal);
    }
}
```

Much better. Now the first loop is warming the cache for the second loop and an increase in overall performance occurs. The optimal block size can differ from processor to processor because cache size is not standard.

Stack, Global, and Heap

Allocate memory with the new operator, add a local function variable, add a static global variable; to an application developer it may all seem like homogenous memory, and in some ways that is true, but the low-level implementation details expose nuances that help you make decisions.

Stack

When you step into a function, instructions push the parameters onto the stack; any variable whose scope exists within the function will be placed on the stack as well. As you load, store, and calculate values within the function, they are likely to remain in the cache because the stack maintains proximity. When a function returns, you are simply moving down the stack.

The stack has the advantage of maintaining spatial locality and temporal coherence. It is always in use, so it tends to stay in cache. Data is grouped well, since all the data used by a function is adjacent.

Of course, stack space is finite. Especially when working with recursive code, minimizing stack usage is important because it will give you better performance.

Global

Global memory is memory that is allocated as part of your program image. Static and global variables are stored here, the only difference being the scope. Global memory is not freed until your program closes, which is a great way to eliminate memory fragmentation—a common cause of cache misses due to a lack of locality.

Typically, the linker allocates global memory based on the order that the linker receives object files. Therefore, items that are frequently accessed together may benefit from being in the same linkage unit (i.e., same .cpp or .c file for C/C++ developers) in order to preserve locality. It can also be possible to specify explicitly where in the image globals are allocated. Check with your specific compiler to see how it handles global variables. Things like profile-guided optimization could affect variable order, too.

One important caveat about sharing global variables occurs when you are accessing variables with multiple threads. Variables that are co-located in memory may suffer performance due to a synchronizing performance problem called *false sharing*. For more on false sharing, see Chapter 13.

Heap

Memory created or freed dynamically uses the heap. For C++ developers, this typically involves a call to `new` or `delete`. C developers will be familiar with `malloc` and `free`. Heap memory is subject to fragmentation over time, based on the allocation pattern, although memory managers work hard to minimize this, which is in itself a possible source of performance loss.

Allocating and freeing memory has a high cost relative to heap or global memory. Memory managers can be very complex. Although the average case can be cheap, sometimes the memory manager will have to request memory from the operating system, reclaim memory from a free pool, or perform other bookkeeping optimizations. These can sometimes be quite costly.

However, when you need dynamic memory, that's a cost you have to pay, but there are many tactics that can help reduce the costs of dynamic memory.

Solution: Don't Allocate

Your authors once sat in on a lecture given by a recent graduate where he discussed topics about the game industry that surprised him in his first days on the job.

On one of his first days writing code, he decided to dynamically allocate memory using the new operator. To his surprise, the keyword caused a compile error. Surprised by his results, he sheepishly asked his boss.

"How do I allocate dynamic memory?"

"You don't," replied his boss.

The company's policy was to remove the new operator and only statically allocate. For devices with limited resources, this can be very effective. But it is quite limiting. Most modern games require dynamic memory management in order to move memory usage from system to system as gameplay changes.

Is there any performance difference between accessing statically allocated memory versus dynamically allocated memory?

Figure 6.6 shows the differences between traversing static allocation and the three access patterns. Notice that dynamically and statically allocated memory achieve very similar performances. Heap Untouched includes data that is slower due to lazy allocation. To ensure that dynamic memory achieves the same performance as global, iterate through the array immediately after allocating the array.

Solution: Linearize Allocation

Consider a particle system. The particles are modeled using many small structs in some sort of list structure. This data is traversed at least once a frame, maybe more if separate passes for position update and rendering happen.

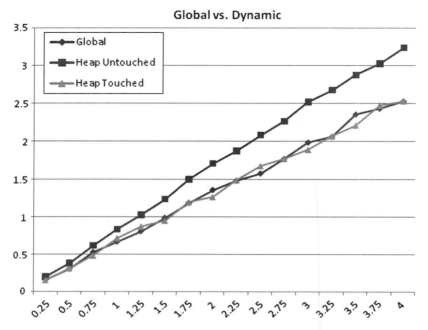

Figure 6.6

The performance of memory types, global and heap, is nearly identical when comparing data memory that has been traversed at least once (Heap Touched). Data that hasn't been fetched at least once is slower.

In the case of a particle system, dynamically allocating particles from the heap can lead to several problems. First, since the structures are small, they may cause fragmentation. The second and much bigger problem is that since they are being allocated dynamically, they can lead to a random access pattern.

If you keep the structs in an array, so that they are always in linear order, you can gain two benefits. First, memory allocation activity is reduced. You always order the array so that "active" particles are at the front. When a particle is freed, you place it at the end of the array and swap the last "active" particle with the now-dead particle in the array. This divides the array into two regions—active particles up front and dead particles at the end.

When you allocate a new particle, you just "reactivate" the first dead particle. You only grow the array when adding more particles. For a continuous particle effect, like spray from a waterfall, this will result in the array growing and staying steady in size. No more allocations and linear access will lead to overall fast performance.

The array approach works less well when the working set varies wildly. For instance, an explosion effect might grow to a high number of particles and then ramp back down. The array approach can be wasteful because most of the time it will be allocating more memory or holding onto more memory than is needed. If you keep a lot of memory in systems that use this approach, you can end up wasting it.

Solution: Memory Pools

Reduce, reuse, recycle! Pooling is designed to maximize efficiency when you are dealing with lots of similar objects. The idea is simple: Maintain a large pool of memory that holds many copies of the same thing. With our particle example, you would allocate, say, a thousand particles up front in a contiguous array. Instead of dynamically allocating particles, you get a free instance from the pool. When you are done with the particle, you return it to the pool.

This is helpful for several reasons. Since all particles are in the same area of memory, the working set will tend to be more coherent (although rarely fully linear). Memory fragmentation will not occur, because the particles aren't being allocated in the same memory space as objects of other sizes.

Most significantly, pooling can be very helpful when the allocation costs are high. Particles are usually lightweight; however, you may find that other items are more complex. If setup costs are high, then pooling objects and not fully destructing them between uses can save a lot of time.

Solution: Don't Construct or Destruct

POS—plain old structures—are structures with no constructor or destructor.

Suppose that you allocate an array of a million points to store mesh data in. The point class has a constructor, which sets its position to some safe value, like (0,0,0). You immediately overwrite these values with data from a file.

The performance problem here is that when the array is allocated, the constructor will be called on each instance. So before you can load data from the file, you have to wait for a million points to get values set on them so they can be immediately overwritten with real data.

If you can avoid these destructor/constructor calls, you can save a lot of time.

Solution: Time-Scoped Pools

Carefully defining the scope in which memory is needed can lead to opportunities for optimization. Many times, code needs to allocate temporary storage. The lifespan of the storage may be just for the duration of a function call or a single frame of rendering.

Often, this temporary data is simple data that does not need to be destructed. For instance, points or primitive types, or pointers that only point to other data in the temporary pool, are all things that can be torn down without destructors being called.

Many games implement pools for the lifetime of the current level. Everything related to the level is allocated from this pool, and when the level needs to be unloaded, the pool is simply discarded, all at once.

Another useful trick is a frame allocator, so named because it gives out memory that is only valid for a single frame (or less). This is a stack from which memory can be allocated on demand. At the start of a function, the position in the stack is noted. Code is executed, and memory is allocated from the frame allocator contiguously. Before the function returns, the stack pointer is reset to where it was at the beginning of the function. At the end of each frame, the stack position is reset to zero.

The allocator is nice because it gives very fast allocations and even faster deallocation. It can be compatible with types that have constructors, but destructors won't be run.

Alignment can be an issue with this (and other) custom allocation schemes. For more information on memory alignment see Chapter 4's discussion on "Alignment and Fetching."

Runtime Performance

The best way to understand memory performance is to do some simple experiments. The next several sections will do just that.

Aliasing

Pointer aliasing occurs when two pointers reference the same address. This is a perfectly acceptable practice, but if the compiler can't rule out the possibility for two pointers to "alias" to the same location, it has to be conservative with its optimizations, typically reloading data from memory more than is needed.

The following test uses two pointer references to the same address.

```
void func( int a[], int *p )
{
    for( int i=0; i<ARRAY_SIZE; i++ )
    {
        a[i] = *p + 5;
    }
}
```

If the compiler can't rule out aliasing, then it has to implement this function by loading *p from memory every time through the loop.

If aliasing is not a risk, then the loop can be optimized. In fact, Visual Studio 2008 implements it with a rep stos instruction, the same as a memset call.

When tested on our standard machine, the unaliased version of the function was roughly 30% faster than the aliased version.

How does the compiler determine when it has to worry about aliasing? Ultimately, it can only make a best guess, and it has to guess conservatively to ensure that the program will work. Some compilers provide keywords for indicating assumptions about aliasing, either that two pointers are not aliased or that they are. For instance, in GCC, you can use _restrict_ to indicate this, while Visual Studio uses _restrict.

If you aren't sure, check the assembly. It will be obvious if the compiler is being careful about aliasing because there will be a lot of extra load and store operations.

Runtime Memory Alignment

Your compiler by default will align structures to their natural alignment by padding with extra bytes. A structure's natural alignment is the alignment of the largest member. For the following structure, which has a double, the natural alignment is eight bytes, which is the size of an IEEE double-precision float.

```
struct eightByteAligned
{
    float m_Float;
    double m_Double;
};
```

Members within a struct are also aligned to their natural alignments. For instance, in eightByteAligned, m_Float will be aligned to an eight-byte boundary because it is at the start of eightByteAligned. There will be four bytes of padding and then m_Double. As a result, eightByteAligned will be 16 bytes long despite only containing 12 bytes of data. Figure 6.7 illustrates some different layout possibilities.

You can use various compiler options to change alignment and packing rules. Sometimes, you may want to pack a structure for minimum space usage, while at other times for best alignment.

Unfortunately, the compiler has less control over alignment at runtime. For example:

```
//function prototype
char* getData();
int* array = (int*)getData();
```

If the function getData() returns a char array, it will be one-byte aligned (meaning any address), therefore, the array has a one–in-four chance that it will be four-byte aligned. If the char happens to be on a four-byte multiple, all is well. Figure 6.8 demonstrates the performance difference this can cause.

If it is not, then depending on platform, OS, and compiler, there will either be a loss in performance or an error. If you have to cast data a certain way for things to work, that's fine, but be aware that it's not optimal.

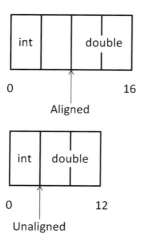

Figure 6.7

Example of possible alignment of a float and double with four bytes' padding (top) and without padding (bottom). Your compiler may have its own approach to this situation.

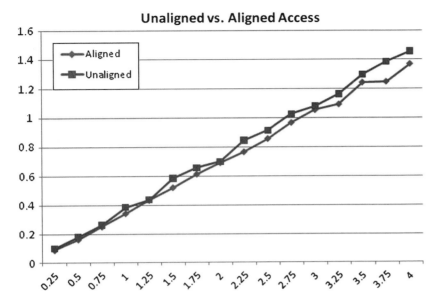

Figure 6.8

Performing addition on 4MB of integer operations shows a slight performance difference between aligned and one-byte offset unaligned data.

Fix Critical Stride Issues

Most CPU caches are set-associative. (A set-associative cache can choose to map a given address to one of N locations.) A set-associative array can have problems when accessing data at certain strides. Similar to how some engine speeds can cause parts of your car to vibrate, these critical strides impact performance by causing the cache to act against itself.

The worst-case critical stride is equal to (number of sets) × (size of cache line).

Consider an Intel Core 2 Duo with an L2 cache size of 2MB. The Core 2 Duo uses cache lines of 64 bytes and is eight-way set-associative.

Therefore, we have 2,048KB/64 bytes = 32,768 cache lines of L2 cache.

These 32,768 lines are organized into eight ways, which gives us 32,768 lines/ 8 ways = 4,096 total sets.

If you were to have a large array of data, and iterate over 64-byte items at a stride of sets × cache line size = 4,096 × 64 bytes = 262,144 bytes, you would only be using eight L2 cache lines for your traversal. Instead of being able to access 2MB of data before blowing the cache and having to fetch from main memory, you would only be able to access 8 × 64 = 512 bytes!

Now, a 262KB stride is a pretty specific scenario, but critical strides can affect you in more pedestrian situations as well.

Consider a one-channel texture that is 4096px on a side with 1 byte-per-channel. In other words, pixels equal bytes. If you were to traverse the first column of this texture, you would load a byte every 4,096 bytes. The first byte of each column won't share the same set, but the first pixel of every 64th row will.

To see this more clearly, consider the math involved in deriving a set from an address.

For simplicity's sake, let's assume our texture begins at address 0×0000. Since addresses are typically represented in hex, we will do the same. Remember 64 bytes in decimal is 0×40 in hex and the number of sets for this example 4,096 in decimal is 0×1000.

To derive the set, use the following formula:

$$\text{set number} = (\text{address / line size}) \% \text{numsets}$$

For address zero, it is obviously set zero, but let's try a more challenging address. Consider the address 0×40000.

$$0 \times 40000 / 0 \times 40 \% 0 \times 1000 = 0 \times 0$$

Where does the critical stride come in? The address 0×40000 is the first pixel of the 64th row of the texture, and shares the same set as address zero. This is an example of critical stride. By fetching the first text in row 0 and then the first texel in row 64, you have used two out the eight ways for set zero. If you were to continue with this stride, addressing 0×80000, 0×120000, and so on, you would quickly use all eight sets. On the ninth iteration with that stride, a cache line eviction must occur.

Because of how the cache is implemented, this is the worst case. Instead of having 2MB of cache available, you're down to 512 bytes. This leaves pre-fetching with very little room to compensate for slow memory. Similar issues occur with other large power-of-two strides, such as 512, 1,024, and 2,048. Figure 6.9 shows the performance of critical stride scenarios.

The best solution for this kind of problem is to pad your data to avoid larger power of two strides. If you know you are only reading memory once, as occurs when streaming music, you can use advanced SSE instructions.

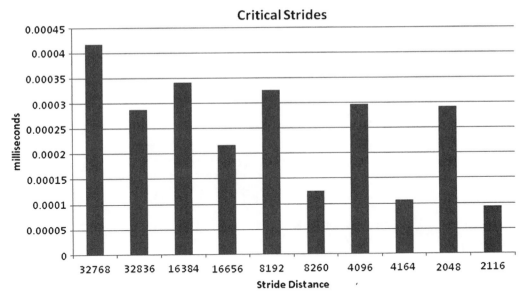

Figure 6.9

Average load time equals total time/number of loads. The source code for this test is available in the Performance Test Harness: "memory/criticalStride." These values will vary significantly, depending on the amount of data traversed and the architecture of your cache.

SSE Loads and Pre-Fetches

Doing one thing at a time faster is good. Doing four (or more) things at the same time is even better. For game developers, that is the basis behind using 128-bit SSE instructions. SSE instructions are an example of SIMD, or Single Instruction Multiple Data, operations. By using SSE instructions, you have access to special hardware that can perform operations in parallel.

Beyond Math with SSE

Typically, we think of SSE instructions as ways to increase math performance, but can SSE instructions offer a boost to memory fetching as well? It's difficult to tell by looking at the following chart in Figure 6.10. Without examining the trade-off of performance vs. accuracy, there is no way to compare apples to apples.

You can also use SSE instructions to provide software pre-fetching. By using software pre-fetching, developers can hint to the memory system in advance of the actual access. Pre-fetching preloads one cache line at a time. When using software pre-fetch calls, developers should, when possible, utilize many loads per software pre-fetch since cache line pre-fetch is not a computationally free instruction.

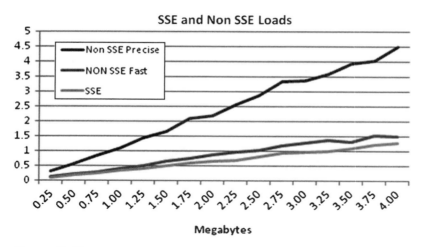

Figure 6.10

In this test, on this processor, SSE loads are significantly faster when using precise floats but only marginally faster than loads when using fast floats. The precision of fast and slow is a configuration setting in Microsoft Visual Studio.

One way to implement SSE instructions is to use intrinsics, which compile to specific assembly instructions. The intrinsic `call_mm_prefetch( char *p, int i )` provides four different types of pre-fetch enumerations:

`_MM_HINT_T0`: Pre-fetch data into all cache levels

`_MM_HINT_T1`: Pre-fetch data into level 2 cache, but not level 1

`_MM_HINT_T2`: Pre-fetch data into level 3 cache, but not level 1 or 2

`_MM_HINT_NTA`: Nontemporal access, loads directly to level 1 cache bypassing other caches

At the very least, we can suggest that use of software pre-fetch requires special care and testing across many processors to ensure reliable performance increases across all processor versions. A simple alternative to using software pre-fetching is to use an access pattern such as linear access forward or backward to ensure best-case use of automatic hardware pre-fetch.

For more information on computing with SSE, see Chapter 8, "From CPU to GPU."

Write-Combined Memory

Accessing memory on a device across the bus from the CPU is problematic. Even if the device's bandwidth is adequate, the bus is even slower to serve requests than main memory. If you are, for instance, updating a vertex buffer in GPU memory, reading data back can introduce significant delays because of the extra roundtrips over the bus.

For this reason, write-combining is implemented. Busses are most efficient when large, contiguous chunks of memory are written; small writes, or interspersed reads and writes, can be much slower. To keep writes big and fast, write-combining buffers are provided in the CPU. If data is written contiguously, then it is cached in the buffer until it can get sent all at once.

A practical example is shown here. Consider the following 32-byte vertex:

```
struct Vert
{
    float m_Pos[3];
    float m_Normal[3];
    float m_TUTV[2];
};
```

If you were to update this vertex, if it were a point sprite in a dynamic vertex buffer, would the following code seem appropriate?

```
for( int i=0;i<numVerts;i++ )
{
    vertArray[i]. Pos [0] = newValueX;
    vertArray[i]. Pos [1] = newValueY;
    vertArray[i]. Pos [2] = newValueZ;
    vertArray[i].m_Norm[0] = vertArray[i].m_Norm[0];
    vertArray[i].m_Norm[1] = vertArray[i].m_Norm[1];
    vertArray[i].m_Norm[2] = vertArray[i].m_Norm[2];
    vertArray[i].m_TUTV[0] = vertArray[i].m_TUTV[0];
    vertArray[i].m_TUTV[1] = vertArray[i].m_TUTV[1];
}
```

Write-combined memory is uncacheable, and doesn't travel through your memory system the way you may be accustomed to. Reads are done from system memory into the L1 cache. Writes are also handled differently. Instead of writing directly back across the bus, they are put into the write-combining buffers.

In the P4 processor, for example, you have six write-combined buffers that are each 64 bytes and act similarly to a cache line. When you update only the position, you are causing partial updates to each write-combined buffer. For example:

```
vertArray[0].m_Pos[0]=1;
vertArray[0].m_Pos[1]=2;
vertArray[0].m_Pos[0]=3;
vertArray[1].m_Pos[0]=4;
vertArray[2].m_Pos[1]=5;
vertArray[3].m_Pos[2]=6;
```

This would produce the following write-combined buffer (unwritten addresses are represented by dashes), as shown in Figure 6.11.

If you were to touch every address, including those whose value you don't update, it would produce a different write-combined buffer and would look like the following example shown in Figure 6.12.

Note that this implementation updates every address.

Now here is where the performance difference occurs. As stated earlier, we have six write-combined buffers in the P4. As we write back values, they are first written to a write-combined buffer. When all of the buffers have been exhausted, a previously used buffer must be evicted.

The rules of eviction are as follows: If you update the entire buffer, a 64-byte burst copies the data across the front-side bus. If the buffer is not completely modified, then the eviction occurs using 8-byte increments.

To recap, from the perspective of writing to nonlocal video memory, it is faster to update all values of the write-combined buffers than it is to partially update the write-combined buffer.

Figure 6.11
Updating only the changed values in 64 bytes of memory that map to one write-combined buffer.

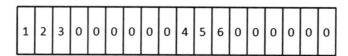

Figure 6.12
Updating and touching changed and unchanged values in 64 bytes of memory that map to one write-combined buffer.

Most applications don't spend a lot of code writing to the GPU. Usually, there are just a few key routines that deal with it. However, if written poorly, those routines can become a major bottleneck. Getting them right is important.

You can also make the GPU update itself, using geometry shaders or render-to-vertex-buffer operations.

Finally, some motherboards or hardware configurations result in write-combining being disabled. If you are doing a lot of profiling, you should make sure it's enabled before optimizing to take advantage of it.

Conclusion

Memory access patterns are a huge part of application performance. While learning all the tricks can take a long time, the basics aren't too complicated. Be sure to keep the following elements in mind:

- **Measure, measure, measure.** The figures in this chapter will differ from processor to processor.

- **You will never eliminate all cache misses.** But you can reduce them.

- **Memory system specifics vary from processor to processor.** Make sure to measure performance on the hardware your users will be using.

- **Do what you can to both conserve memory and access it linearly.** Linear access of contiguous, efficiently packed memory is the fastest option.

Remember, at some point you will reach a physical limitation that will be hard to overcome. Even cached memory takes time to read.

When this happens, don't forget that the fastest memory is the memory you don't touch—look for an algorithmic-level optimization that is cache friendly and reduces memory access. If your working set is small enough, you won't need any of the techniques we've discussed in this chapter.

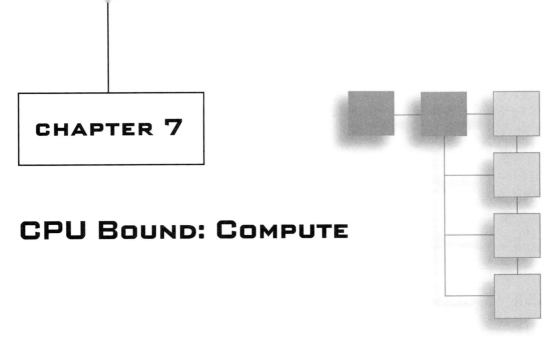

CHAPTER 7

CPU BOUND: COMPUTE

Compute bound programs are limited by the speed of internal operations of the CPU such as math, logic, or branching.

In many ways, this chapter contains the most "traditional" optimization discussions. How many of us have wondered at a really concise, optimized rendering loop? (See Michael Abrash's *Graphics Programming Black Book.*) Or studied the best way to do substring matching? (See Michael Abrash's *Zen of Code Optimization.*) Or researched highly efficient math operations? (See John Carmack's excellent inverse square root implementation. It is described at http://betterexplained.com/articles/understanding-quakes-fast-inverse-square-root/ and also in "Understanding Quake's Fast Inverse Square Root," a paper by Chris Lomont.)

However, if you have a single memory stall (as discussed in Chapter 8, "From CPU to GPU"), you've just lost thousands or millions of possible operations. You could wait dozens of milliseconds for a mass storage device to read a few bytes of data (see Chapter 12, "Mass Storage"). Or if you block on network IO (see Chapter 13, "Concurrency"), you could be waiting seconds for a packet!

All this is to say that you should make sure that your computation is the bottleneck by profiling before you spend much time optimizing it.

It's important for you to take advantage of the specialized capabilities of your target CPU(s). In the 1980s, the main distinguishing factor between supercomputers like Crays and standard mainframes was not raw computing speed. It was that the Cray had specialized hardware for doing certain operations extremely quickly. Seymour Cray's systems had support for vector operations, the forerunners of today's modern SIMD instruction sets such as MMX, SSE, and Altivec. Identifying and using special hardware capabilities for maximum performance is a key technique for speed.

There are many basic techniques that will help you get high performance, which this chapter will cover in detail. We will discuss how to deal with slow instructions, the basics of using SIMD to maximize speed, and what your compiler will and won't do for you. After reading this chapter, you should have a basic set of techniques to apply when faced with slow computation.

Micro-Optimizations

What is your favorite optimizing compiler? Have you even heard of an optimizing compiler? Back in the day, you would have had a compiler, and then, if you so desired you might have bought a better compiler that would perform optimizations. Now, it's likely that the compiler you own does plenty of optimizations—even free compilers do. Today's compilers perform very robust optimizations, such as link-time optimizations that optimize between object files.

If you want to start an argument, you could discuss either politics in a D.C. bar or micro-optimizations in a blog. As you will recall from Chapter 1, micro-optimizations are detail-oriented, line-by-line performance work. Hand-writing assembly, tweaking the order of specific operations, and the like all fall under this umbrella.

A program in a high-level language like C++ has many layers of abstraction above actual hardware operations, which is great since coding at the hardware level is hugely inefficient. The compiler converts C++ code into machine code that the processor converts into micro-code at runtime. Because of this, the net effects of changes on an individual line of code are difficult to predict without also knowing the exact compiler version, settings, and processor used to run the program.

Let's use the perf Test Harness test "compute/loopunrolling/unrolledEF" and vary the compiler settings on our copy of Visual Studio (any version from 6 on) to illustrate how the compiler's assembly can vary. Using the fast floating-point model (/fp:fast) yields significantly different assembly than if we used the precise floating-point model (/pf:precise).

The x86 architecture can do floating-point math in 32-, 64-, and 80-bit mode, and setting the compiler's floating-point model controls both how the internal

CPU precision is set, as well as whether or not extra instructions are added to perform explicit rounding or error checking. Compare the assembly listings in Listing 7.1.

```
// fp:precise
fld    dword ptr [eax-4]
add    eax,10h
sub    ecx,1
fadd   dword ptr [esp+8]
fstp   dword ptr [esp+8]
fld    dword ptr [esp+4]
fadd   dword ptr [eax-10h]
fstp   dword ptr [esp+4]
fld    dword ptr [eax-0Ch]
fadd   dword ptr [esp+0Ch]
fstp   dword ptr [esp+0Ch]
fld    dword ptr [eax-8]
fadd   dword ptr [esp+10h]
fstp   dword ptr [esp+10h]


// fp:fast
fld    dword ptr [eax-4]
add    eax,10h
sub    ecx,1
faddp  st(3),st
fld    dword ptr [eax-10h]
faddp  st(2),st
fadd   dword ptr [eax-0Ch]
fld    dword ptr [eax-8]
faddp  st(4),st
fstp   dword ptr [esp+10h]
```

Listing 7.1

With floating point model `fp:precise`, the compiler generates assembly in a manner that preserves accuracy; the `fp:fast` is using less accurate means but provides a significant increase in performance. Both implementations begin with the same C++ code of a loop performing addition. For reasons of length, the C++ code is not shown here.

As you can see, the floating-point model has a big impact on how much work gets done and in what way—in precise mode, our snippet has eight stores/loads. Fast mode does half as many. Not bad for changing a flag.

The code in the performance test "compute/fp_model" generates the previous assembly. Running the test in precise and fast mode shows that the flag can make a significant difference. On a test machine, the precise mode was 3.17 times slower than fast mode.

This example provides you with a simple example to understand how a micro-optimization may yield performance gains. More examples of micro-optimizations, and specifically floating-point optimizations, can be found throughout this entire chapter.

Compute Bound

When you find that your application is CPU bound, the next step is to determine whether you are compute or memory bound. You will want to use a profiler that can read the CPU counters to do this; see Chapter 4 for an overview of tools. Chapter 6's "Detecting Memory Problems" section discusses how you can distinguish between memory and compute bound applications.

Basically, if your application is CPU bound and not bound by memory or instruction fetching, it is bound by computation. You can confirm this by looking at the code identified as a hotspot. If it is doing a lot of arithmetic operations, not loads or stores, you are probably looking at a computational bottleneck. If the number of cache misses for the suspicious code is low, that's another supporting condition.

Lookup Table

Optimization has been described as the art of trading time against space in the search for speed. Lookup tables (and related techniques) are the most direct instance of this trade. They trade memory for performance by storing the results of calculations in memory and doing a lookup in the table instead of performing the calculation.

The classic lookup table example is speeding up sin/cos. Many older games didn't require high accuracy in their trigonometric equations, so they would approximate sin/cos in, say, 1,024 steps by having an array 1,024 entries long containing precalculated values. Then when they needed to calculate sin/cos, they would simply look up in the table, saving a lot of computation.

Unfortunately, the gap between memory fetch performance and calculation has only grown. As a result, lookup tables are less often the obvious choice for performance.

Memory Speed versus Computation Speed

Herb Sutter has a great article called "The Free Lunch Is Over," which discusses how memory speed and computation speed have grown over the past several decades. He discusses the implications for program design and performance. You can read it at <http://www.gotw.ca/publications/concurrency-ddj.htm>.

If the penalty of cache misses exceeds the performance gain from skipping the calculations, then the lookup table is useless. Fetching calculations from a large table may evict other values, resulting in compulsorily cache misses for upcoming instructions. It's likely that the use of a lookup table will result in a random memory traversal pattern, which we learned in Chapter 6 is a bad case for automatic hardware pre-fetching and is likely to cause frequent cache misses.

The best case for lookup tables is when they are small enough to stay cache resident, and then they can save you a large amount of computation. Use a lookup table when the table is small, when access to the returned calculations maintains spatial locality, or when the amount of calculation saved is worth the price of cache misses. In other words, you should test your lookup table's performance compared to simply calculating the values you need. Make sure to take into account varying cache sizes of different hardware targets.

Memoization

An alternative to lookup tables is memoization. *Memoization* is a specialized form of caching that stores the results of computations for reuse. In both approaches, you end up with a table storing results you can quickly look up, but memoization generates that table dynamically.

The basic idea behind memoization is that when you complete a calculation, you make a "memo" to yourself noting the inputs and outputs of the calculation. For instance, suppose that you wanted to calculate the Fibbonaci sequence. Each successive number in the Fibbonaci sequence is made up of the sum of the previous two numbers. Or more mathematically:

```
F(0) = 0
F(1) = 1
F(n) = F(n−1) + F(n−2)
```

Suppose that you implemented this by using a simple recursive function that computes the Nth value.

```
int fibonacci(int n)
{
     if(n==0) return 0;
     if(n==1) return 1;
     return fib(n-1) fib(n-2 );
}
```

This will give you the correct results, but very slowly since there are many function calls and redundancy. You can speed things up quite a bit by using memoization.

```
map<int, int> fibonacciMemos();

int initialize()
{
     fibonacciMemos[0] = 0;
     fibonacciMemos [1] = 1;
}

int fibonacci(int n)
{
     // Check for a memo about this number.
     map<int,int>::iterator i = fibonacciMemos.find(n);
     if(i == fibonacciMemos.end())
     {
         // Calculate the fibonacci number as we would normally.
         int result = fib(n-1) + fib(n-2);
         // Store the result for future use.
         fibonacciMemos[n] = result;
         // And return.
         return result;
     }
     // Look it up and return.
     return fibonacciMemos[n];
}
```

The performance gains you see are dependent on the time it takes for the memory reads vs. the time involved in the calculation. If the memory lookup you create (the map in the above example) is hardware cache friendly, the savings will almost always validate the effort of implementation. For an example of an ideal memory lookup for memorization, refer to the perf-TestHarness test "compute/fibonacci." The memoization example in this case is ideal, and the performance increase is in the hundreds of percents. Your mileage on other memoization opportunities may vary depending on the cache friendliness of your requests.

A common extension to this technique is to cap the memo storage space, making it a cache. For instance, perhaps only the most recently accessed 1,024 memos will be kept. This is useful for more complex calculations that can give larger results. You will want to profile carefully to make sure that you are striking the right balance of cache vs. calculation.

Another useful technique is to make memoization work with larger or more numerous input parameters. A key gating factor on the performance of memoization is the cost of looking up the right answer. If you have a hundred string parameters, it might become very costly to do this. There are many solutions, but the most common ones are either nested hash tables or combining the multiple input parameters into a single key that supports quick comparisons. Make sure that you handle collisions correctly in the latter case.

A practical example of memoization is the post-TnL cache on the GPU, which we'll discuss in Chapter 9, "The GPU." This cache significantly reduces the number of times the vertex shader must be run.

Function Inlining

The goals of abstraction and performance often conflict. An abstracted codebase will have lots of little functions and classes, which can make it easier to extend and maintain, but it will cost in performance because of the overhead of making lots of little function calls. Removing a little abstraction in a compute bound routine can pay big dividends.

Function inlining occurs when the compiler (or developer) takes the body of a function and replaces calls to that function with direct execution of the body code. For example:

```
int cube(int i){return i*i*i;}
int main(int argc, char* argv[])
{
    for(int i=0; i<100; i++)
        printf("%d\n", cube(i));
}
```

Could be rewritten as:

```
int main(int argc, char* argv[])
```

```
{
    for(int i=0; i<100; i++)
        printf("%d\n", i*i*i);
}
```

This is beneficial since calling a function has overhead. It depends on your calling convention, but function calls commonly include the following steps:

1. Push function parameters on the stack.

2. Create a new stack frame.

3. Save any currently used registers.

4. Allocate local variables.

5. Execute the function.

6. Release local storage.

7. Restore saved registers.

8. Restore the stack.

With function inlining, these steps are eliminated or reduced, and the CPU can spend its time doing productive work rather than doing bookkeeping. In addition, inlining can offer more opportunities for the compiler to optimize code, since it can mix the inlined code with the surrounding function's code for better performance.

Sounds good, but similar to other optimizations, there are some catches. First, bear in mind that function inlining is another space vs. time trade-off. Instead of having a single block of machine code for that function that everything jumps to, you are essentially replacing the few bytes it takes to call that function at each call site with the actual machine code implementation of the function. This increases executable size, which isn't necessarily bad by itself (people have lots of RAM and disk space), but carries another, more subtle problem.

Inlining increases the working set of instructions, which means that there is effectively less room in the instruction cache, because it has to store duplicates of the same code.

Of course, inlining by hand is a huge maintenance nightmare. It makes a lot more sense to let the compiler do it, which it will generally do on its own when it feels inlining makes sense. You can also hint that you'd like a method or function to be inlined by using the `inline` keyword.

How compilers handle inlining differs, so let's use the Visual Studio 2008 compiler documentation to explore how Microsoft's compiler interprets the standard.

There are two major decisions a compiler must make before inlining a function. First, it performs a cost/benefit analysis. Among other things, this is based on the size of the function to be inlined. The best candidates for inlining are functions that are small, fast, and called frequently from only a few call sites. If the compiler believes this code would be faster left as a function call, then inlining does not occur.

There are also some situations where inlining isn't readily possible. For instance, if a virtual function is called in a situation where the specific type cannot be inferred, then the function cannot be inlined (since the specific implementation will only be known at runtime). Function pointers also invalidate inlining attempts for a similar reason.

Recursion is incompatible with inlining, since the compiler would have to either solve the halting problem or produce a binary of infinite size. (Turing introduced the halting problem, but Stroustroup noted that inlining recursive code requires that the compiler solve it.) There's typically a small laundry list of cases for every compiler where inlining is not possible. Check the compiler docs for details.

If all these conditions are met, the function will be inlined.

You can use the `__forceinline` keyword to disable the cost/benefit analysis and force a function or method to be inlined whenever possible, subject to the restrictions mentioned previously. This compiler heuristic is pretty good, so unless you have strong performance numbers to back it up, don't go sprinkling `__forceinline` around your codebase, because it's liable to hurt more than it helps.

In general, the guideline with inlining is to let the compiler deal with it unless you can find evidence that you need to step in.

Inlining versus Inline Assembler

Do not confuse function inlining with the inline assembler, which allows you to write assembly code from within higher-level languages. Function inlining uses `—asm` blocks to notify the compiler of the use of assembly.

Also confused are function macros and function inlining. They have some similarities, but in general, function inlining is a much better choice. Macro expansion is a purely lexical operation, which can lead to strange side effects. Let's clarify with an example. In the following code, cubei and cube produce different answers:

```
#define cube(x) (x)*(x)*(x)

inline int cubei(int i){return i*i*i;}

int main(int argc, char* argv[])
{
    int i=0,j=0;
    int k = cube(++i);
    int l = cubei(++j);
    return 0;
}
```

The cubei function will evaluate its arguments (++j) once and return an answer of 1. The cube macro will evaluate its argument each time it is used in multiplication and return 6. For this reason, unless you actually want lexical expansion, stick with functions.

Another reason to stick with functions is that debuggers are usually line oriented, and will not let you step easily through or see the contents of macros, since they are unexpanded in the source code view. Meanwhile, inline functions will be treated more intuitively, and are easier to debug.

Branch Prediction

Out-of-order execution allows you to have multiple instructions in flight at the same time. Parallel execution can give major performance wins. However, it does complicate something, namely branching.

Branches come in two varieties: *conditional* and *unconditional*. Unconditional branches are easy to handle; they always jump to the same instruction, no matter what. As a result, they don't affect out-of-order execution.

Conditional branches, however, pose a problem. The branch can't be taken until any instructions that affect the decision are finished executing. This introduces "bubbles," periods of halted execution, in the execution pipeline. Instruction reordering can help to avoid bubbles, but it's still a problem.

To get around this, most CPUs predict which way the branch will go, and start speculatively executing based on the prediction. Some branches will be hard to guess, but a lot of them look like this:

```
for(int i=0; i<100; i++)
    doWork();
```

In 99 out of 100 times, the branch in this loop is going to repeat. A lot of the time, branches will always go the same way. If the CPU only guessed that the branch would go back for another loop, it would be right 99% of the time—not bad for a simple strategy!

If the CPU mis-predicts a branch, it just discards whatever work it guessed wrong and carries on. This wastes a little bit of work, but not much, because a branch prediction miss is roughly equivalent to the depth of the CPU pipeline (Intel Software Optimization Guide). A successful branch prediction is free, like on the P4, or very low, like predicted, taken branches on the Pentium M.

The processor's ability to predict a branch is dependent on the branch prediction algorithm the processor uses and the predictability of the branch. Generally, the less random a condition is, the less likely the processor will miss a branch. Some processors can support periodic patterns for branch prediction, while others will not. A condition that is 50% randomly true or false is completely unpredictable and likely to cause the most branch prediction misses. Branch prediction often uses a branch target buffer to store historical data on which way branches have gone. This can give a major accuracy improvement for predictions.

After you've identified a hot spot that is bottlenecked by branch mis-predictions, there are several techniques you can use to help reduce misses. The cost of a single cache miss is many times greater than a branch mis-prediction, so make sure that you have correctly identified your bottleneck.

What can you do to help reduce prediction misses? The following sections discuss this issue.

Make Branches More Predictable

Consider the following code inside a function:

```
if( condition[j]>50 )
      sum+=1;
else
      sum+=2;
```

Using VTune to perform a rough guide of performance on a Core 2 Duo with Visual Studio 2008, we found that when myArray is initialized with random numbers...

```
myArray[i]=rand()%100;
```

...as opposed to an initialization that uses numbers less than 50, such as...

```
myArray[i]=rand()%10;
```

…the latter resulted in considerably slower execution time. The random initialized conditions performed roughly 3.29 times slower than the nonrandom branch. As usual, numbers will vary based on your specific situation.

Remove Branches

Another option is to simply remove branches. In some cases, you can avoid traditional, bubble-causing conditionals and use instructions that are designed to pipeline more effectively, like CMOV or some SSE/MMX extensions. Some compilers will automatically use these instructions, depending on their settings.

You can also convert some branch-based operations into more traditional arithmetic operations. For instance, you could rewrite:

```
if(a) z = c; else z=d;
```

As:

```
z = a*c + (1−a)*d;
```

This will completely remove the need for branching. You will notice that it does at least double the cost of the "branch," since both sides need to be calculated and combined, so you need to measure the benefits carefully. On a micro level, this sort of approach can be problematic. On a higher level, the same concept can bear fruit more reliably. For instance, if you can write your conditionals so that 90% of the time they branch the same way, it helps the CPU predict the execution path correctly.

Profile-Guided Optimization

Some compilers (GCC 4 and newer, MSVC2005 and newer) support profile-guided optimization. (GCC refers to this as "feedback-guided optimization.") PGO helps with branches in a couple of contexts. Branches the compiler generates for things like virtual function call dispatches and switches will be optimized for the common case. Because PGO will optimize every case, it won't be guaranteed to help speed up a bottleneck, but it will give you an overall boost.

Loop Unrolling

Back before compilers would unroll a loop for you, programmers noticed that unrolling a loop achieved better performance than leaving it rolled. Let's start by explaining what loop unrolling is via a simple example:

```
int sum = 0;

for( int i=0;i<16;i++ )
{
    sum +=intArray[i];
}
```

This loop will execute 16 times. That means that you will have 16 addition assignments and 16 iterator updates. You will also execute 16 conditional statements. For every iteration of the loop, you must perform a conditional branch and an increment.

Unrolling this loop might look like this:

```
int sum=0;

for( int i=0;i<16;i+=4 )
{
    sum+=myArray[i];
    sum+=myArray[i+1];
    sum+=myArray[i+2];
    sum+=myArray[i+3];
}
```

This version appears to dedicate more cycles to work (addition) and less to the overhead of updating the loop. The key word here is "appears." The compiler does some interesting things behind the scenes.

Your compiler is looking for opportunities to enhance performance, and when it finds those opportunities, it rewrites the code behind the scenes to make it faster and better suited to the CPU. These two snippets of code generate the same assembly in Visual Studio 2008 (although different settings may generate different code). Their performance is identical (see Listing 7.2).

```
//unrolled Loop
mov   esi,dword ptr [eax-8]
add   esi,dword ptr [eax-4]
add   eax,10h
add   esi,dword ptr [eax-0Ch]
add   esi,dword ptr [eax-10h]
add   edx,esi
sub   ecx,1
jne   unrolledLoopPerfTest::test+14h (419EF4h)
```

```
//Rolled Loop
mov   esi,dword ptr [eax-8]
add   esi,dword ptr [eax-4]
add   eax,10h
add   esi,dword ptr [eax-0Ch]
add   esi,dword ptr [eax-10h]
add   edx,esi
sub   ecx,1
jne   rolledLoopPerfTest::test+14h (419EB4h)
```

Listing 7.2

Both the unrolled and rolled loop generate the same assembly implementation for an integer loop.

Intel's "The Software Optimization Cookbook"[1] suggests the following optimization to the unrolled loop. It reduces data dependencies, which allows for more instruction level parallelism.

```
int sum=0,sum1=0,sum2=0,sum3=0;

for( int i=0;i<16;i+=4 )
{
     sum+=myArray[i];
     sum1+=myArray[i+1];
     sum2+=myArray[i+2];
     sum3+=myArray[i+3];
}

sum =sum+sum1+sum2+sum3;
```

As you can see, the code is effectively doing four sums in parallel and then combining the results. If you check out Chapter 13, "Concurrency," you will see how this approach leads naturally into true thread-level parallelism. It also leads to another valuable idea, that of SIMD instructions, such as SSE. It should be obvious how a single instruction that does four adds in parallel could be used to rewrite this loop.

One important wrinkle is dealing with leading and trailing data. This example is working with a fixed number of values. But what if it had a variable number of values to add? You could do any multiple of four with the previous loop, but you'd have to do something special to mop up the last 0–3 values:

```
int sum=0,sum1=0,sum2=0,sum3=0;

// Mask off the last 2 bits so we only consider
```

```
// multiples of four.
const int roundedCount = myArrayCount & (~0x3);
for( int i=0;i<roundedCount;i+=4 )
{
    sum+=myArray[i];
    sum1+=myArray[i+1];
    sum2+=myArray[i+2];
    sum3+=myArray[i+3];
}

sum =sum+sum1+sum2+sum3;

// Finish up the remaining values.
for(;i<myArrayCount;i++)
    sum += myArray[i];
```

For the trailing cleanup code, there are plenty of options to keep your speed up. For instance, you could use a `switch` statement and have cases for zero, one, two, and three remaining values. As long as you have plenty of values in `myArray`, the speed of the cleanup values won't be a bottleneck.

But what if you're using SSE and all the values have to be aligned? If you accept arbitrary arrays, there's no guarantee that they will be aligned for SIMD. (You can usually assume that the floats will be at their natural alignment, meaning that if there are seven or more, there will be at least one SIMD-able block.) The solution is to have leading and trailing cleanup blocks that deal with the unaligned segments, leaving a big juicy chunk of aligned data for SIMD to churn through.

```
int sum=0,sum1=0,sum2=0,sum3=0;

// Deal with leading unaligned data.
int i=0;
while(i<myArrayCount)
{
    // Check to see if we can move to the aligned loop.
    if(isAligned(myArray+i))
    break;
    sum += myArray[i++];
}

// Fast, aligned-only loop.
for( int i=0;i<myArrayCount&~0x3;i+=4)
    AddSSE(myArray+i, counters);
```

```
// Finish up the remaining values.
for(;i<myArrayCount;i++)
     sum += myArray[i];
```

In Figure 7.1, you can see how good the compiler is at optimizing simple loops. The light columns are times for versions compiled without compiler settings turned on, and the dark columns are times for versions with compiler optimization turned on. As you can see, there is a marked improvement in unrolled enhanced floating-point performance and all integer implementations.

Floating-Point Math

Floating-point math has been a longstanding hot topic for game developers. At first, having it at all was out of the question. At best, you could do a few thousand integer operations per frame. As time went on, hardware-supported floating point became available, but it was still slow. Eventually, it became possible to do a lot floating-point operations (FLOPs) if you were careful to treat your compiler and hardware just so.

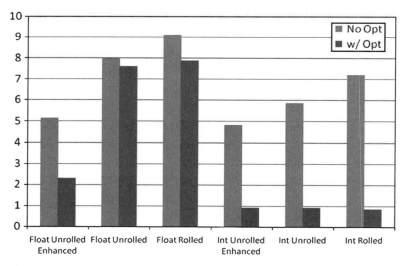

Figure 7.1

The differences between the different loop configurations are more apparent when optimizations are turned off. When turned on, implementations differ slightly on integers, but show a marked improvement on floating-point implementations. In other words, the compiler is able to analyze and optimize many of the loops to the same high level of performance despite the varying code. Time is in milliseconds.

Nowadays, you don't have to be quite as careful, but there are still some pitfalls. We're going to go into them both as a practical matter and as an opportunity to show how compiler flags can affect runtime performance and behavior. Even if floats aren't a problem for you, you're sure to run into some compiler behavior down the line that is similar.

The compiler in Visual Studio 2005 and 2008 includes the ability to reduce the precision of floating-point operations for faster performance by setting the compiler option `/fp:fast`. (Note, you can also do this in the Code Generation page of the compiler settings.) Figure 7.2 shows the performance difference between these flags. The documentation for this capability explicitly points to video games as a good example where precision may not be the ultimate goal.

Slow Instructions

When describing a CPU instruction's performance, the two main characteristics are latency and throughput. *Latency* is the number of clock ticks a given instruction takes. For example, the latency of a floating-point multiply on the Pentium M is 5 clock ticks. Divide on the Pentium M is 18.[2]

Throughput is always less than or equal to latency. For example, floating-point multiply throughput of the Pentium M is 2, which means that after 2 clock ticks, the execution unit can begin doing the next multiply. Divide's throughput matches its latency at 18; therefore divide must finish completely before begin-

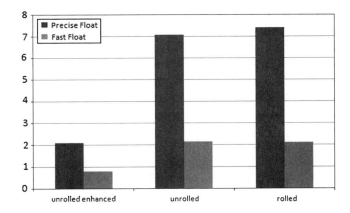

Figure 7.2

Floating-point model fast shows a significant performance increase over floating-point model precise for the loop unrolling floating-point tests.

ning the next. However, if you're considering breaking out the instruction latency tables and optimizing your instruction order, think again. In most cases, the compiler will know more about the CPU than you do, and it will be able to automatically order the instructions as well or better than you can. Unless you are late in development and looking at a specific bottlenecked routine, it is probably not the right time to spend a ton of time optimizing for slow instructions. In fact, even if you insert inline assembly, the compiler will still often reorder it for better performance.

The Importance of Measurement

Intel says in a processor optimization guide: "Due to the complexity of dynamic execution and out-of-order nature of the execution core, the instruction latency data may not be sufficient to accurately predict realistic performance of actual code sequences based on adding instruction latency data. In the old days, it was often possible to calculate ahead of time how a core would handle execution of some assembly code with good precision. Now, CPUs are complex enough that it's often more effective to do measurements and optimize based on observed values.

Make sure that you've checked the following things before jumping into assembly reordering:

- You're using the right algorithm. There's no point optimizing an algorithm if there's a better one.

- Cache misses aren't a bottleneck. A cache line fetch across the front side bus is more expensive than the slowest instruction.

- The compiler isn't set to do something poorly. Try setting some compiler settings to different values. Sometimes, specific combinations will make the compiler emit poor code—switching something up might make your problem disappear. And you should definitely make sure that you're optimizing a final binary, not a debug build.

With that out of the way, here are several techniques that can come into play when you start running up against slow floating-point performance.

Square Root

Square roots can be costly. They are often used for distance calculations. As a result, a program can easily end up taking many square roots every frame. A common trick is to do comparisons in distance-squared space, such as:

```
if( distanceSquared > lodDistance*lodDistance)
```

This trick trades maintenance (and sometimes memory, if you store distances as squared values) for performance. If you're finding that you're spending a lot of time in sqrt(), this can be a worthwhile trade.

Another option is to use your own square root approximation. You can trade speed for accuracy. There are several options. This method uses the integer representation of 1.0f and bit shifting to approximate a square root. A test of this method is available in the test "compute/bitwise/square_root/bit" and achieves significantly better results on a standard test machine.

```
int temp = *(int*)&floatVal;
temp -= FLOATING_POINT_ONE_POINT_ZERO;
temp >>= 1;
temp += FLOATING_POINT_ONE_POINT_ZERO;
return *(float*)&floatVal;
```

If you are calculating inverse square roots—for instance, for normalization—a good option is the method Carmack used in *Quake III: Arena*.

```
float InvSqrt (float x){
    float xhalf = 0.5f*x;
    int i = *(int*)&x;
    i = 0x5f3759df - (i>>1);
    x = *(float*)&i;
    x = x*(1.5f - xhalf*x*x);
    return x;
}
```

This method ends up being quite a bit faster than square root, at the cost of some performance. You can read a thorough treatment of the implications of this method in the 2003 paper "Fast Inverse Square Root" by Chris Lomont from Purdue University. Lomont reports it as 4x faster than the traditional (1.0/sqrtf(x)) and within 0.001 of true values.

Bitwise Operations

Because computers operate in binary, a working knowledge of bitwise manipulations is a powerful programming tool. Often, a few quick operations can elegantly replace what would otherwise be complex and slow code. Familiarity with this bag of tricks can save you time and pain.

For instance, suppose that you want to round a number to a multiple of 4. You could do it like this:

```
int rounded = (inNumber/4)*4;
```

which will work for the general case, but it involves a multiply and a divide, two fairly costly operations. But with a little bit of bit magic, you can do it this way:

```
int rounded = inNumber & ~3;
```

(Notice that, as with most of the tricks in this section, this will only work for powers of 2.)

This has two benefits. First, it's a bit faster, and second, once you get used to it, it's a more precise representation of what you want—you want to set certain digits to zero.

The most common demo of bitwise operations on the context of optimization is replacing multiplication/division by constant powers of two with a bit shift. For instance,

```
int divided = inNumber * 4;
```

Becomes:

```
int divided = inNumber << 2;
```

However, this is generally not worth your while to type, because any compiler will do this optimization internally. If you know that you will only ever be dividing/multiplying by a variable power of two, you can get a benefit, since if you do:

```
int divided = inNumber * variable;
```

The compiler normally can't infer that the variable will only be a power of two. That's only worthwhile if you're compute bound. Integer multiplications are fast. Do yourself a favor and use bit manipulation when it gains you some real convenience and power, not just a perceived performance win.

Useful Bit Tricks

We tested some popular bit level tricks and analyzed their performance. Run the compute/bitwise tests to see how these tricks perform on your computer.

Bitwise Swap

Instead of creating a temporary variable to swap two integers, use three bitwise exclusive ors. It's not faster but it can be useful in some situations. You must also ensure that variable X is not the same address as variable Y.

```
X^= Y; Y^= X; X^= Y;
```

Bitmasks

If you have several bools, you can pack them into a single byte or integer for better coherency. Assign each value a bit and test with bitwise-and, thusly:

```
isFlagSet = someInt & MY_FLAG;
```

You can easily save memory footprint for a struct or class by using flags as shown instead of bools. The main benefit is that it dramatically increases cache coherency while keeping the cost of checking for a flag cheap. Raymond Chen has some thoughts on "The Cost-Benefit Analysis of Bitfields for a Collection of Booleans" on his blog, "The Old New Thing" at <http://blogs.msdn.com/oldnewthing/archive/2008/11/26/9143050.aspx>.

```
// Enums are a good place to store flags.
#define BIT(x) (1<<x)
enum
{
    Flag0 = BIT(0),
    Flag1 = BIT(1),
    Flag2 = BIT(2),
    Flag3 = BIT(3),
}


// Example of setting and reading flags.
unsigned char flags = Flag1 | Flag3;
if(flags & Flag2) doSomething();


// We can clear a flag with by bitwise and-ing with the inverse of that flag.
flags &= ~Flag2;


// We can set a flag by bitwise or-ing it in.
flags |= Flag3;


// You can also clear/set/test multiple flags at a time:
flags |= Flag1 | Flag2;
flags &= ~(Flag2 | Flag3);
if(flags & (Flag1|Flag2)) ifFlag1OrFlag2WereSet();
if(flags & (Flag1|Flag2) == (Flag1|Flag2)) ifFlag1AndFlag2WereSet();
if(flags & ~Flag3) ifAnyOtherThanFlag3WereSet();
if(flags & (Flag1|Flag2) == Flag1) ifFlag1IsSetAndFlag2IsNot();
if(flags == Flag1|Flag3) ifOnlyFlag1AndFlag3AreSet();
if(flags != Flag2) ifAnyConfigurationExceptOnlyFlag2IsSet();


// Some more advanced tricks:
if(~(flagA ^flagB) == (Flag1|Flag2)) ifFlag1And2AreDifferent();
if(flagA | flagB == (Flag2|Flag3)) ifBetweenAAndBFlag2And3AreSet();
```

Fast Modulo

If performing modulo arithmetic on powers of two, use the bitwise-and operator.

```
X & 255; //is the same as X%256
```

In other words:

```
X%Y = X&(Y-1) iff Y is a power of 2.
```

Even and Odd

Using bitwise-and, you can determine if a variable is even or odd.

```
(X & 1) == 0; //is the same as X%2==0
```

This generalizes to any power of 2, which is useful for generating checkerboard patterns (for example, X & 2, X & 3).

Absolute Value

Generate an always positive value of a given signed integer. This is for 32-bit integers; for 64 bits, you need to use a constant of 63.

```
(X ^(X >> 31)) - (X >> 31);
```

Comparing Signs

Determine if two signed integers share the same sign.

```
X ^Y >= 0
```

Getting Next Higher Power of Two

```
unsigned int v; // compute the next highest power of 2 of 32-bit v
v--;
v |= v >> 1;
v |= v >> 2;
v |= v >> 4;
v |= v >> 8;
v |= v >> 16;
v++;

return v;
```

Fast Log2

```
const float v; // find int(log2(v)), where v > 0.0 &&
             // finite(v) && isnormal(v)
int c;       // 32-bit int c gets the result;
c = *(const int *) &v;
c = (c >> 23) - 127;

return c;
```

Further Tricks

A great site for learning more of these sorts of bit twiddling tricks is "Bit Twiddling Hacks" by Sean Eron Anderson, located at http://graphics.stanford.edu/~seander/bithacks.html. It has tricks like counting numbers of set bits, conditionally setting/clearing bits without branching, and more.

Be aware that bit tricks rely on the format of signed numbers. For a standard x86 processor, all this will work, but if you go to more exotic hardware you will have to be aware of the bit encoding that integers and floats use to know if the same tricks still apply. In general, all the tricks for unsigned integers will work anywhere.

In some cases, bit tricks can even act as vectorization. For instance, www.stereopsis.com/ has some great discussions about doing stuff this way. Especially look at the "FPU Tricks," "Double Blend Trick," "Fast log2," and "Fast P3 Memory Access" discussions.

Datatype Conversions

Processors natively support several different data types (signed/unsigned integers of various widths, half/single/double floats, SIMD formats, flags, etc). Because of this, data frequently needs to be converted from one format to another. Although good design can minimize this, it's impossible to write a program of any complexity without conversions.

However, conversions can be expensive. The standard for C++ states that when casting from float to integer, values are to be truncated. For example, 1.3 and 1.8 are converted to 1. A compiler might implement this truncation by modifying the floating-point control word from rounding to truncation, which is a slow process. If the compiler can use SSE instructions, it avoids costly modification of the floating-point control word.

Intel's "The Software Optimization Cookbook" suggests a rounding technique that uses a magic number and the structure of floating point numbers to approximate the truncation.

```
float f+=FLOAT_FTOI_MAGIC_NUM;
return (*((int *)&f) - IT_FTOI_MAGIC_NUM) >> 1;
```

In Visual Studio 2008, even with optimizations turned off and floating-point model set to precise, the compiler uses the SSE conversion, eliminating the need for modifying the floating-point control word.

Conversions from float to integer are more costly than from integer to float. On our standard machine, the magic number method, listed as ftoi_fast in the performance harness, showed slightly slower performance than the SSE version compiled by Visual Studio 2008. Figure 7.3 compares several methods for converting from integer to float.

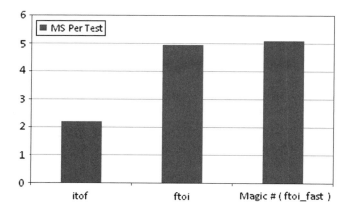

Figure 7.3

Comparison of execution time for different methods for converting from float to integer. Time is in milliseconds.

SSE Instructions

Vector instructions have a long and distinguished history in the realm of high performance computing. From the early days of vector processing with Cray to the latest SIMD instruction sets like SSE and LRB, vector ops have been the key to speed. SSE uses dedicated hardware registers capable of performing a single instruction on multiple data (SIMD) to achieve parallelism.

Time to rewrite your math library for the Nth time? Well, if it was written sometime in the past decade, it probably already takes advantage of SIMD. If you use the D3DX functions bundled with DirectX, they already take advantage of SSE. However, simply rewriting your math library isn't going to be your biggest win.

The best place for SSE is going to be when you have a whole algorithm you can SIMDize. When you can stay exclusively in the SSE registers for an extended period, you can often get large performance gains.

The remainder of this section focuses on opportunities for compute wins. For a discussion of SSE's memory streaming and cache management capabilities, see Chapter 6, "CPU Bound: Memory."

History

The quest for a multimedia friendly processor is a difficult one. Typically, multimedia processors, like Sony's Cell, attempt to reach this goal by providing enhanced support for vector processing. Intel's SSE instruction set represents the most widely accepted means for introducing hardware accelerated vector processing into widely distributed software.

History of Vector Processing

Intel is not the only source for vector operations; most other CPU architectures have their own instruction sets. The history of vector processors is pretty interesting, because it is motivated entirely out of a desire for performance. See "Vector Processors" on Wikipedia for a good overview.

With each version of the SSE instruction set, the capabilities and in some cases data type support increases. The first version of SSE instructions were integer only; today's instruction set provides functionality for floats, doubles, integers, long integers, and bit fields.

Basics

How can you put SSE to work for you? You can access the instructions directly via assembly. But most of the time, you will use intrinsics, special functions provided by the compiler that always compile to SSE instructions. The most convenient option is to use a library that deals with SSE for you. In addition, some compilers will go above and beyond to translate your standard C code into SSE instructions through a process called *auto-vectorization.*

In Chapter 6, we mentioned data alignment and the effects on runtime performance of memory. Data alignment issues are important with SSE instructions since the design of the hardware relies on it for execution. Failing to use 16-byte alignment for SSE instructions and 8-byte alignment for MMX will lead to a crash due to hardware fault. Special allocation functions are available to ensure alignment. There are system-provided aligned-allocation functions, but many developers implement their own by allocating the number of bytes needed plus the value of the alignment number and offsetting to the first 16-byte aligned address.

Example: Adding with SIMD

Let's examine a simple array traversal to show how a typical vectorized C/C++ implementation looks.

First, you have to do a bit of overhead work to be able to use the SSE intrinsics. These macros use the _ _mm128 primitive as inputs. So your first task is to load your data from your C style array or structure, into the _ _mm128 primitive. This is relatively simple to do with the following code:

```
_ _m128 sseVec = _mm_load_ps( &m_Vector );
```

m_Vector must be 16-byte aligned memory. For more on how to align memory, see the following sidebar.

Allocating Aligned Memory

To allocate static memory, you can use a compiler directive in front of the member you would like to align. Visual Studio and GCC use different compiler directives to achieve this. You can make your code work on both compilers by using the following definitions:

```
#ifndef __WIN32__
#define _align16_ __attribute__((align(16)))
#else
#define _align16_ __declspec(align(16))
#endif
```

Now that you have defined align16, you can use it to tell the compiler to align the memory automatically.

```
__align16__ float m_Vector[4];
```

Or:

```
__align16__ struct Particles
{
      float m_Position[4];
}
```

To dynamically allocate aligned memory, use the mm_malloc call (unless your memory manager provides a better path). You can access this call by including #include <xmmintrin.h>. To allocate 100 floats in an array that are 16-byte aligned, use the following function:

```
(float*)_mm_malloc( 100 * sizeof(float),16);
```

If you need to implement your own aligned alloc, then you need to allocate a block of requested_size + alignment-1 and then offset from the beginning of the returned block to the first aligned byte (i.e., (allocated_block + alignment) & ~(alignment-1), assuming alignment is power of 2 in size). You can also look for other standard aligned-allocation functions like memalign or posix_memalign.

The update loop in a very basic form of a particle system may look like the following:

```
_align16_ struct Particle
{
      float position[3];
      float velocity[3];
}

for( int i=0;i<m_NumParticles;i++)
{
```

```
        pParticle* pPart = particleArray[i];
        pPartposition.x += pPartvelocity.x;
        pPartposition.y += pPartvelocity.y;
        pPartposition.z += pPartvelocity.z;
}
```

An obvious enhancement would be to do the addition using SSE. Instead of six loads, three adds, and three stores, you could do two loads, one add, and one store. The code for this approach would look something like this:

```
for( int i=0;i<m_NumParticles;i++ )
{
        pParticle* pPart = particleArray[i];
        AddSSE( pPart->position,
        pPart->velocity,
        pPart->position );
}

void AddSSE( float* vec1, float* vec2, float *out )
{
        __m128 a = _mm_load_ps( vec1 );
        __m128 b = _mm_load_ps( vec2 )
        __m128 c = _mm_add_ps( a, b );
        _mm_store_ps(out, c );
}
```

While this works, it's not a very efficient use of SSE intrinsics since there is a lot of overhead for just one "add" call. Ideally, you would like to reduce the load and store calls required for an entire particle system update. Particle systems are much more complex than this simple example, and there will likely be more than just this simple position update. There's no need to load and store every time you want to use a single SSE instruction.

The solution requires some structural changes to the particle system. The first change is to redesign the particle structure from an array of structures (pParticle->[i]position) to a structure of arrays (pParticle->position[i]). For more on this conversion, see Chapter 6's discussion on AOS vs. SOA.

After your structure is in SOA format, you will traverse your loop four at a time. Keep in mind that the arrays for the structure must be 16-byte aligned. The enhanced code looks like the following:

```
_align16_ struct Particle
```

```
{
    float posX[100];
    float posY[100];
    float posZ[100];
    float posW[100];
    float velX[100];
    float velY[100];
    float velZ[100];
    float velW[100];
}

for( int i=0;i<m_NumParticles/4;i+=4 )
{
    pParticle* pPart = particleArray[i];
    pPart->position += pPart->velocity;
    __m128 posXvec = _mm_load_ps( pPart->posX[i] );
    __m128 posYvec = _mm_load_ps( pPart->posY[i] );
    __m128 posZvec = _mm_load_ps( pPart->posZ[i] );
    __m128 posWvec = _mm_load_ps( pPart->posW[i] );

    __m128 velXvec = _mm_load_ps( pPart->velX[i] );
    __m128 velYvec = _mm_load_ps( pPart->velY[i] );
    __m128 velZvec = _mm_load_ps( pPart->velZ[i] );
    __m128 velWvec = _mm_load_ps( pPart->velW[i] );

    posXvec = _mm_add_ps( posXvec, vecXvec );
    posYvec = _mm_add_ps( posYvec, vecYvec );
    posZvec = _mm_add_ps( posZvec, vecZvec );
    posWvec = _mm_add_ps( posWvec, vecWvec );

    //remainder of particle update
}
```

Switching to this format is useful, especially if you plan on having a lot of batch calculations. While CPUs can do speculative execution, it's always nicest to give them large streams of data to process in fixed ways. This is part of the secret to GPU's incredible stream processing performance. (See Chapter 13, "Concurrency" for the other part of the secret.)

The final approach to this particle system contains several other challenges. After updating the particle, a copy from CPU memory to a vertex buffer (which is in nonlocal video memory) must occur. That copy is on one particle at a time instead of four at a time. Doing so ensures that you don't copy inactive particles to the renderable particles. We will leave that portion of this particle system as an exercise for the user. Of course, if you are implementing a particle system with heavy performance requirements, you will want to put it on the GPU or use concurrency. (Chapter 13 discusses using concurrency, and Chapter 16 discusses how to run general-purpose code on the GPU.)

Trusting the Compiler

Compilers are smart. You can't rely on them to do exactly what you want at any given place in the code, but in aggregate, they do a pretty good job. As a programmer, you don't have the time or motivation to look for a hundred little optimizations in every line of code, but the compiler has plenty of energy for that purpose.

Some developers are very suspicious of their compilers. And indeed, some compilers are worth being suspicious of. As part of your basic profiling work—benchmarking and identifying bottlenecks—you will quickly get a sense of whether you can trust your compiler, because if it isn't being smart, you'll catch lots of performance sinks. If you're using a recent version of a big name compiler, like GCC, Intel, or Visual Studio, it'll probably do pretty well (even if you have to tweak some options to get there).

Throughout the writing of this book, we've included tests to go along with our examples. The ability to write these tests has been challenging due to the fact that it is usually very hard to write wasteful code. Many times, the compiler surprised us by removing code we were hoping to use as our baseline.

No matter where you stand on the issue, it's difficult to argue that compilers have been doing anything but improving. Newer features, such as Visual Studio's profile-guided optimization, perform profiles on your executable and compile your program based on the collected data. Take a little time to get to know your compiler, and you will be pleasantly surprised.

Removing Loop Invariant Code

One of the most basic optimizations is the removal of invariants such as that inside of a loop. An invariant operation is one that occurs with every iteration, when only one is necessary. This test is available by viewing test `"compilerTest/ invariant."`

```
int j=0;
int k=0;
for( int i=0;i<100;i++ )
{
     j=10;
     k += j;
}
```

In this example, setting j=10 isn't the only invariant. The whole loop returns a constant value, and most compilers will reduce it to that constant, producing code equivalent to:

```
k = 1000.0f;
```

Consolidating Redundant Functions

The test "compilerTest/sameFunction" shows an interesting optimization. The code follows:

```
void test()
{
     gCommon +=TestLoopOne();
     gCommon +=TestLoopTwo();
}

float TestLoopOne()
{
     float test1=0.0f;
     for( int i=0;i<1000;i++ )
     {
          test1 += betterRandf();
     }

     return test1;
}

float TestLoopTwo()
{
     float test2=0.0f;

     for( int i=0;i<1000;i++ )
     {
          test2 += betterRandf();
```

```
    }

    return test2;
}
```

In this code, both `TestLoopOne` and `TestLoopTwo` do the same thing. The compiler recognizes this and removes `TestLoopOne` and forwards all references to the assembly generated for `TestLoopTwo`. Why does this happen? It's an optimization introduced as a side effect of C++ template support. Because templatized classes often generate the same code for different types, the compiler looks for functions with identical assembly, and in order to reduce overall executable size, removes the redundancy. This can add up both in terms of instruction cache efficiency and binary size.

Loop Unrolling

As described previously, compilers are good about tuning loop unrolling for best effect. While your compiler can do many things, it can't predict the future. A lot of optimizations won't occur because of the possibility of what could happen— even if it is unlikely. For example, let's take another look at the example listed earlier in the loop invariant section. If k was instead a global variable accessed by another thread, then the compiler would not fully optimize the loop. Since the variable is global, and therefore accessible to others, the value of k may change partially through the loop, changing the result.

Cross-.Obj Optimizations

Today's compilers have the ability to optimize between object files, and this process is known as *whole program optimization.* It takes longer, but it "flattens" the cost of calling between linkage units, as if your whole program were in one big C file. As a result, things such as inlining work a lot better.

Hardware-Specific Optimizations

While some compilers offer hardware-specific settings, a human can typically make better decisions about your platform than the compiler. However, this information doesn't help PC developers who are trying to build their game for thousands of PC configurations. For console development, understanding every last detail of your target machine will help you discover every nook and cranny of computing capability. (See Chapter 14, "Consoles," for more information on optimizing for consoles.)

If you are one of the lucky few game developers who get to choose your PC platform (such as kiosk games), then you may be in the same good graces as the console developer. If you are not, consider using the CPUID assembly call (and other system query methods) to extract more information about the PC at runtime. Using this data, you can create a single interface and multiple implementations for critical parts of your program where generalities aren't enough. These decisions may include things such as detecting the processor, cache size, or presence/absence of instruction sets like SSE.

For raw performance tuning, like choosing between high/medium/low rendering capabilities, you may want to simply run a brief benchmark at install time and allow players to adjust the settings later as needed.

Conclusion

CPUs are getting ever faster, but when you run out of computing power, it's time to optimize. Lookup tables, inlining, dealing with branch prediction, avoiding slow instructions, and SIMD instructions are techniques you can use to enhance the performance of your code. Modern compilers will make the most out of code that doesn't specifically target performance.

With good profiling techniques, careful design, and iterative improvement, even the worst compute bound application can shine, but don't forget, computing power has improved much faster than general memory fetching.

Works Cited

[1] Gerber. (2005) *The Software Optimization Cookbook.* Intel Press.

[2] Intel. (2001) *Intel Pentium 4 and Intel Xeon Processor Optimization.*

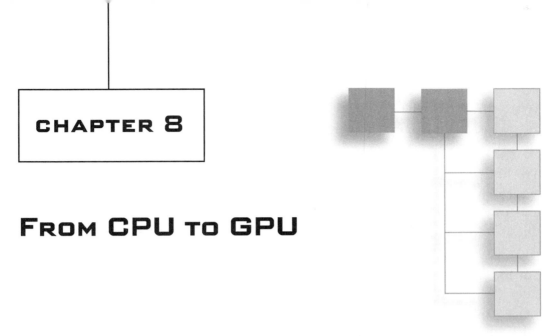

CHAPTER 8

FROM CPU TO GPU

Writing good rendering code is challenging because of the many changing variables. For most game projects, the art at the start of the project is nothing like the final art. The scenes get more cluttered and complex. Many more materials are present. Vistas are larger, and gameplay also has to happen sometime during execution.

Never mind that a major new OS might drop, new GPUs will become available, and drivers will be updated over the course of your project. For example, Microsoft does quarterly updates to DirectX. They aren't big, but you do have to test against them. OpenGL might be more stable, but there are still driver updates many times a year.

All these factors affect your game, but more importantly, it can change your performance picture quite a bit. If a driver update makes a specific case slow, you might be sunk without issuing a patch or doing some serious refactoring. Scary stuff!

Beyond all this, you have to know who your target audience is and what sort of hardware they will own when you release your game. You have to choose which of the veritable buffet of rendering APIs and capabilities you can and want to support. And all this might change over the course of a project, too.

You also have to choose a graphics API. DirectX 9 and DirectX 11 are the main options in the Windows world, while everywhere else you get to choose between a couple of flavors of OpenGL (or perhaps even a proprietary API). You might need to ship with support for a software renderer, like Pixomatic from RAD, WARP from Microsoft, or SwiftShader from TransGaming. If you are really cutting edge, you might implement your own renderer on top of OpenCL or CUDA!

The bottom line is that you must have a foundation in your code that will meet the changing needs of your project. You need to structure your architecture carefully, not only to be prepared to meet the performance needs of the project, but also the compatibility, porting, and scalability requirements.

We will go into a detailed discussion of getting maximum performance on the GPU in the following chapters. This chapter is about how to write your renderers so that you will survive that knowledge. Michael Abrash's *Graphics Programming Black Book* is a big, thick book, and mostly about how, while working on *Quake*, John Carmack and Michael Abrash kept completely rewriting their renderer for maximum performance. The state of the art is slower moving than that nowadays, but not by much.

One closing thought before we move into the meat of this chapter: Any time you, as a graphics programmer or optimizer, need inspiration, check out what the demo scene is doing. They can create works of art using nothing more than a few KB of data and clever hacks. There are hundreds of incredible techniques that have come out of that space due to the extremely tight requirements they face.

Project Lifecycle and You

We discussed how optimization fits with a project's lifecycle in a previous chapter. Let's revisit it very briefly as it relates to optimizing rendering.

There are many big changes that happen to rendering code as it goes from early project to late project. In the early phases, it does not have to work 100% right or be 100% stable. The art load is light, both in terms of model complexity and the sheer number of objects in the scene. Gameplay and the other subsystems that will strain the performance picture haven't been fully fleshed out.

By the time you hit the end of the project, the following has happened:

- Your game is being run on a GPU that was not on the market when you started the project.

- Rendering is 100% right and 100% stable. Getting this right can require some costly operations.

- The artists have gone nuts and put a unique material (with its own shader) on every item in the game. You now have 100x the state changes you started with.

- Gameplay and other systems have grown to require 100% of the CPU per frame.

How do you stay sane through all this? With careful preparation from day one of the project. And if you come in late—God help you, and try to get as much of our advice in as you can!

Points of Project Failure

Let's start by talking about common performance problems that projects are suffering from by the time they ship. If you have shipped a few games, these will come as no surprise. If you haven't, take heed and realize that you can't fix everything up front. It is better to take these problems as they come and spend your time when you need to. The main points of project failure when it comes to rendering are synchronization points, capability management, resource management, global ordering, instrumentation, and debugging capabilities.

Synchronization

A single synchronization point can cause huge performance loss. The GPU is a deep pipeline, taking rendering commands and resources in at one end and spitting out complete frames at the other. If you do something that depends on output, you have to wait for the pipeline to clear out before you can proceed.

Certain state changes have high overhead. For instance, a new pixel shader won't be able to take advantage of hardware that is already processing a shader program. The GPU will need to wait for the old shader to finish before loading the new shader into the memories of the multi-processors.

Worse than state changes are readbacks. A readback is when you lock a resource on the GPU and read data back from it. The data flow is optimized for pushing content from CPU to GPU, not the other way around, and this can often be very slow.

Locking the framebuffer or depth buffer, especially, has dire performance consequences. Not only must the pipeline be flushed, but all rendering also has to cease while the data is being read. If you are lucky, the drivers will copy it all back into a buffer and give that to you while other rendering is going on. However, this requires very careful coordination to pull off, since programs usually don't submit render commands while locking a resource.

Or you might be computing some vertex positions on the CPU and streaming them to a vertex buffer. If you're not careful, you might write code that stores temporary values (for instance by using *=) in the buffer, causing an extremely slow readback. Your authors worked on a project where we were doing that, and just by using a local temporary instead of the VB's memory, we saw a manyfold speedup in one of our inner loops.

If you are frequently locking something, you should consider just locking it once. The cost for locking any given resource is the initial stall while the GPU synchronizes with the CPU and the lock is acquired. If you lock again immediately thereafter, the synchronization work is already done, so the second lock is cheap. It's very smart to minimize the number of locks you acquire on a resource—doing a single lock per resource per frame is the best rule of thumb.

Caps Management

Another crucial piece for any good renderer is capability management. Capabilities, or *caps* as the DirectX 9 API names them, describe what a given card can do. In addition to binary questions like "Can I do wireframe?" there are some scalars you will probably want to know about, like "What is the highest level of MSAA supported?" or "How much video RAM is available?"

These sorts of things are essential to know because every card and vendor works a little differently, and not just in terms of varying video RAM. OpenGL and DirectX imply, by their nature as standardized APIs, that you can write rendering code once and have it run everywhere. While they certainly make that scenario easier, anyone who tells you your rendering code will always work on every card and computer is a liar.

It is not uncommon for some vendors to ship drivers or hardware that completely breaks in certain cases. Or for hardware/drivers to report that capabilities are available, but not to mention that they are very slow. On OS X, if you use an unsupported GL feature, it will switch you to a software implementation—talk about falling off the fast path!

Bottom line—you need to have a flexible system for indicating what cards need fallbacks or other work-arounds, as well as more mundane things like what level of PS/VS is supported or how much VRAM there is. This is very useful during the time period immediately surrounding launch—it's easy to add special cases as you run into them and push updates.

Resource Management

A lot of games, especially PC games, are unpleasant to play because of their resource management code. It might take them a long time to load things to the card. They might be wasteful of VRAM and perform badly on all but the highest-end systems. They might break during device resets when switching out of full-screen mode, or when resizing the game window. Level changes might result in resource leaks.

A big cause of performance problems is failing to get resource management right! We'll talk about what's needed in the "Managing VRAM" section that follows.

Global Ordering

Ordering your render commands is crucial for good performance. Drivers and GPU do not have good visibility into your scene's specific needs, so they mostly have to do what you say in the order you say it. And reordering render commands on the fly isn't likely to be a performance win, even if it could be done reliably due to the overhead of figuring out the optimal order.

Every computational problem becomes easier when you add constraints, and figuring out optimal render order is no exception. It's much, much cheaper for you to submit things properly.

It's worthwhile to think about the kind of rendering order that might be important. Maybe you want to draw all your reflections and shadow maps before drawing the main scene. Maybe you want to draw opaque stuff front-to-back and translucent stuff back-to-front. Maybe you want to sort draws by material or texture in order to reduce state changes.

Games have shipped doing awful things, like switching the render target in the middle of the frame to draw each reflection. So you can certainly get away with it, at least on the PC. But in those scenarios, the developers had to pay a high price. On consoles, the overhead of changing render targets can make this prohibitive. It's better to address the problem up front.

We'll discuss a flexible system to help deal with these sorts of sorting issues later in this chapter, in the "Render Managers" section.

Instrumentation

Good instrumentation means good visibility into your code. Renderers have lots of moving parts. You need to know which ones are moving! If you don't have a way of seeing that you're doing 10x too many locks per frame, you'll never be able to fix it.

The best thing here is to add a counter system and note important operations (like locks, draw calls, state changes, and resource creations/destructions). Tools like PIX and NvPerfHUD can also do this, but onboard tools are great because they are always available, even on your artist's or tester's computer.

Debugging

When you are debugging graphics code, tools like NvPerfHUD, PIX, gDE-Bugger, BuGLe, and GLIntercept are essential. One of the best things you can do is intelligently support their APIs for annotating your app so that it's easy to include the annotations in your rendering stream when appropriate, without always requiring the tools to be present. Don't forget your trusty profiler, either, because you can often spot rendering hotspots by looking for unusual numbers of calls to a block of code, API calls, or driver modules that take a large percentage of execution time (for instance, when locking a buffer).

Many projects have delivered subpar products because the developers didn't have an easy way to see what their code was (or wasn't) doing. When debugging complex rendering code, visibility into what's going on behind the scenes is key. Otherwise, you cannot make intelligent decisions—you're flying blind!

You also need tools in your engine to cross-check that what your code thinks it is doing is what is really happening, as reported by PIX, etc. Some generally useful tools include a command to dump a list of all known resources, a way to see what's in all your render targets, and the ability to toggle wireframe/solid rendering on objects. There are a ton of other possibilities if you have laid out your code sensibly.

Make sure that you have meaningful error reports that dump enough information so that you can interpret garbled reports from artists/testers. It's also smart to put warnings in if performance boundaries are exceeded, to help keep people from blowing the budget when building content.

Managing the API

Now that we've laid out some of the major problem areas for graphics coders, let's talk about what you can do to help deal with them. The first step is dealing with the API. Whether you are working with DirectX or OpenGL, there are a lot of things you can do to simplify life and prevent problems before they start to be a barrier.

Assume Nothing

The best rule with any rendering API is to assume nothing. Keep it at arm's length and use a minimal subset. When developing *Quake*, Carmack used a minimal subset of OpenGL, and for many years after, no matter what else didn't work, vendors would be sure to test that *Quake* ran really well on their hardware. As a result, staying on that minimal subset helped a lot of games run better.

Even on today's APIs, which are more mature and reliable than they were in those days, it still makes sense to find the common, fast path and use that for everything you can.

GL has GLUT and Direct3D has D3DX. GLUT and D3DX are convenient helper libraries that make it easier to get started with both APIs. However, they are not necessarily written with performance or absolute correctness in mind. (GLUT's window management code can be buggy and unreliable, while D3DX's texture management code can be slow and inefficient.) We highly recommend either not using these libraries at all, or if you do, being vigilant and ready to ditch them at the first sign of trouble. With a few exceptions, the things these libraries do can be done readily in your own code.

For more complex operations, like some of the mesh simplification/lighting routines in D3DX, you might consider running them offline and storing the output rather than adding a dependency in your application.

Build Correct Wrappers

Make sure that every basic operation you support—like allocating a vertex buffer or issuing a draw call—happens in one and only one place. This tremendously simplifies problems like "finding that one vertex buffer that is being allocated with the wrong size" or "preventing draw calls during a device reset." It also makes it easy to be sure you are doing the right thing in terms of calling APIs the correct way, doing proper error handling, consistently using fallbacks, and so on.

Having everything happen in only one place gives you yet another benefit. When you do encounter a problem in the hardware or with the driver, it makes it trivial to work around the problem.

You may want to wrap every single API call in routines that do error checking and validation on their behavior. Having wrappers also makes it easier to do useful things like log every call to a text file—a lot of data, but a very useful trick when you are trying to track down a rendering bug.

Wrappers also help a lot because they make it much simpler to port your rendering code from API to API or from platform to platform. Even large incompatibilities can be localized to a single file or method.

State Changes

State changes are a big part of the performance picture for rendering code. Advice to avoid too many is a perennial part of every GPU vendor's "best practices" talk. A state change happens whenever you change something via the rendering API, like what the current texture is, what the fill mode is, or which shader is in use. Newer rendering approaches, such as deferred shading, are designed to (among other things) reduce state changes, but it is difficult to remove them entirely.

One very useful trick is to use your API wrapper to suppress duplicate state set calls. Depending on the API and platform, API calls can range from "a relatively cheap, in-process call" to "very costly; requires calling kernel mode driver code." Even in cheap cases, suppressing duplicate calls is easy and reduces work for the driver. Just track each state's value and only call the API to set it if the new value passed to the wrapper is different.

Some drivers will actually batch similar states for you if they are called near to each other. For example, state changes A, B, A, B will actually submit to the hardware as A, A, B, B, thus reducing the overall stage change count by half.

Draw Calls

State changes tell the graphics card how to draw, but draw calls (DX's `Draw*-Primitives` or GL's `glDraw*` call) are what trigger actual work. Typically, the drivers defer all work until a draw call is issued. This helps reduce the cost of duplicate state changes (although they still have a noticeable cost).

The net result is that when you are profiling, you will typically find that your draw calls are where most of your graphics API-related time is going. This is largely due to work that the driver has to do to queue up all the commands so the GPU will render, which is not to say that a draw call itself doesn't have noticeable costs. Figure 8.1 shows the time in milliseconds that it takes to draw frames with varying number of draw calls. For comparison, we show two scenarios: no state changes (the best case) and varying the texture bound to sampler zero. Both cases draw to a very small render target—64px square—to minimize the impact of fill-rate while requiring the card and drivers to actually process the change. As you can see, there is a nice linear trend. Texture changes between draws are about triple the cost of straight draws.

However, this also suggests an upper limit. Every additional piece of state that changes consumes additional mspf. You cannot budget your entire frame for draw call submission. Suddenly, spending 5mspf on draw calls seems very generous. For a very simple scene with only textures changing between draw calls, you can do perhaps 6,000 draw calls. But if you are changing your shaders, changing render target, uploading shader constants, and so forth, that will quickly drop off to less—only one or two thousand calls.

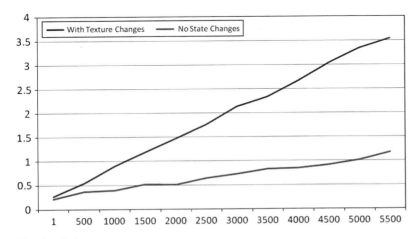

Figure 8.1

Time in milliseconds (Y-axis) for varying number of draw calls (X-axis). Notice that changing state for each draw (in this case, the active texture) dramatically increases the cost of each draw call. Each draw call only draws a few pixels in order to minimize actual work the GPU has to perform.

A symptom of draw call issues is clearly visible in Intel's VTune. When too many draw calls exist, the driver consumption of the CPU is extraordinarily high. If VTune's module view doesn't show high levels of utilization in the driver (usually a .dll file with either an NV or ATI in its name), then draw calls aren't your problem. If the driver does show a relatively high utilization and draw call numbers are in the 2000+ range, then your issue is quite clear—your application is CPU bound, which means the GPU is starving.

State Blocks

To remove the need to make dozens or hundreds of calls to the driver to modify the state between draw calls, it's possible to use state blocks. A state block is a group of related states that are all set at once, reducing GPU and driver workload. So, for instance, you can predefine values for all the states on a texture sampler at startup, and then instead of making a dozen calls to completely set it later, you can simply assign the state block.

One thing to be aware of with state blocks is that support for them can vary, especially on older or lower-end hardware. In some cases, they are emulated by the driver because it simply goes through the values in the state block and sets all the states normally. In this case, simply reducing state changes (as discussed elsewhere) will give you better performance.

As always, make sure to test on your target hardware to make sure that state blocks are a good fit. If the hardware doesn't support it, the drivers may emulate it more slowly than you could do it yourself.

Instancing and Batching

Are we stuck with less than a thousand objects? By no means.

For simpler objects like text, particle effects, motion trails, user interfaces, and similar low-poly objects, a common technique is simply to put all the objects into a single dynamic vertex buffer, transformed into world space or screen space as appropriate, and draw them with a single draw call per material. This works well for some scenarios, but it breaks down in more complex cases.

Instancing is a technique that allows you to resubmit the same geometry many times with different parameters, automatically. In short, instancing moves the overhead of draw call submission to the GPU. There are two different versions of instancing and each has positive and negative side effects.

- **Shader Instancing**: Constant instancing builds on dynamic instancing by moving the multiplication from the CPU to the GPU. A stream of instanced data accompanies the vertex data through the use of constants. This technique is sensitive to hardware constant minimums. Since attribute data may exceed that of the space available for constants, developers may need to break rendering into several draw calls. This is a fair trade-off in many cases and may reduce the number of draw calls from many to several. This technique is still memory intensive.

- **Hardware Instancing**: Hardware instancing is a feature of shader model 3.0 hardware. It achieves many of the positive elements of the other techniques with one major drawback—it requires shader model 3.0 hardware. Hardware instancing uses one data stream that contains a mesh. The second data stream contains attribute information. Using the `SetStreamSourceFreq` call, we are able to map vertex data to instance data. This method is both CPU and memory friendly. The instancing isn't free, however, and some cards may have overhead in pre-vertex parts of the GPU. In NVIDIA's PerfHUD, you may notice high levels of utilization in the vertex assembly unit.

Render Managers

The most obvious way to write a renderer is to have a bunch of objects that look something like this:

```
Class MyRenderableObject
{
    Matrix worldXfrm;
    VertexBuffer myMesh;
    void onRender()
    {
      Graphics->setTexture("red");
      Graphics->setBuffer(myMesh);
      Graphics->setTransform(worldXfrm);
      Graphics->draw();
    }
}
```

Then, for each visible object, the scene-drawing code calls `onRender` and off you go.

Naturally, over time, each object's rendering code gets more and more complex. If an object requires a reflection, it might do something like this:

```
void onRender()
{
     Graphics->setRenderTarget(myReflectionTexture);
     drawSceneForReflection();
     Graphics->setRenderTarget(NULL);
     // Draw the object normally using the reflection texture.
}
```

Aside obviously awful things like the previous example, each object ends up with slightly different rendering code for each specialized kind of drawing it does. Your rendering code ends up mixed in with your gameplay and other code. And because each object is working independently, with no global knowledge of the scene, it becomes very difficult to do something like optimize mesh rendering in general—you can only do fixes to each object.

What makes a lot more sense is to create render managers. They have a manager-specific way to submit items for rendering—for instance, a mesh + transform + material for a mesh render manager, but a particle render manager might just need a point in space for each particle. They have common interfaces for sorting and drawing, so that the core renderer can call them all equally. In other words:

```
class RenderItem;

class IRenderManager
{
     virtual void sort(RenderItem *items, int count)=0;
     virtual void render(RenderItem *items, int count)=0;
}

class MeshRenderManager
{
     RenderItem *allocateRenderItem(Mesh &myMesh, Material &myMaterial,
                                    Matrix &worldXform);
     void sort(RenderItem *items, int count);
     void render(RenderItem *items, int count);
} gMeshRenderManager;

MyObject::onRender()
{
     submitRenderItem(gMeshRenderManager.allocateRenderItem(mesh,
                      material, xfrm);
}
```

As you can see, now the object that is being drawn can concern itself with describing what it wants drawn, and the `MeshRenderManager` deals with how to draw it quickly and correctly.

Render Queues

An important piece in the example code shown earlier is the `RenderItem` and the sort/render calls. You notice everything works in terms of lists of `RenderItems`. Well, this is actually very useful when you want to do things like optimize render order. Look at the definition of `RenderItem`:

```
struct RenderItem
{
     float distance;
     IRenderManager *manager;
     unsigned int key;
     void *itemData;
}
```

You'll notice a couple of things. First, it is a 16-byte structure, so it is very cache friendly. Second, there is data to help with sorting, but most of the data for rendering is stored in `itemData`. With just this small amount of structure, you can handle most sorting quickly and easily.

Because you know what the manager is for each item, you can put opaque and translucent `RenderItems` into separate lists. You can do this either from explicit knowledge about the manager (for instance, all particle effects are probably translucent), or by querying it when creating the `RenderItem` (since it will have to know how each `RenderItem` is drawn).

Once that is done, you can easily sort by the distance field (which stores distance to the closest point on the object) if you want front-back/back-front ordering, or by grouping items by manager and letting the manager `sort()` them for maximum efficiency (whatever that means for that manager). For efficiency, the manager can encode sort-related data into the key field and only access whatever it stores in `itemData` when actually rendering.

Allocation overhead can be a problem, so we recommend pooling the memory used for `itemData` (per manager) and for `RenderItem` (per scene).

There are several variants on this idea, mostly relating to the packing. For instance, *Quake 3 Arena* encodes the *entire* render command into a single four-byte value. Forsyth recommends using a 64- or 128-bit value, so there's room for a pointer if needed. The approach we've outlined is nice because it is a little easier to follow and extend. With very tight packing there's a lot of range management required in order to avoid exceeding what you can address with (say) four bits. Of course, it can be worth it when you need your render sorting to really scream.

Since this makes sorting a great deal more flexible and extensible, and completely separates scene traversal and determining what needs to be rendered from the actual API calls required for rendering, it is a major building block for all sorts of rendering improvements. Two obvious improvements are keeping a queue per render target and the targets in a list with dependency information, so that you can easily arrange to touch every RT only once, and to buffer all the render queues so rendering can happen in a second thread.

Managing VRAM

We've covered some of the major concerns when dealing with your rendering API. The other major piece of any renderer is resource management, which is what this section covers.

In rendering terms, a resource is anything you allocate from the rendering API. It could be a state block, a vertex or index buffer, a texture, a shader, one or more shader constants, a query/fence, or a half dozen other things. Specifically, it is something you have to allocate from the API, use for rendering, and release during the course of rendering.

Getting resource management right is a big pain, but it is essential for good performance. There are two contexts in which performance is important: at device reset time, and during normal rendering. The following sections cover dealing with those contexts.

Dealing with Device Resets

Device resets can happen in both GL and Direct3D programming, although the causes and promises related to them are different. Basically, a device reset occurs any time you need to tear down everything you've allocated for rendering and re-create it. In Direct3D this can happen whenever the OS feels like it (or more commonly when you switch resolutions or windowed to/from full screen, or the user switches to another program), and you generally lose most of your data and have to re-upload it. OpenGL is better about preserving data across resets, but it operates similarly.

Good performance during a device reset is important because of the user experience it creates. If a player's IM program pops up and steals focus from the game, the game needs to be snappy about it; otherwise, the user will become frustrated. When the game starts up and goes to full screen, it needs to be quick so the user knows what is happening. If the program is slow/buggy, the user is less likely to play it.

To deal with device reset, you need to know about every resource you have allocated from the device, and you have to take resource-type-specific steps to preserve it across the reset. The simplest way to do this is to have a base class for your resources that knows what device allocated them, has callbacks for the resource type to implement for device lost/device found, and maintains itself on a per-device list. Then, when a reset happens, you just walk the list, call lost on everything, do the device reset, and when you come back, call found.

You may need to keep copies of some resources in system-memory backing store or regenerate procedurally generated content! Thankfully, dealing with device resets is well documented in both DX and GL, so we don't need to go into the specifics here.

Resource Uploads/Locks

Runtime is the other situation where resources have a big performance contribution. There are three basic guidelines here, and they all revolve around doing exactly what you have to do and no more.

- **Minimize copies**: Copying 4MB of texture data onto the card is bad; copying it once in system memory and again to the card is even worse. Look for and avoid extra copies. The only time you should do them is when you need the data on a physically different chunk of RAM (like on the GPU).

- **Minimize locks**: This is also crucial. Whenever possible, lock buffers *once*, write each dword *once, in linear order, immediately* and then unlock it and move on. We'll cover this in more detail in the following chapters, but it's worth mentioning here.

■ **Double buffer**: This isn't appropriate for every situation, but if you have data that is changing frequently (once or more every frame), double buffer it so the card has more time to process each frame before it moves on. In some cases, the driver does this for you.

Resource Lifespans

One key to dealing with resource allocations efficiently is to figure out in what timeframe they will be used. Using different allocation strategies for different lifespans can pay big dividends. Consider breaking things down into these three scenarios:

■ **Per-frame usage**: Keeping a special shared buffer for vertices/indices that are only going to be used once in a frame and then discarded can give you big wins. By reusing the buffer every frame and batching uploads into bigger transfers, you can regain a lot of the performance loss caused by small draws (of <100 triangles).

■ **Dynamic resources**: These are buffers that are kept around for multiple frames, but changed once every frame (or relatively often). Typically, you allocate these with different flags in order to let the driver be more intelligent, although most drivers detect usage patterns and move data around appropriately.

■ **Static resources**: These are buffers that are locked and written to once and never changed again. Often, by hinting this to the driver, the driver can be more efficient about keeping them on the card and available for fast access.

Look Out for Fragmentation

Fragmentation can rapidly reduce how much of the GPU's memory you can work with. It can be worth it to round all allocations to powers of two in order to make it harder for fragmentation to occur. Do some tests. If you centralize all your allocations, it becomes much easier to do these sorts of changes. The worst-case scenario is finding out a change like this is required, and realizing that you have no wrapper around the API's resource allocation/deallocation calls.

Other Tricks

Here are a few other tricks that will be helpful in managing the performance characteristics of your game.

Frame Run-Ahead

An important factor that can affect perceived performance of a system is frame run-ahead. The drivers will try to buffer commands so that the GPU always has a constant stream of work, which can lead to it running behind the CPU by several frames. At 30Hz, the user might press a button, experience one frame (32ms) of latency until the CPU processes the effect and issues the commands to display the result, and then two or three frames (64 –96ms) before the commands are visible onscreen. Suddenly, you have an extra 100ms of latency, making your game feel loose, unresponsive, and generally laggy.

When you are running interactively, you will want to make sure you prevent this behavior. The easiest way to do so is to force synchronization at certain points. This is a great opportunity to reverse your optimization knowledge. Usual tricks here include issuing a command like an occlusion query or a fence that you can use to determine where the GPU is in executing your commands, or locking a 1px square texture that is touched as part of the rendering process and reading back a pixel from it.

When you profile your code, you'll see that the GPU or CPU is waiting on these synch points, but that's probably fine. If you find that one is consistently waiting for the other, it might be an opportunity to scale up the work you're doing on the resource that is waiting.

Lock Culling

When culling is working properly, it is invisible. There should be no way to tell that you are drawing everything in the scene, as opposed to drawing only what is needed, except by comparing frame rate. This makes it easy for culling to be broken, since if it "mostly" works, then it is possible you would never know.

A useful technique to fight this is to add a flag to your application that locks the camera information used for culling, i.e., prevents it from being updated. In combination with some debug visualization (like showing bounding boxes of culled items and the frustum of the camera), it becomes trivial to turn on the flag and then freecam around your world to confirm visually that only stuff in the frustum is being drawn.

Stupid Texture (Debug) Tricks

Texture sampling is an infinitely useful tool. You can lock your textures to 1px in size to check on fill-rate. But there are a lot of other possibilities, too.

You can visualize which mipmap levels are in use by generating a texture with a different color in each mip level; for instance, red at level 0, green at level 1, blue at level 2, etc. Then just play your game and look for the different colors. If you never see red, you can probably drop a level or two on your mips and save some VRAM. Many engines automate either mip visualization or even mip in-use detection for you, so check before you add something like this.

For checking alignment and sampling issues, checkerboard textures of all varieties are extremely useful. A 1px checker pattern (every other pixel set) makes it easy to tell if you are sampling on texel centers; if you're right, you get a pretty checker pattern, and if you're wrong, you get a gray blob. Larger checks are good for checking alignment. (For instance, suppose that a model should be using 16px square regions of the texture; if you put a 16px checkerboard on it, it will be easy to spot if you are crossing boundaries that you ought not cross.)

Some graphics hardware also has precision limits when you are drawing very large UV ranges or very large pieces of geometry, and a checkerboard texture will make it easy to spot any errors in calculation because they'll show up as artifacts in the checker pattern. The fix there is usually to make sure that you're drawing data that's approximately the same size as the screen, rather than many times larger.

Gradients are also very useful. For instance, a texture where you map (U,V) to the (R,G) color channels makes it easy to see if your texture mapping is working correctly. When you're generating texcoords procedurally, generating a gradient based on position can make it easy to spot if transforms that should be identical across draw calls really are identical.

In the brave new world of pixel shaders, you can do most of these tricks with a few instructions in your pixel shader instead of generating a texture.

Conclusion

In this chapter, we've presented a survival guide for anyone who is tasked with writing or working with a renderer. We've covered the major areas that are essential for good performance and proper functioning, and we've outlined specific problems that cause projects to fail, as well as tips and tricks to help make development easier. Our focus so far has been on how to co-exist peacefully with graphics drivers and treat the CPU well. The next few chapters will discuss the specifics of GPU and shader performance.

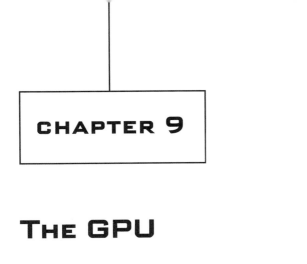

CHAPTER 9

THE GPU

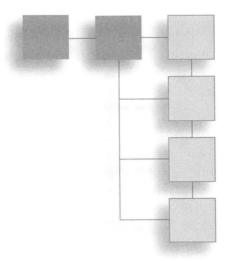

At this point, you've run through the techniques in the preceding chapters (especially Chapters 6, 7, and 8) and determined that the GPU, not the CPU or another resource, is your bottleneck. Fantastic! Optimizing the GPU can be a lot of fun.

As always, you will want to measure carefully after each change you make. Even if the GPU were initially the bottleneck, it might not be after a few optimizations. Be sure to keep your mental picture of your game's performance up to date by regularly measuring where time is going.

Direct3D vs. OpenGL vs. Proprietary APIs

This chapter focuses primarily on Direct3D. The basic concepts are the same, and you will find most of the `PerfTestHarness` tests are readily portable. Why don't we also cover OpenGL and other APIs? Because we want to focus on high-level concepts.

What does it cost to clear the screen or draw with a certain number of textures active? How do you identify a performance bottleneck? When is it appropriate to optimize the CPU and when the GPU? All of these things are the same under both APIs—just the details shift slightly.

In general, for a given generation of hardware, Direct3D has provided a cleaner interface. OpenGL has more precisely exposed the features of cutting-edge hardware, but at the cost of a more complex API.

Another important consideration is that if you are developing for a more exotic system, it will have a proprietary rendering API. So you will have to adapt anyway, depending on where and what you code.

Let's not get bogged down in religious wars. In the end, it comes down to understanding the basics of profiling and the flow of data in the system. Master these, and you will be able to optimize any rendering system on any hardware.

Optimizing GPU performance is fun because it varies so much. The general rule is always the same—draw only what is needed. But the details shift. Each generation of graphics hardware changes the performance picture. Each generation of games has more required of it by its audience.

Categories of GPU

You can break GPUs into three broad tiers. *Fixed function* GPUs have no or limited programmability. They can only apply textures or do other shading or transformation calculations in certain fixed ways, which is what gives them their name. You most often find these cards in cheap consumer hardware—low-end game consoles, portable devices, and budget systems. The Nintendo DS, the pre-3Gs iPhones and iPod Touches, and the Wii all fall into this category.

We consider programmable GPUs to be *shader* GPUs. These are so named because they can run user shader programs to control various parts of the rendering process. Programs are run at the vertex, pixel, and geometry level. Nearly every card made by any manufacturer in the past decade supports shaders in some way. Consoles like the Xbox 360 and PS3, and nearly all desktop PCs, have cards that fall into this category.

Finally, there are *unified* GPUs. These are pure execution resources running user code. They do not enforce a specific paradigm for rendering. Shader Model 4.0 cards fall into this category—recent vintage cards from ATI and NVIDIA, for the most part. At this tier, the capabilities of the hardware require special consideration, which we highlight in Chapter 16, "GPGPU."

Each tier of GPU can perform the operations of the preceding tier. You can exactly emulate a fixed-function GPU with a shader GPU, and a shader GPU can be exactly emulated with a unified GPU. But each tier also adds useful functionality and allows you to operate under a less constrained set of assumptions when it comes to optimizing.

The decision as to which tier of hardware to target will be determined by your game's target audience. If you are developing a Wii game, your decision is made for you. If you are developing a PC game, you will need to do some research to see what level of graphics hardware your audience has. Targeting the latest and greatest is a lot of fun from a development perspective, but it can be unfortunate for sales when only a few users are able to run your game well!

Sometimes, it is worthwhile to optimize for income. And it is always nicer to develop on lower-end hardware and find at the end that you have done all the optimization you need, instead of developing on high-end hardware and finding you have major performance issues to resolve at the end of your project.

3D Pipeline

The rendering pipeline in 3D cards has evolved over the years. Figure 9.1 shows the last few generations of the Direct3D pipeline, from DirectX 8 through 10. As you can see, there has been a heavy trend from fixed-purpose hardware to having nearly every part of the pipeline be programmable.

Chapter 4, "Hardware Fundamentals" goes into more detail, but, in general, work flows from the top to the bottom of the pipeline. Each point of added programmability (shown as elliptical circles in Figure 9.1) makes it easier to build complex visual effects. These points also provide opportunities to tune performance.

I'm GPU Bound!?

How do you tell if you're GPU bound? To summarize quickly, if you see that you're spending a lot of time in API calls, especially draw calls or calls to swap/present the framebuffer, it's likely that the CPU is waiting for the GPU to finish drawing.

Look Out for Micro-Optimization

Be aware that every vendor implements its cards differently. While they all have to support the same API features and give similar rendering output, each vendor has his own designers, patents, and hardware manufacturing processes. They compete continuously on features and prices, pushing the limits of the state of the art. As a result, the internals of how any given rendering feature works can vary tremendously from vendor to vendor, or even cards from different generations of the same vendor.

What does this mean when you are profiling? If your code is going to run on multiple video cards (as the typical PC game must), you cannot afford to optimize too closely for any one card. A good strategy is to identify a few specific worst-case scenarios to focus on. Any programmer can get his game to run well on a $300 video card (or as is more common these days, two $300 video cards working in parallel), but if you are going to spend time on micro-optimization that will help your game, do it against the common, low-end graphics cards.

Tools like PIX, PerfView, Intel's GPA, GPU Perf Studio, and others (discussed in Chapter 3, "The Tools") will analyze the GPU's performance statistics. If you see

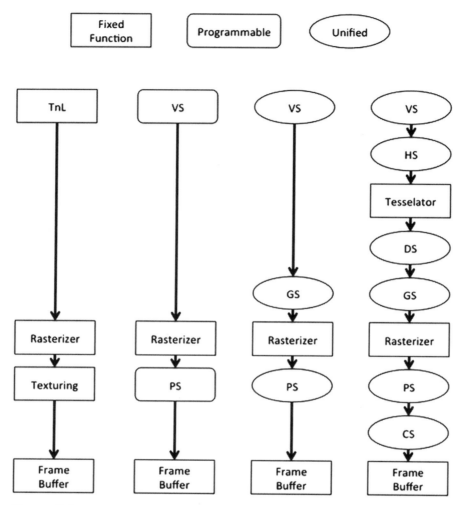

Figure 9.1

Evolution of graphics pipelines. From left to right, DirectX 7, DirectX 8.1, DirectX 9, and DirectX 10/11. Not shown, the shift in fundamental capabilities of the hardware from fixed to shader-based to fully programmable hardware.

that you have zero GPU idle time and high CPU idle time, it's another clear indicator that you are GPU limited. These tools will give you a clear idea of what is taking up the most time on the GPU.

If you know you are GPU bound, the next step is to look at where the time is going, and to do that you have to look at what is going on in the source of rendering a frame.

What Does One Frame Look Like?

A frame can be visualized as a series of events taking place on the GPU. Each event, determined by your API calls, is data being copied or processed in some way. Keep in mind that the GPU maintains a queue of commands to execute, so the actual results of an API call might not be calculated until several previous frames' worth of rendering are completed.

In the case of PIX, you get a direct visualization of the event execution on the timeline view. In the absence of a PIX-like tool, you can infer the behavior with careful timing. There are also ways to force synchronization (discussed in Chapter 8).

All this is to say that your goal as a GPU optimizer is to identify the events that are taking up the most execution resources and then optimize them. It's the Pareto Principle at work again—20% of GPU activity tends to take up 80% of time and space. Of course, sometimes you will find a situation where the workload is even. In that case, it will be a slow grind to reduce drawing and find enough small wins to get the performance win you need.

Front End vs. Back End

Are you limited by geometry or pixels? You can break the pipeline into a front and back end as an aid to optimization. The front end deals with setting up triangles and other geometry for drawing, while the back end handles processing pixels, running shaders, and blending the results into the framebuffer.

How do you test to see which half is the bottleneck? It's easy—vary the workload for one half and see if overall performance varies. In the case of the GPU, the simple test is to reduce the render target size. You can do this most simply by setting the scissor rectangle to be just a few pixels in size. All geometry will still have to be processed by the front end, but the vast majority of the work for the back end can be quickly rejected.

```
// Make a one pixel scissor rect.
RECT testRect = {0, 0, 1, 1};

// Set the scissor rect.
pD3DDevice->SetScissorRect(testRect);
pD3DDevice->SetRenderState(D3DRS_SCISSORTESTENABLE, true);
```

Notice that we chose a scissor rectangle more than zero pixels in size. Graphics cards do have to produce correct output, but if they can save processing time, they will. So it is reasonable for them to optimize the zero-size scissor rectangle by simply ignoring all draw operations while the scissor is relevant. This is why it is essential to measure on a variety of cards because not all of them use the same tricks for gaining performance.

Warnings aside, it should be pretty clear if the front end (geometry) or back end (pixels) is your bottleneck by the performance difference from this quick test. If there is a performance gain, then you know that per-pixel calculations are the bottleneck.

Back End

You will notice the subsequent sections here are organized based on whether they are related to the front end or the back end. We will start from the back, where pixels are actually drawn, and work our way to the front, where draw commands cause triangles to be processed. Because the later stages of the pipeline tend to involve the bulk of the work and are also easier to detect and optimize, we'll start with them.

Fill-Rate

Fill-rate is a broad term used to refer to the rate at which pixels are processed. For instance, a GPU might advertise a fill-rate of 1,000MP/sec. This means it can draw one hundred million pixels per second. Of course, this is more useful if you can convert it to be per frame. Say you want your game to run at 60Hz. Dividing 1,000MP/sec by 60Hz gives a performance budget on this theoretical card of 17MP/frame.

Another consideration is overdraw. Overdraw occurs when a given location on the screen is drawn to more than once. You can express overdraw as a coefficient. If you draw to every pixel on the screen once, you have the ideal overdraw of one. If you draw to every pixel on the screen 10 times, you have an unfortunate overdraw of 10. Since most applications draw different content to different parts of the screen, overdraw is rarely a whole number.

Many graphics performance tools include a mode to visualize overdraw. It's also easy to add it on your own—draw everything with alpha blending on and a flat transparent color. Leave the Z test, culling, and all other settings the same. If you choose, say, translucent red, then you will see bright red where there is lots of overdraw and dim red or black where there is little overdraw.

Finally, you should consider your target resolution. You can express your target resolution in megapixels. If you are targeting 1,920 × 1,080, then you are displaying approximately 2.0 megapixels every frame. This is useful because, combined with average overdraw, target frame rate, and fill-rate budget, you have a relationship that governs your performance.

```
GPU fill rate / Frame rate = Overdraw * resolution
```

You can plug in your values and solve to see how much overdraw you can budget per frame.

```
1000MP/sec / 60Hz = Overdraw * 2MP
17MP/frame = Overdraw * 2MP
Overdraw = 8.5
```

Now you know that, from a fill-rate perspective, you cannot afford more than 8.5x overdraw. That sounds pretty good! But you shall see as we move through the next few sections that even a generous budget can get used up very quickly.

Render Target Format

The first factor that directly impacts fill-rate is the format of your render target. If you are drawing in 16-bit color, fewer bytes have to be written for every pixel. If you are writing each channel as a 32-bit floating-point value, a lot more data must be written. On PC hardware, the best-supported format is R8G8B8A8, and it's a good place to start. Extremely narrow formats can actually cause a performance loss, because they require extra work to write. Sometimes, you need wider formats for some rendering tasks. If you suspect that the bottleneck is reading/writing the framebuffer, vary the format. If you see a performance change, then you know that the format is a bottleneck.

We'll look at the implications of varying pixel formats later in the section, "Texture Sampling."

Blending

The first factor that can consume fill-rate is blending. Enabling alpha blending causes the hardware to read back the existing value from the framebuffer, calculate the blended value based on render settings and the result of any active textures/shaders, and write it back out.

In our test results shown in Figure 9.2, we found that drawing alpha-blended pixels consumes approximately 10% more fill-rate on our NVIDIA GTX 260.

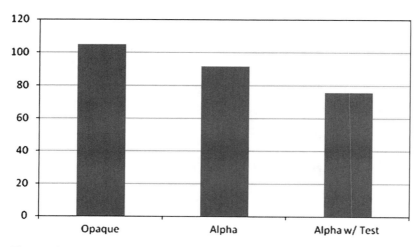

Figure 9.2

Comparison of drawing a fixed number of opaque, alpha tested, and alpha blended pixels. A small test texture was active while drawing.

Enabling alpha testing gained even more performance, although that will vary depending on your art.

There are several strategies you can use to reduce the cost of translucent objects. The first is to draw them as opaque. This gets you the fastest path.

The next is to use alpha testing if you need *transparency* not *translucency*. (Transparency means you can see through parts of an object, like a chain link fence, while translucency means light filters through the object, like a stained glass window.) Alpha testing is also good because it is compatible with the Z-buffer, so you don't have to do extra sorting to make sure alpha-tested geometry is drawn at the right time.

Finally, you can go to approximations. There are a variety of order-independent, depth-sorted translucency techniques available (all with limitations, all with a high performance cost). Sometimes, dithering is an option. Distant translucent objects could be drawn as opaque to save fill-rate, too.

You can tell if blending is your bottleneck by a simple test—disable alpha blending and draw opaque! If you see a performance gain, your bottleneck is alpha blending.

Shading

The performance implications of pixel shaders are so big that we had to devote Chapter 10, "Shaders," to fully consider them. On most fixed-function hardware available to PCs, the relative cost of none, flat, and Gouraud shading is minimal. (If you are targeting a more limited GPU, like on a mobile device, you may want to run some quick tests.)

Texture Sampling

Textures can cost a *lot* of fill-rate! Each texture sampled to draw a pixel requires resources to fetch data from memory, sample it, and combine into a final drawn pixel. The main axes we will consider here are *texture format, filter mode,* and *texture count.* In the case of programmable GPUs, the "combine" step will be discussed in Chapter 10, while in the case of fixed-function GPUs, the combine step is implemented in hardware and is usually overshadowed by the cost of the texture fetches.

Figure 9.3 shows the performance effects of various texture formats. You can see that 16- and 32-bit textures are the cheapest, while DXT1 gives pretty good performance at nearly 80% memory savings. Performance doesn't quite scale linearly with bit depth, but that's a good approximation.

Filtering is a little harder to analyze because it can be affected by the orientation of the rendered surfaces. To combat this, in our measurements of various texture-sampling modes (shown in Figure 9.4), we adjusted our test geometry to get a good distribution of samples and sizes. The same random seed was used for each run of the test to get comparable results.

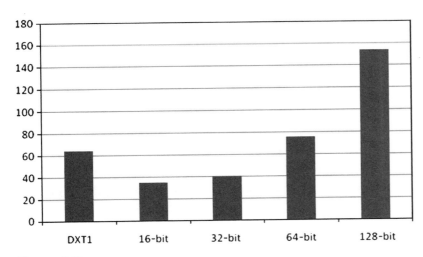

Figure 9.3

Comparison of fill-rate when drawing geometry using textures with different sized pixels.

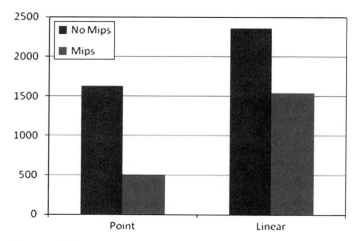

Figure 9.4

Comparison of various sampling modes with mipmapping on and off. The test geometry was drawn at random orientations to ensure realistic results.

As you can see, enabling mipmapping is a major performance win. Turning on linear sampling almost exactly triples the cost per pixel, but it is a major quality win.

Figure 9.5 shows the performance drop from sampling more textures. As you can see, it gets worse and eventually plateaus.

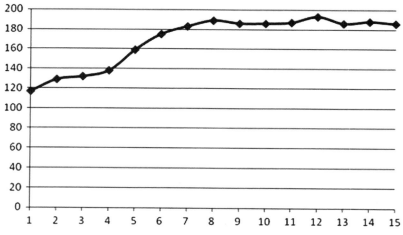

Figure 9.5

Comparison of performance (Y-axis, in milliseconds) with varying number of active textures (X-axis). Bilinear filtering and mipmapping were enabled for all textures.

Bear in mind that with shaders you can do dependent or conditional texture samples, which can dramatically alter the performance picture. We'll discuss this wrinkle in the next chapter.

If you suspect that texture sampling is a bottleneck, the best test is to replace all your textures with a single small 4x4 test texture and disable samplers where possible. Because such a small texture easily fits in the GPU's texture cache, you should see a significant speedup. If so, you know that texture sampling is your bottleneck.

Z/Stencil Culling

The Z-buffer is a major tool for increasing rendering performance. Conceptually, it is simple. If the fragment to be drawn to a given pixel is farther than what is already drawn there, reject it. GPU manufacturers have since introduced two major enhancements.

First, you have *hierarchical Z*, which is where the GPU maintains a version of the Z-buffer data that can be hierarchically sampled. This allows the GPU to reject (or accept) whole blocks of pixels at once, rather than testing each individually. API and vendor documentation go into the specifics of how this is implemented for each GPU, most importantly covering what, if any, settings or actions will cause hierarchical Z to be disabled. All GPUs on the PC market today support it, so we will not be doing any tests targeting it specifically.

Often, the hierarchical structure degrades as drawing occurs, so it is necessary to reset it. This is done when a Z-clear is issued. The usual Z-clear at the start of rendering is sufficient.

Second, you have *fast Z writes*, which are enabled by disabling color writes. When this mode is active, the GPU skips most shading calculations, enabling it to draw significantly faster. Why is this useful? If you draw the major occluders in your scene with fast-Z before drawing the scene normally, it gives you an opportunity to reject many pixels before they are even shaded. Depth tests occur at the same place in the pipeline as alpha tests, giving significant savings when the depth tests can reject pixels.

The stencil buffer can also be used for culling (among other operations). Stencil tests occur at the same stage in the pipeline as depth and alpha tests, allowing for very fast pixel rejection.

Clearing

Clearing the framebuffer is an important operation. If the Z-buffer and stencil buffer aren't reset every frame, rendering will not proceed correctly. Depending on the scene, failing to clear the color channels will result in objectionable artifacts. Clearing is another commonly accelerated operation, since setting a block of memory to a fixed value is an embarrassingly parallel operation.

Generally, you should only issue `clears` at the start of rendering to a render target. A common mistake is to issue `clears` multiple times, either on purpose or due to bugs in code. This can quickly devour fill-rate. Generally, applications are not bound by the performance of `clears`, but the best policy is to make sure that you clear no more than is strictly necessary for correct results.

Front End

The front end is where geometry and draw commands are converted into pixels to be drawn. Performance problems occur here less often, but they still happen. Don't forget to run the stencil test at the beginning of the chapter to determine if the front or back end is your bottleneck!

If the front end is a bottleneck, there are three main potential causes: vertex transformation, vertex fetching, and caching, or tessellation. Most of the time, scenes are not vertex-bound because there are just so many more pixels to render. But it can happen.

In general, fewer vertices are better. You should never be drawing triangles at a density of greater than one per pixel. For a 1,080p screen, this suggests that more than 2MM triangles onscreen at a time is more than you need. Of course, your source art is liable to have an extremely high polygon count, so you should be using LOD to reduce workload at runtime.

Vertex Transformation

Vertex transformation is the process of converting vertex and index data fetched from memory into screen coordinates that can be passed to the back end for rasterization. This is the compute part of the vertex performance picture, where vertex shaders are executed. On fixed-function cards, where vertex processing isn't programmable, there are usually lighting, texture coordinate generation, and skinning capabilities.

You can test whether vertex transformation is a bottleneck very simply: simplify the transformation work the GPU must do. Remove lighting calculations, replace texture coordinate generation with something simple (but not too simple, as simply writing out a fixed coordinate will favor the texture cache and alter performance elsewhere), and disable skinning. If there's a performance gain, you'll know that vertex transformation is a bottleneck.

On fixed-function hardware, usually all you can do is disable features to gain performance. On old or particularly low-end programmable hardware, be aware that the vertex programs may be run on the CPU. This can shift your system-level loads rather unexpectedly, as work that should be on the GPU is done on the CPU. We will discuss optimizing vertex shaders in Chapter 10.

Vertex Fetching and Caching

Index data is processed in order, and vertex data is fetched based on the indices you specify. As you will remember from Chapter 6, "CPU Bound: Memory," memory is slow. The GPU can fight this to a certain degree. Indexed vertices are not hard to pre-fetch. But there is only limited cache space, and once the cache is full, pre-fetching can't hide latency.

As you know, geometry is submitted to the GPU in the form of primitives. The most common types are triangle lists and triangle strips. Strips have the benefit of having a smaller memory footprint, but the bigger issue by far (see Figure 9.6) is

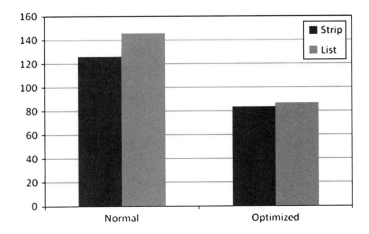

Figure 9.6

Performance of various primitive types representing the Stanford Bunny, drawn in cache-friendly order and in random order.

how many cache misses are encountered while the vertices are being fetched. Maximizing vertex reuse is crucial, and most 3D rendering libraries include code for optimizing vertex order. Of particular interest is the D3DXOptimizeVertices call from D3DX and "Linear-speed Vertex Cache Optimization" by Tom Forsyth, 2006, at http://home.comcast.net/~tom_forsyth/papers/fast_vert_cache_opt.html.

There are two other major considerations for performance in this area. First, index format. The two options here are 16-bit and 32-bit indices. See Figure 9.7 for a comparison of performance with these options. Note that not all cards properly support 32-bit indices.

The other consideration is vertex format, specifically vertex size. By reducing the total dataset that must be processed to render a mesh, you can gain some performance. Figure 9.8 shows the variation for different vertex sizes. As you can see, there is a cost for large and odd vertex sizes.

Tessellation

The final major performance bottleneck is tessellation. More recent GPUs with DX11 tessellation capabilities can alter, delete, and emit new geometry via geometry shaders. We will discuss this capability in more detail in the next chapter.

Many older GPUs feature different tessellation capabilities, but unless you are targeting a specific card, they are not flexible or powerful enough to warrant

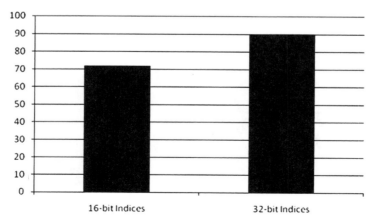

Figure 9.7

Performance of a cache-friendly Stanford Bunny with 16-bit and 32-bit indices.

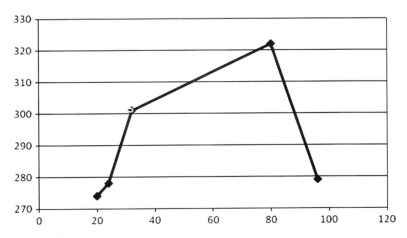

Figure 9.8

Performance of a cache-friendly Stanford Bunny with varying vertex sizes of 20, 24, 32, 80, and 96 bytes. Notice that footprint is a factor, but so is alignment (96 is better than 80).

spending the time on custom art and one-shot code. It's better to spend the effort to make your game run well on many GPUs and systems.

Special Cases

In addition to the main pipeline discussed previously, there are several other wrinkles that can affect your performance.

MSAA

Multisample antialiasing is a technique for supersampling an image. Originally, it was done by rendering the scene at a high resolution and downsampling. Now more exotic techniques are used, with varying performance implications. The specific details are interesting, but beyond the scope of this book. What is relevant is that MSAA can significantly affect fill-rate.

Lights and Shadows

Lighting and shadows can be a major performance problem in all but the simplest scenes. They do not have a simple fix. Lighting can require a lot of data to get right. Shadows can stress the entire rendering pipeline, from CPU to vertex processing to pixel processing, because they often require drawing the whole scene from multiple viewpoints every frame.

A survey of all the rendering techniques for lighting and shadowing is well beyond our scope, and it would probably be obsolete as soon as it was printed. Instead, we'd like to give some general guidelines.

Remember that *lighting quality* is a matter of perception. Great art can make up for minimal or nonexistent lighting. Humans have an intuitive understanding of lighting, but what looks good and serves the purposes of gameplay doesn't necessarily have anything to do with the physical reality of the game space. (*Illustrative Rendering in Team Fortress* 2 by Mitchell, Francke, and Eng has an interesting discussion of the trade-offs here in section 5.)

In general, consistency is the most important attribute for lighting to have. It should not have discontinuities or obvious seams. The human eye is very good at noticing that, say, a whole object becomes dark when it cross through a doorway, or that different parts of a character are lit differently with seams between them. People will accept very simple lighting calculations if they do not have objectionable artifacts.

Take advantage of the limited scenarios your game offers to cheat. You can design your levels and other assets so that performance drains and problematic cases never occur. It will be a temptation to implement a total lighting solution that deals with every case well. Resist this. Determine the situations your game has to support and make sure they work well. Ignore the rest.

Ultimately, *lighting calculations* are done for every pixel on the screen. They might be interpolated based on values calculated per vertex. They might be calculated based on some combined textures or with multiple passes that are composited. They might be done in a pixel shader. In the end, multiple light and shadow terms are combined with material properties to give a final color for each pixel on the screen.

This brings us to the first performance problem brought by lighting: It can require you to break up your scene and your draw calls. If you are using the built-in fixed-function lighting, a vertex shader or a pixel shader, each object will require a different set of constants (or a call to set the lighting properties). For small mobile meshes, like those that make up characters, vehicles, and items, a single set of constants can hold all the information needed to light that object. But for larger objects, like a terrain or a castle, different parts of the object will need to be lit differently. Imagine a castle lit by a sunrise with dozens of torches burning in its hallways.

It is generally cost prohibitive to render every light's effect on every object in the scene, so most engines maintain a lookup structure to find the N closest lights.

This way, if only four lights can be efficiently considered for a material, the four most important lights can be found and supplied for rendering.

For larger objects, it can make sense to calculate lighting as a second pass. If the lit area is significantly smaller than the whole object, redrawing just the affected geometry can be a big savings. In some cases, just the triangles affected can be streamed to the GPU dynamically. For more complex meshes, this can be cost-prohibitive, so an alternative is to group geometry into smaller chunks that can be redrawn without requiring per-triangle calculations.

While lights are important, *shadows* are the interaction between lights and objects, and they bring a lot of realism to any scene. Shadowing is generally implemented by rendering depth or other information to a texture and then sampling that texture in the shaders of affected objects. This consumes fill-rate when rendering, as well as introducing the overhead of rendering to and updating the texture(s) that define the shadows. As alluded to earlier, this is essentially a second (or third or fourth or fifth) scene render.

The nice thing about shadows is that they do not require the fidelity of a full scene render. Post-processing effects are not needed. Color doesn't matter—just the distance to the closest occluder. A lot of the overhead of sorting, of setting material properties, and so on can be avoided.

In the end, lighting systems are built on the primitives we have discussed already in this chapter. There is a lot to say about lighting and shadowing in terms of getting good quality and performance, but once you know how to fit them into your optimization framework, it becomes a matter of research and tuning to get the solution your game needs. The optimization process is the same as always. Find a benchmark, measure it, detect the problem, solve, check, and repeat.

Forward vs. Deferred Rendering

The biggest game changer, as far as performance goes, is deferred rendering. The traditional model is forward rendering, where objects are composited into the framebuffer as rendering proceeds. If you were to take a snapshot of the framebuffer after each render call, it would look pretty much like the final frame (with fewer objects visible).

In deferred rendering, normals, material types, object IDs, lighting information, and other parameters are written to one or more render targets. At the end of this process, the rich buffer of data produced is processed to produce the final image displayed to the user. This significantly simplifies rendering, because even scenes with many lights and shadows can be processed in a uniform way. The main problem a forward renderer faces, with regard to lighting, is getting multiple shadows and lights to interact in a consistent way.

But creating the data for the final deferred pass is not cheap. It requires a very wide render target format or multiple render targets. A lot of fill-rate is consumed when moving all this data around, and the shader for the final pass can be costly. In general, though, deferred rendering acts to flatten performance—it is not great, but it doesn't get a lot worse as scene complexity grows.

MRT

We've already discussed rendering to wide render targets. It is also possible to render to multiple render targets at the same time. This is referred to as *MRT*. It can be a useful technique for deferred shading, for shadow calculations, and for optimizing certain rendering algorithms. However, it does not come without cost.

MRT is not available on all hardware, but when it is available, it's a clear win, as Figure 9.9 shows.

Conclusion

A GPU is a complex and multifaceted beast, but with care, research, and discipline, it is capable of great performance. From API to silicon, GPUs are

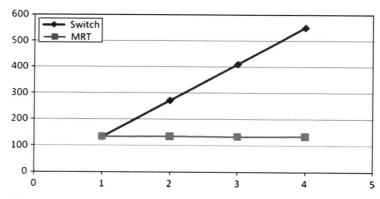

Figure 9.9

Comparison of performance when rendering to multiple targets by switching between targets and using MRT.

designed to render graphics at incredible speed. In this chapter, we covered the GPU pipeline from the performance perspective, and shared tests, performance guidelines, and recommendations for getting the best performance from each stage. Don't forget to run the performance test harness on your own graphics hardware. The best way to get great performance is to measure, and the test harness is the easiest way to do that.

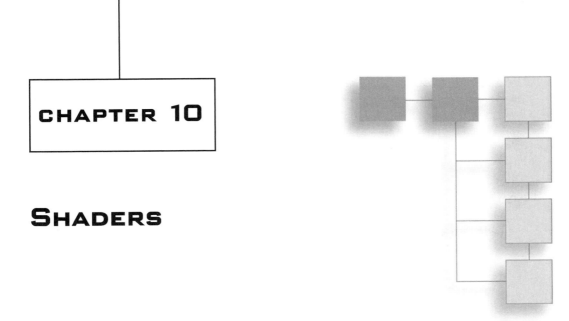

CHAPTER 10

SHADERS

The secret to great graphics lies with shaders. Good art is always a requirement, but good shaders let good art shine (or glow, shadow, occlude, reflect, refract, or sparkle). You'll find an abundance of articles and books on writing and integrating shaders into games.

In this chapter, we'll explore the different factors that control shader performance, as well as explore how to detect and fix bottlenecks in your shaders. In doing this, we build heavily on the preceding two chapters, Chapter 9, "The GPU," and Chapter 8, "From CPU to GPU." Make sure that you've read them first.

A quick aside on our methodology for the tests in this chapter. Every video card has different performance characteristics, which tend to change with each driver revision. If you need to know exact specifics for a card, you need to re-run the tests for the card and driver that are relevant for your exact situation. However, we have normalized the data shown—all the tests were run with the same card (NVIDIA GTX 260) with the same total amount of fill (0.5 gigapixels). You can expect the broad relationships shown to apply to most cards, but remember that the basis of optimization is good measurement of your application's actual performance.

Always remember the big picture. You want your shaders to run as tightly as possible, but the nature and complexity of your game's scenes will have a bigger impact on performance. Make sure that you are doing the right thing before spending a lot of time optimizing.

Shader Languages and Compatibility

There are several languages for writing shaders, depending on API, hardware, and programming languages. They are all largely similar, coming in two varieties: high level and low level. The high-level languages are all C/C++-like, with special extensions for vector operations, for indicating how to connect shaders, and a small built-in library of functions implemented by the GPU hardware. The low-level languages are a rich form of assembly that is mapped directly to the machine code executed by the GPU by the driver.

Behind the scenes, GPU manufacturers map all these available languages to the same core capabilities of the hardware and drivers, making them very similar in terms of syntax, capabilities, and performance. Because this book focuses primarily on the Direct3D side, we will only briefly cover other languages. On to our survey:

- **HLSL:** Microsoft's shader language; this is the one used in Direct3D across all Direct3D hardware. It is compiled to shader assembly before being uploaded to the GPU, where it may be processed further into native microcode before being executed. It is probably the most well-known and best-supported option. It's used in Direct3D's Effects material framework.

- **Cg:** NVIDIA's cross-platform shader language, which is similar to HLSL in most regards. Used in CgFX, it's a material framework similar to Direct3D's Effects system.

- **GLSL/GLslang:** The OpenGL Shader Language. A high-level language for programming shaders for OpenGL, similar to Cg and HLSL.

- **PixelBender:** Adobe's shader language, embedded in Flash and the Creative Suite (Photoshop, AfterEffects, etc.). It can run multithreaded on the CPU or on the GPU.

- **Direct3D Assembly:** The low-level representation to which HLSL and other Direct3D-compatible languages compile; sometimes shipped to avoid compile times, allow low-level tweaking, or target very low-end programmable hardware.

- **ARB Assembly:** Exposed through the ARB_vertex_program and ARB_fragment_program OpenGL extensions. It fills a similar role to D3D assembly. Before ARB assembly extensions were available, a series of proprietary extensions, mostly from NVIDIA and ATI, allowed access to the capabilities of the hardware.

- **Texture Combiners:** The earliest programmable hardware was not general purpose, and could only perform a limited number of texture samples and arithmetic operations. This was exposed via texture combiners, a series of stages that could be programmed to combine texture data in predetermined ways. If you are targeting fixed-function hardware, it may support programmability under this guise. The pixel shader capabilities in shader model 1.0 are designed to map to texture combiner capable hardware.

If you need to target multiple shader languages, one tool to consider is MojoShader, available from icculus.org/mojoshader. It is an open source, zlib-licensed library, which can take compiled HLSL assembly for SM1-3 and automatically convert it to target various GL shader extensions. It's used by *Unreal Tournament 3*, among others.

Shader Assembly

Just as high-level languages like C and C++ map to low-level assembly, high-level shader languages map to shader assembly instructions. Let's look at a minimal example (shown in Listing 10.1).

Listing 10.1

Comparison of HLSL (right) and Corresponding Shader Assembly (left).

```
// Parameters:
// bool $bTexture;
// sampler2D MeshTexture;
// Registers:
// Name            Reg Size
// ---------------------------
// $bTexture       b0   1
// MeshTexture     s0   1
//
  ps_3_0
  dcl_color v0
  dcl_texcoord v1.xy
  dcl_2d s0
  if b0
    texld r0, v1, s0
    mul oC0, r0, v0
  else
  mov oC0, r0
endif
// approximately 8 instruction slots used
// (1 texture, 7 arithmetic)
```

```
PS_OUTPUT RenderScenePS(
          VS_OUTPUT In,
          uniform bool bTexture )
{
  PS_OUTPUT Output;
  // Look up mesh texture and modulate
  // it with diffuse.
  if( bTexture )
      Output.RGBColor =
                  tex2D(MeshTexture,
                      In.TextureUV)
                  * In.Diffuse;
  else
      Output.RGBColor = In.Diffuse;
  return Output;
}
```

As you can see, the shader assembly (just like with x86 assembly) gives you a very detailed view of what is going on behind the scenes. You can see some interesting details, too. For instance, you can see that there is a register dedicated to the output color, oC0, and that conditionals are implemented directly in the assembly.

With a more complex shader, you could quickly tell if your HLSL were being mapped properly to the assembly. Although shader compilers are getting better and better, sometimes small changes to the high-level shader can lead to much better efficiency in the resulting assembly. It's always worth a look to be sure that the shader is doing what you think it should. Notice that the compiled output conveniently includes an instruction count among other information.

Using fxc
_____

With the DirectX SDK, a tool called fxc is available to compile your shaders from the command line. fxc can be found in the bin folder of the DirectX SDK. It has many uses, but most significantly, you can use it to get an approximate idea of the complexity of the shaders you are running. The command line to generate the example in Figure 10.1 is simple:

```
fxc /T ps_3_0 /E RenderScenePS BasicHLSL.fx
```

Of course, fxc /? will give you full information on all its arguments, but a quick summary is as follows:

/T ps_3_0—Specifies the shader model to target, in this case, a SM3.0 pixel shader.

/E RenderScenePS—Specifies the entry point for the shader, the function at which to start execution.

BasicHLSL.fx—The most important argument is the FX file to compile, of course.

fxc has many other features commonly found in compilers. You can have it print the source lines that correspond to a given block of assembly. You can have it emit debugging information or optimize more or less aggressively, too. There are many other fancier and nicer tools out there, but in many situations fxc is all you need.

_____

Full Circle

By this point, you should be having flashbacks to Chapters 6 and 7, "CPU Bound: Memory" and "CPU Bound: Compute," where we discussed optimizing code for the CPU. While GPUs change the performance picture significantly, once you get down to the shader level, many CPU optimization techniques become very relevant.

The main difference between CPU and GPU code is that GPU is architected to be embarrassingly parallel. Memory access is aggressively restricted to certain well-defined operations (i.e., texture sampling), and programs are kept very small and independent so that many instances can be run in parallel. And, at least when programming within DirectX or OpenGL, these programs are only executed in specific contexts, removing a lot of bookkeeping overhead and infrastructure that the user would otherwise need to implement.

You can also run general-purpose computations on the GPU (see Chapter 16, "GPGPU," for more details), and if you do, many of these restrictions are lifted and a more general programming model is available. In most cases, this is not a good choice for applications that need to render 3D graphics because it brings too much complexity back up to the surface.

Find Your Bottleneck

After you've followed the process in Chapter 5, "Holistic Video Game Optimization," to determine that the GPU is your bottleneck, you'll want to run through Chapter 9 in order to figure out which part of the rendering pipeline is slowing you down. There's no sense in optimizing your shaders when disk access is slowing you down! You should always benchmark and measure before proceeding with further optimization work.

To quickly recap, you can test if pixel shading is your bottleneck by reducing the number of pixels you draw (for instance, by reducing resolution or by setting a scissor rectangle), test if vertex processing is your bottleneck by reducing the number of vertices that are drawn, and test if geometry shaders are your bottleneck by reducing the amount of tessellation that is performed. You have to test these in order (pixel, vertex, geometry), as each affects the ones that follow in the pipeline. In other words, reducing vertex load tends to also reduce the number of pixels that are drawn, so you have to test pixels first.

Once you suspect a programmable part of the GPU's pipeline, the next step is to isolate the specific shader that is taking up time and determine at how you can optimize it. The remainder of this chapter runs through various potential performance problems and how they can be detected and optimized.

Memory

Just like on the CPU, GPUs have (relatively) slow memory access. The advantage of the GPU is that it is running dozens or hundreds of "threads," so it has more opportunities to do useful work while waiting for data to be fetched. Chapter 9 gave some starting guidelines for memory, specifically to reduce vertex and pixel sizes when possible and make sure that data is in cache-friendly order. See the discussions on vertex and texture formats, and the discussion on vertex cache optimization in Chapter 9 for more detail on these points.

Let's briefly consider how each type of shader interacts with memory. We are broadly considering Shader Model 4 here; lower shader models have more restrictions.

- Geometry shaders are fed a limited set of data relating to a primitive. They can emit one or more new primitives.

- Vertex shaders are given one vertex and output one vertex.

- Pixel shaders are passed interpolated attributes, based on where on the triangle they are located, and output one or more color values to be blended into the framebuffer.

In addition, depending on what shader model is supported, all the shader types have access to a variety of constants and textures provided at draw call time. For instance, on recent hardware, you can sample textures from your vertex shader or even your geometry shader.

Inter-Shader Communication

The "shared data" between the various shaders can affect performance, but only in limited ways. The only trade-off is time for space. Passed attributes, like texture coordinates or normals, all consume resources. If they can be packed more tightly, taking up fewer attributes, it can be possible to gain back some performance. This is not generally a performance problem, but if you have many attributes, it can be worth a try.

Texture Sampling

Texture sampling is the biggest source of memory access problems in shaders. Without care, it can lead quickly to major performance problems. The two major factors that affect shader performance are number of samples and the depth of dependent reads. We discussed varying the number of active samplers in the last chapter, but we've re-created the test using a shader in Figure 10.1.

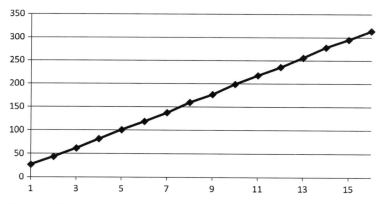

Figure 10.1

Performance (Y-axis, ms) varies with number of textures sampled (X-axis, number of active samplers).

Depth of dependent reads is the trickiest option by far. It is like a data dependency (as described in Chapter 6) with a vengeance, since by definition it is causing a round trip to VRAM to fetch texture data, plus the additional overhead of filtering. Let's explore dependent reads by way of a quick example:

```
float4 read1 = tex2D(sampler1, texCoord1);
float4 read2 = tex2D(sampler1, read1.xy);
float4 read3 = tex2D(sampler2, read2.xy + float2(0.2, 0.2));
float4 read4 = tex2D(sampler2, texCoord2);
```

This sample has four texture reads, with results stored in read1 through read4. You will notice that read2 depends on the result of read1 and read3 depends on read2. Only read1 and read4 can be fulfilled without prior access to texture data. Because of this, you can say the depth of dependent reads in this shader is three and the longest chain of reads is three long (read1   read2 -> read3). For a visualization of how dependent reads can affect performance, see Figure 10.2.

For many effects, dependent reads are a necessity. Suppose that you are doing a BRDF lookup based off a normal, which is in part determined by values from a normal map. In this case, if performance is a problem, the solution isn't to avoid dependent reads at all costs, but to try to fill in the latency hole created by the dependent reads. Suppose that it takes 100 cycles to sample a texture. In this example, assuming no compiler optimizations, it would take 400 cycles to finish sampling all the textures, plus the time to add two float2s for read3 (a few more cycles).

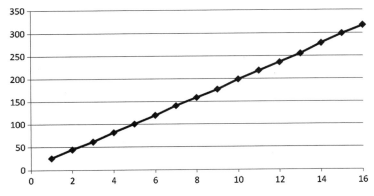

Figure 10.2

Performance (Y-axis, ms) varies with the number of textures sampled in a dependent chain (X-axis, number of active samplers). Notice that performance slows more rapidly than with independent samples.

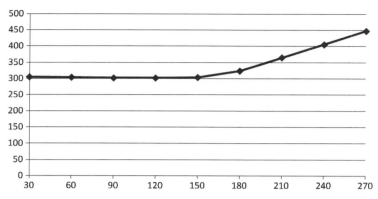

Figure 10.3

The performance (Y-axis, ms) varies with the number of mixed math operations (X-axis, number of operations, a mixture of add and multiply instructions). Notice that until around 180 math operations, performance is dominated by the fixed load of 16 dependent loads the shader is doing in parallel. Texture loads are a great deal more expensive than math operations.

The shader compiler is smarter than this, though, and it will reorder your code so that read2 is fetched before you calculate the texture coordinate for read3. This helps hide the latency of the fetch for read1, and since it puts read1 and read4 in parallel, it reduces your total execution time to 3ms. There is still a latency hole, but you're closer to filling it. We did a real performance test exploring this, shown in Figure 10.3.

If you had more math that did not depend on the value of read2 and read3, the compiler would automatically move it farther ahead to help hide the latency of those reads. Ideally, by the time all the other calculations were done, the values of read2/read3 would be ready to go and execution could proceed without any delay at all. Keep this in mind when optimizing. Sometimes, all you can do is take advantage of the performance that is available, rather than reducing your footprint! See the performance test in Figure 10.4.

The number of samples is simple in comparison. You can test if that is the performance issue by replacing the textures with 1x1 dummy textures, as discussed in Chapter 9. If raw texture throughput, not data dependency, is your problem, then there are a few options:

- **Reduce reads.** This is the no-brainer option, but it's worth looking at! Do you really need all the data that you're fetching? Can you calculate some of it instead?

- **Pack data.** Artist created textures often don't use the alpha channel. Maybe you could use all that free storage to save reading from a secondary texture. Or maybe you could store your normal map in just two channels and use the other two for specular and detail map intensity, instead of taking up three whole textures.

- **Reduce bandwidth.** As shown in the last chapter, texture format can greatly increase the amount of bandwidth that rendering takes. Are you using 32 bits when 16 would do? Are you using floating-point formats? They can consume a lot of bandwidth very quickly.

- **Optimize for the cache.** If you are frequently reading pixels in strange patterns, you might be missing the cache. Caches assume that you want to read adjacent pixels. If you're reading out of order (for instance, your Gaussian blur should read pixels from top to bottom or left to right, not in a scrambled order), you will lose this benefit, potentially leading to major performance loss.

The bottom line is that GPUs are very, very good at reading and filtering texture data. With a little care, you can maximize that performance and have your shaders screaming along. But if you aren't careful, you can spend all your time waiting on memory, and not doing productive work.

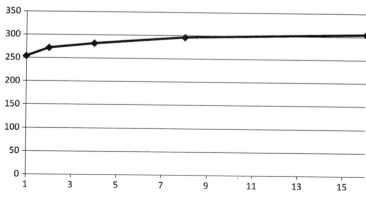

Figure 10.4

Performance (Y-axis, ms) of shader doing 16 total samples. Reads are grouped into dependent chains of length 1 through 16, length corresponding to the X-axis. Notice that the length of the chain directly correlates to performance loss.

Compute

Your shaders might be compute bound! (See Chapter 7, "CPU Bound: Compute.")

The easiest way to check if this is the case (*after* checking that texture sampling isn't the bottleneck) is to stub out a lot of your math—everything except what is necessary for basic rendering. Figure 10.5 shows how math operations correlate to shader performance.

Most vertex shaders are a matrix transform with a lot of secondary calculations bolted on. Pixel shaders can always be reduced to a single `return float4(1,0,1,0);`. After this is done, see if you have a performance gain. If you do, then you are set for a nice session of shader math optimization.

There are several major options for reducing compute load in shaders. We will run through them in the next few sections. Many of them are similar to or depend on concepts discussed in Chapter 6, so be sure to go back and review if anything is unfamiliar.

Hide Behind Latency

We don't usually encourage cowardice, but in this case, it might be just the thing. Texture reads are high-latency, but as we discussed in the texture section, if your calculations are dependent on them, they can't begin until the read completes. Make sure that the shader compiler is reordering as much calculation as possible to take place before the result of the texture read is used. On a high level, this

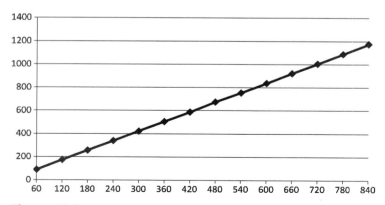

Figure 10.5

What the performance looks like (Y-axis, ms) as the number of math operations (X-axis, instruction count) is varied. Like a CPU, math is much faster than memory access.

means moving the bulk of your calculations to take place before the `tex2D` call and making sure that none of the parameters for the `tex2D` depends on those calculations. In other words, make sure that you are maximizing instruction level parallelism. See Figure 10.3 for an example of how much performance you could be leaving on the table.

Sacrifice Quality

Maybe you don't really need a full precision sin/cos for that lighting calculation. A dot product might give you enough quality for the ranges that you care about. As long as there is no obvious aliasing, users are unlikely to notice that lighting isn't exactly right.

Additionally, consider pushing terms up the shader hierarchy. Does everything really need to be calculated in the pixel shader? Maybe some of the beefier terms could be moved up into the vertex shader and interpolated linearly by the hardware. Perhaps there are some complex values that simply could be stored in a constant and updated at the start of every draw call by code running on the CPU.

Trade Space for Time

If you have a complex equation, like a BRDF or a lighting curve, which only has a few input values, consider moving it out into a lookup texture. It will add some latency but if you are compute bound, hopefully there is other work that can be done while the data is being fetched. If the lookup texture is small enough, it will stay in the texture cache, reducing read latency tremendously. Figure 10.3 is helpful in estimating the trade-off point for this.

Sometimes, a complex term can be stored as part of an existing texture. For instance, an irradiance map might store direction and intensity of incoming light. If your lighting equation immediately calculates a new term from that data, which doesn't vary based on other parameters of the scene, you could simply store the result of that term in the texture rather than recalculating it all the time. Or, if all your shaders are taking an object space normal map for a static object and converting it to world space, maybe a prudent step would be to simply store world space normals in the first place.

If you are already fetching data from the texture, then moving data into an unused part of it is essentially performance for free—you are paying for the whole pixel whether or not you are using all of it.

Flow Control

Flow control is a fairly important feature used by many shaders. A loop can help in a number of ways, but performance is usually not one of them. Programmatically they are quite useful (especially for anything that is iterative), but they should be used with caution. A shader with multiple `for` loops can stall as a result of each loop getting executed and holding up the execution of the rest of the shader. Please note that this as an extreme example. Looping can help to make code easier to read and more portable. The issue is about the execution of the loop. Older versions of HLSL must unroll the loop for execution. Newer versions (SM3) may not need to do so. It depends on whether the loop is static or dynamic.

The following HLSL code for a static loop:

```
for (int i=0; i<5; i++)
   Output.RGBColor = g_MeshTexture.Sample(
                        MeshTextureSampler,
                        In.TextureUV) * In.Diffuse;
```

Generates this in assembly:

```
SM2:
    texld r0, t0, s0
    mul r0, r0, v0
    mov oC0, r0
SM3:
    texld r0, v1, s0
    mul r0, r0, v0
    mov r1, c0.y
    rep i0
    mov r1, r0
  endrep
  mov oC0, r1
```

If the code is changed to be a dynamic loop (SM3 feature) as follows:

```
for (int i=0; i<Var; i++)
   Output.RGBColor = g_MeshTexture.Sample(MeshTextureSampler, In.TextureUV) *
                                       In.Diffuse;
```

The following assembly is generated:

```
texld r0, v1, s0
  mul r0, r0, v0
```

```
mov r1, c1.x
mov r2.x, c1.x
rep i0
  if_lt r2.x, c0.x
    add r2.x, r2.x, c1.y
    mov r1, r0
  endif
endrep
mov oC0, r1
```

Proper branching can help speed up code, but there are some pitfalls to be aware of. Instead of doing a particular operation, you can skip it as well as the rest of the shader. Static branching is pretty nice because it will do the comparison during compile or between shader execution. The only real penalty for static branching is that code is not completely inline (jumps occur based on the branch). Dynamic branching, on the other hand, will branch based on variables during shader execution. There are performance penalties for doing each compare (to figure out whether to branch or not), and the performance can alter based on what executes after the branch. It should be noted that dynamic branching does a compare per vertex/primitive/pixel (depends on the type of shader) and can start to add up quickly.

Constants

Constant variables are a special kind of variable in DirectX. Basically, they are variables that are stored in registers or buffers and are constant during the execution of the shader, as opposed to a true variable, which is updated during execution. It is important to understand that the API limits don't necessarily reflect what is optimal. For example, shader model 3 hardware is required to support 256 vertex shader constants. Most architectures store shader constants in caches or registers. Fixed constants can sometimes get compiled right into the shader. But there may be a performance cliff if you exceed available space.

Indexed constants may not be able to be allocated in cache or registers because the true value is not known until the index is looked up. These would show as something like c0[a0.x] in the disassembly statements. Thus, just because the disassembly shows that values are being stored in registers doesn't mean that they are truly using hardware registers.

In Direct3D 10, the idea of constant buffers (cbuffer) was introduced. Instead of individually updating constants, the whole buffer(s) can be updated. However, this can work against you. If your two most commonly updated constants are in separate cbuffers, you can cause a lot more work than is really needed. Constants should be grouped into constant buffers based on frequency of update. For example:

```
cbuffer UpdatePerScene
{
  float Constant_1;
  float Constant_2;
  float3 Constant_3;
  float4 Constant_4;
  float4 Constant_5;
};

cbuffer UpdatePerFrame
{
  float Constant_6;
  float3 Constant_7;
  float3 Constant_8;
  float4 Constant_9;
  float4x4 Constant_10;
};
```

In Direct3D 9, most hardware vendors optimize their drivers to store constants in whatever registers or caches that will fit. In Direct3D 10, due to the constant buffer model, the optimization falls to the developer. The organization of those buffers can be optimized to allow for the registers/caches mentioned in the Direct3D 9 portion to be used.

Direct3D 10 also introduced the concept of a texture buffer (tbuffer). This is similar to a constant buffer, but it is optimized for random access of large numbers of constants. Tbuffers are a mixed bag, because they rapidly increase memory footprint and cause cache misses. On lower-end hardware, they can be a significant performance drain. You can test if they are a bottleneck by reducing your constant footprint and seeing if performance increases.

Runtime Considerations

Shaders bring a lot of power to your application. However, there are a few areas of your game's infrastructure that they will affect. They won't necessarily show up as bottlenecks in your profiler, but they will cost you in terms of code complexity and maintenance.

The first area is *shader compilation*. All shaders are compiled to some degree when you load them (unless you are targeting a platform with a single GPU and unrestricted APIs, like a console). Even shader assembly is converted to the GPU's native microcode. But more often, applications ship with HLSL or GLSL or another high-level language, which is compiled at load time. This is more flexible, and makes it easier for driver updates to improve performance, but it can take a while to process all the shader code. Keep an eye on your load times. It might be beneficial to cache the compiled form of your shaders to simplify loading time.

The second area is *shader count*. Early programmable GPUs could not have multiple shader programs in flight, meaning that changing the active shader required a flush of the shader execution units. More recent GPUs can have different shader programs executing simultaneously, but there is still a penalty to having a lot of shaders in a single scene. It puts more strain on the shader instruction cache, and it means more state changes, too.

There are three general schools of thought with regard to shader count. First is the *ubershader* approach, which is to write a single master shader with many conditionals that can be toggled for all the different materials in the world. This can work, but all the conditionals introduce overhead, and it can be difficult to maintain due to the many interactions in the single shader.

Second is the *programmatic* approach, where shaders are constructed on the fly from small fragments of shader code based on higher-level descriptions of materials in the scene. This is more complex to develop because it requires a lot of infrastructure and an intricate synthesis engine, but it gives leaner shaders.

Finally, there is the *hand-written* approach, where technical artists and coders work together to develop custom shaders for each scenario that the game requires. On the surface, this sounds like more work. But in practice, games tend to rely heavily on just a few high-quality materials with great tweakability—if artists are given the right knobs, they can make the world look good.

There are other options for reducing shader count, too. The biggest cause of shader count explosions is not the basic materials, but all the interactions in the world between lights, shadows, and materials. If you must have # of basic materials * # of light types * # of shadow types, you not only have a major increase in shader programs, but also a lot of complexity in the shader setup between draw calls.

With deferred shading, you can use the same basic shaders for all of the objects in the world, a few shaders for light and shadow accumulation, and finally a material shader to do the final rendering pass. It reduces a multiplicative explosion in shader count to an additive growth. Of course, it does require more renderer complexity and fill-rate, so for scenes with simple lighting and shadowing, it may not be worth it.

The final consideration is *effects frameworks*. These are libraries like the DirectX Effects Framework, CgFX, or ColladaFX. They are supported by tools like NVIDIA's FX Composer. They provide a high-level language for describing how geometry, pixel, and vertex shaders can be combined to render a given material. They are very flexible ways to build complex, modular ways.

However, effects frameworks are usually more oriented toward ease of use and flexibility than performance. They are also usually closed source. You will notice that most game engines (Unreal 3, Source, Unity3D, Torque, Gamebryo) all have their own material/effects rendering systems. Because managing shaders and materials is such a key part of the performance picture, it turns out that relying on third-party libraries is a bad idea. They make it hard to debug code or performance problems. They are usually tricky to integrate tightly into a rendering pipeline. They don't usually support all platforms. And they can make it very easy for artists to introduce performance problems by copying and pasting example code from the Web.

There is no harm in using an effects framework to get your game off the ground. And it may be that you can get all the way through QA to shipping with that, depending on the needs of your game and the maturity and options of the library. But we highly recommend abstracting your material system so that if you need to swap effects frameworks or move to your own solution, you have the freedom to do so without a major rewrite of your game.

Conclusion

Optimizing shaders can be a lot of fun. The techniques are similar to those used for optimizing CPU-executed code, with special considerations around texture sampling, constants, and available resources. Because all of the operations are massively parallel, there's great feedback when you get performance up. Find a good benchmark, identify the specific shaders that are hurting performance, and go nuts!

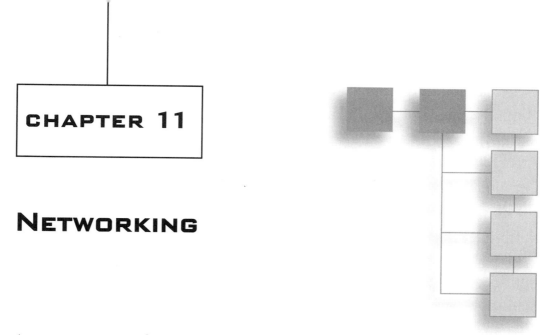

CHAPTER 11

NETWORKING

As mass storage performance is dominated by the physical attributes of the disk, a networked application is dominated by the network link over which it is operating. Every other part of a computer is at least an order of magnitude faster than its network connection.

Writing good networked game code requires embracing the limitations and problems inherent in networked communications. You have to know what is really going on behind the scenes in order to get good results. Despite this, it is possible to build compelling, rich networked worlds with limited resources.

Fundamental Issues

There are three fundamental issues when it comes to networking: throughput, latency, and reliability. *Throughput* you are already familiar with from previous discussions—the rate at which data is transferred. *Latency* is the time for a message to travel from one end of the connection to the other. *Round trip time* (RTT) is the time for a trip to one end of a connection and back.

Reliability is an issue that most other types of hardware don't present. If you draw a triangle with the graphics card, either it works immediately, or it is time to reboot. If you write some data to memory, it just works. If you want to read something from disk, you generally don't have to worry about any complex error scenarios.

Network data transmission is a different story. Not only can packets be out of order, but they can be corrupted, truncated, or even lost! At its lowest level, you might never know what happened to a packet you've sent.

Any successful networking system has to handle these issues.

Types of Traffic

Nearly every operating system ships with an implementation of Berkeley Sockets. On Mac and Linux, it is a derivative of the original implementation. On Windows, there is WinSock, which is a superset of the Berkeley API. There are a few other variant technologies, but in general, when it comes to networking, Berkeley has set the standard.

The first distinction in networking is in regards to reliability. You can either handle it yourself, or leave it up to the operating system. This is the difference between UDP and TCP. In UDP, the User Datagram Protocol, you can send and receive datagrams, but there is no concept of a fixed connection. Datagrams may be lost, received multiple times, delivered out of order, corrupted, or fail in many other ways. If you want your data to be sent reliably or in a specific order, you have to do it yourself. On the other hand, the true nature of the network is exposed to you, and you have a lot less OS involvement in the process.

TCP, the Transmission Control Protocol, lets you send data as if you were working with a file stream. Data is sent in order with guaranteed delivery. On the other end, the networking stack (typically provided by the OS but sometimes by software running on the network card itself) ensures that data is also received by the application on the other end in the same order with nothing missing. This is done at some cost to efficiency.

Another distinction in networking is between client/server architectures and peer-to-peer. Different games use different approaches in this area. Depending on the type of game and number of players, one or the other might give better results. This is a discussion well outside the scope of this performance-oriented chapter, so we encourage you to review the resources mentioned at the end of this chapter if you want to learn more.

Those are the basics. Now we'll talk in some more detail about types of reliability and how they play out in a real-time game networking context.

There are two main conditions for thinking about network transmission: reliability and order.

Data delivery can be reliable or unreliable. Reliable means that, unless the connection completely fails, the data will arrive on the other side. Unreliable means that any specific piece of data might be lost, although the success rate is usually quite high.

Delivery can be ordered or unordered. Ordered delivery ensures that if you send messages 1,2,3, they will arrive in that order. If packets arrive out of order, data is buffered until the missing pieces arrive. Unordered delivery means that data is processed in the order it is received, so our example might arrive 3,1,2 or in any other order.

This gives us a nice four-quadrant diagram:

Ordered, Guaranteed	Unordered, Guaranteed
Ordered, Unguaranteed	Unordered, Unguaranteed

In the next few sections, you'll see that different types of game traffic fall into different quadrants.

One point to understand is that TCP is implemented in terms of raw datagram delivery. In other words, it sits on top of the functionality that the UDP layer exposes. So you can do everything that TCP does in your own protocols, with the added benefit that you have much more direct control over what is going on.

At the end of this chapter, we will discuss various middleware, some open source and some closed source, which can help you on your way to having a working networked game.

Game State and Events

We've described how raw data delivery works—how to get buffers of bytes from place to place on the Internet in different ways. Once you have the ability to control how your data flows, you can move on to discussing the different delivery needs for different kinds of data. The two main types of data for game networking are events and most-recent-state data.

Events are discrete messages you want to send, like chat messages or events such as a lightning strike in-game or a signal indicating the end of the round. They are basically equivalent to remote procedure calls (RPCs). They are often ordered and reliable. A game will usually have many different kinds of network events that are sent.

Most-recent-state data is what makes the game go around, and they're a big optimization opportunity. Most games have a lot of objects that need to be approximately consistent on all the nodes in the network, and for which only the current state is relevant.

A good example is a door. You can model it as a single bit, and players only care about whether the door is currently open or closed. Suppose that you have a maze with thousands of doors in it. You assign each door a shared ID that is the same between client and server. Then, as doors change state, you send the latest state in unguaranteed, unordered packets. If a packet is lost, it's not a big deal—just note that you need to resend whatever updates were in that packet, and when you do resend, send the latest state. If packets are duplicated or received out of order, you need to use information from your protocol to reject the old or already-processed data. In the case of TCP, this is easy; in the case of UDP, it's slightly trickier.

This not only works for doors, but it also works for nearly everything else in a game world. Colors of trees, locations of power-ups, and even the position and status of other players can all be tracked this way.

The only situation that this approach is not good for is when you need to simulate exactly the behavior of a game entity on every peer. Most recent state only gives approximate results. For instance, the player character that a client controls needs to exactly match, at every tick, the player's input. Otherwise, control feels loose and laggy, cheating is possible, and artifacts may occur, such as remote players walking through walls.

The solution is for the client to send a stream of its moves to the server. Then the server can play them back to mimic the client's moves exactly. The server, if it is authoritative, can also send a full precision update of the player character's state to the client in every packet, so the client has the best and freshest information. (You can replace client with "player's node" and server with "the other peers" if you are working in a P2P environment.)

Bandwidth and Bit Packing and Packets, Oh My!

Before we move on to what data gets sent, let's talk about *how* it should be encoded and *why* encoding matters. The previous section presented a networking strategy—a bunch of small chunks of data encoding various pieces of game state. And even if your networking doesn't work with exactly the same types of data, it probably still has lots of small pieces of data being transmitted—this is typical in games. Lots of small packets means lots of overhead.

First, ***bandwidth drives fidelity.*** That is, the more effectively you can use your bandwidth, or the more bandwidth you can use, the more state updates you can send. The more updates you can send, the more consistent the world state will be for everyone. In the ideal case, everyone would be able to get full precision world state information in every packet. But this is rarely possible, so the system must be able to send as much game state as possible in every packet.

You want your updates to be as small as possible. How do you do this? The basic tool at your disposal is how you pack your data. At minimum, you want a bit stream where you can write values with varying numbers of bits. That way, if you have a flag, it only takes one bit; if you have a state that can have one of four values, you only need two bits. You should be able to encode floats with varying precision as well. Things like health often don't need more than seven or eight bits to look correct to clients, even if you use full floats internally. Integers often fall into a known range, and can be encoded more efficiently (and validated) with this knowledge.

After you use a bitstream to pack your data, you can add all sorts of interesting encoding techniques. See Figure 11.1 for a visualization of how the approaches

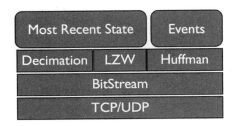

Figure 11.1

View of the game protocol-encoding stack. At the lowest level is the network transport that transmits bytes. Above this, the bitstream, which allows bit-level encoding. Above this, various context-specific options like LZW, Huffman encoding, or decimation. And on top, the various kinds of updates that your game sends.

will layer. Huffman encoding is useful for strings. You might also want to have a shared string table that you can index into instead of sending full strings. You can use LZW compression for bulk data. There are more advanced techniques like arithmetic coders that can take advantage of statistical knowledge of what data looks like.

The smaller your updates are, the more you can send in each packet, the more effectively you can prioritize them, and the better your user's experience will be.

Second, *prioritize data intelligently.* With each packet, you want to start filling it with the most important data and only send less important data if you have space. With most recent state data, you want a heuristic that not only takes into account how long it has been since each object has been updated, but also how close it is to the player and how important it is for game purposes. A projectile moving toward the player at high speed is a lot more important than a vehicle driving slowly away in the distance.

Third, *only send what you must.* This saves bandwidth and prevents cheating. Checking can take a little work, but if you have any sort of zone, potentially visible set, or at a minimum a frustum, it works out pretty well—you only need to be mostly accurate to cut down on the worst offenses. You could also cast rays from the player's eye position to potentially networked objects to determine if they should be considered visible. Skipping updates for invisible objects has big benefits. Ideally, the client will have no idea what is happening in the world other than what is directly relevant for the player, which saves on both bandwidth and on processing power.

Culling (i.e., only sending what you must) is different than prioritizing updates. In the case of low priority updates, you may still want the object to be known to the client. For instance a tree might be very low priority but still relevant. On the other hand, even though the movements of an enemy on the other side of a wall are highly relevant to a player, you might want to purposely omit information about it from the network stream until it is very nearly visible to the player, to prevent cheating.

There are a few other things to keep in mind with your packets. Make sure they are not too big. The maximum safe size for general Internet traffic is about 1,400 bytes—any bigger and you risk packets getting lost, corrupted, or truncated. A quick explanation of this limit: the MTU for Ethernet traffic is 1,500 bytes. Since most of the Internet runs over Ethernet, it is a good base size to plan around. If you then subtract some space for headers, compression/transmission overhead, etc., you end up with 1,400 bytes. Choosing this size also gives you some wiggle room if you end up needing to go a few bytes over sometimes.

Make sure that you send packets regularly. Routers allocate bandwidth to those who use it. If your bandwidth usage varies over time, routers tend to give bandwidth to other users. So the best policy is to send packets of fixed size at a fixed rate. For instance, you might send an 800-byte packet 10 times a second, using 8KB/sec of bandwidth. You can tune this based on player connection, server load, and many other factors.

Using fixed bandwidth/packet rate also exposes potential problems immediately for users. So instead of letting them get into the game, start doing something, and then experiencing bad play when the link becomes saturated with updates, if they can't support the required traffic levels, the game fails immediately.

How to Optimize Networking

Optimizing your networking code follows the same cycle—profile, change, and measure again—as every other kind of optimization work. The bottlenecks are quite a bit different, though. Computation is usually not a bottleneck because the network link is so much slower. Usually, you are optimizing for user experience, which means minimizing latency and maintaining fidelity.

The first order of business is getting the OS to do what you want. Most applications just want to get bits from one end of a TCP connection to another in bulk—for instance, an FTP client—they don't want to deal with the innards of the transport. The OS caters to this by default, but there is a cost in latency.

If your network IO thread is also your main game thread, you want to use nonblocking IO, so that you can do other productive work like drawing frames while waiting for your data to arrive. This is done on most operating systems by setting a flag—`fcntl` or `ioctl` are the usual APIs. `write()` and `send()` return once the data is in the queue to transmit, but `read` and `recv` can either wait until data is available to return, or return and indicate that no data was available. If the connection is set to be blocking, they will wait, which makes simple protocols work properly by default, since the connection acts just like a normal file stream. If the connection is set to nonblocking, then the application can detect that there is no new data and intelligently deal with it.

And that is the key to performant networking—*dealing with it*. The key to good networking performance is embracing the fundamental issues of networking. The

OS will attempt to isolate you from this by buffering and delaying data so it looks like a linear stream, which is quite counter to what's happening behind the scenes.

Speaking of buffering, if you are working with TCP, you need to be aware of Nagle's Algorithm. Sending many small packets increases networking overhead, as the overhead for a TCP packet is about 40 bytes—41 bytes for each byte of network traffic is pretty useless! John Nagle's enhancement is to combine writes so that full packets are sent. The flag that controls this is TCP_NODELAY (part of POSIX, so present on all OSes), and if you want to have more control over how your TCP packets are sent, it's wise to set it.

However, trying to get TCP to do exactly what you want can be a fool's errand. Sometimes, you'll have to make do with TCP. But in most cases, it's better to implement your own solution on top of UDP, because in addition to things like Nagel's algorithm, there's an unspecified amount of buffering and processing that happens not only in the networking stack in the operating system, but also potentially at every node along the route between you and the peer you are connected to. Traffic shapers and intelligent routers can buffer or even modify data en route based on the whims of network administrators. Virus scanners will delay delivery until they can determine that the data is free of viruses. Because TCP is easier to understand and work with on a per-connection basis, it is more often molested en route to client or server.

UDP is a much better option in terms of control. Because it is connectionless, most routing hardware and software leaves it alone, choosing either to send it or drop it. The bulk of Internet traffic is over TCP, so UDP often flies below the radar. Since it foregoes a stream abstraction, it's not as easy to modify, either. It also directly exposes the nature of networked data transfer to you, so that you can intelligently handle lost, delayed, or out-of-order data.

Another issue that frequently comes up with networking is the desire to do more than there is bandwidth available to do. This is one of the main reasons why compression is such a well-developed field. For your typical telecommunications giant, bandwidth is a major limiting factor—the more phone calls they can fit on an intercontinental fiber optic link, the better their bottom line.

Compression lets you trade computing power, quality, and latency for reduced bandwidth usage. For instance, you can run a raw image through JPEG and get a much smaller representation of nearly the same thing. But you must have the whole image ready for compression to start, and you also have to wait for it to finish before you can send it.

The best way to optimize for bandwidth usage is to add some (or use existing) counters that count how many bytes or bits each type of data is using—a simple network profiler. From there, you can easily identify the largest consumer and work on reducing it, either by sending it less often or by making it take less data when you do send it.

Another source of performance overhead is the cost per connection. This is, of course, more of a concern for servers, although P2P nodes can be affected, too. For most networked services, sufficient popularity is indistinguishable from a denial of service attack. So you need to consider the costs related to each connection, both during the connection process as well as while the connection is active.

The risk during the connection process is that the server can allocate resources for that connection before it is sure it is a valid user. With poorly designed code, an attacker can initiate a large number of connections cheaply, using up all the server's resources. Even in legitimate cases, a client might be unable to fully connect due to high traffic or firewalls, and keep retrying, wasting resources.

A good solution is to use client puzzles, small computational problems that clients must give the solution for before they are allowed to continue connecting. The server doesn't have to maintain any state per clients until they solve the puzzle, so it's very difficult for a DoS situation to occur.

Computational complexity and resource use when connections have been made are also important. If every connection takes up 100MB of RAM, you won't be able to support as many users as if each one takes 100KB. Similarly, if you have algorithms that are $O(n^3)$, it will directly impact your ability to scale user count. Optimizing algorithms is well-trodden ground at this point in the book, so the only advice we need to add is to make sure you profile any networked application under heavy load. A good journaling system can be very useful in doing this.

Watch out for DNS lookups. Resolving a host name such as www.google.com to an IP address can be costly. The default APIs (`gethostbyname`) can block for a very long time (seconds to minutes) if they are trying to connect to an unknown host or one with slow name resolution. This isn't a big deal for, say, a command line tool like ping, but for an interactive application it can be a big problem.

The common solution is to put DNS lookups on their own thread so that they are nonblocking. There are libraries and often OS APIs for doing asynchronous DNS lookups, too.

Embrace Failure

Any game can run well on a fast connection to a nearby server. The real test is what happens when a few packets get lost, or the player is on a bad connection, or there's a misbehaving router in the way. The trick to good networking is embracing failure.

- **Assume high latency:** Test with an artificial delay in your packet transmission/reception code. Latency of 100ms is a good starting assumption for hosts on the same coast as the player (Valve's source engine, for instance, is configured with this assumption), and some players will encounter latency up to 500ms. You'll have to figure out yourself where the bar is in terms of playable latency for your game, but make sure the system won't break due to short-term problems—even the best connections can have bad days (or milliseconds).

- **Expect packet loss:** If you are using UDP, add code to randomly drop packets. Loss rates of 20% are not unheard of. Packet loss tends to be bursty, so your system should be able to tolerate occasional periods of 20–30 seconds where no packets are received at all. (TCP, of course, will simply buffer and resend.)

- **Everyone is out to get you:** A lot of the time, denial of service attacks are planned by hostile hackers. But they are also indistinguishable from periods of high demand. Bugs can also cause DoS scenarios, such as a client who doesn't respect the timeout period between reconnections. Be paranoid and check everything. A good practice is to figure out what the worst thing that a client/peer could do, assume the client/peer will do it, and fix your code so it won't break in that scenario.

Lie to the User

One of the best ways to give users a great networked experience is to lie to them, blatantly and continuously. No, we don't mean about your age. We mean about the state of the game.

The human eye is drawn to discontinuous or abrupt movement. If something jerks or pops, it gets attention. If something moves smoothly, even if it doesn't move quite right, it's less likely to get attention.

To this end, you want to interpolate and extrapolate whenever you can. If you get a position update for an object, smoothly move the object to that position rather than setting it immediately resulting in a pop. If you don't get updates for something with predictable movement, you want to extrapolate via a client-side prediction until you get an authoritative update from the server.

This approach is known as *dead reckoning*. Since many objects tend to move in a reliable pattern, you can use heuristics on many different aspects of the physics for a given object. Linear interpolation may meet your needs for most cases, but if you still aren't getting what you are looking for, try making educated guesses about the future path due to current velocity, mass, angular velocities, or drag. The more data you use, the better you can guess. But be careful, the longer you wait for the update, the more likely you are to have big errors in your guess. Correcting the "guess" can lead to unnatural movement, popping, or even frustrated players.

Typical Scenarios

Most networking scenarios break down to one of the delivery types we mentioned previously. Let's go through a few common situations.

Asset Download

A lot of games, even single player games, need to have updates or patches. An MMO might need to stream world resources. Or a game might need to interact with Web services. All of these are situations where you want bulk, guaranteed delivery of in-order data.

The most common solution is to use TCP. In many cases, if that's all you need, HTTP is a good choice. Libraries like libcurl make it easy to add this functionality. For mass delivery of static data, HTTP is also great because it's easy to deploy to a server farm or a content delivery network.

Content delivery networks, like CloudFront by Amazon or Akamai's network, are server farms run by third parties, and are optimized for delivering large amounts of static content. Typically, they charge by the gigabyte of delivered content, and they include an API for uploading your own content to the service. They replicate data out to thousands of servers, eventually reaching edge servers. These edge servers use fast connections and geographic proximity to deliver fast downloads.

Streaming Audio/Video

Streaming audio and video in real time is more challenging. Imagine a game with voice chat (or even video chat). The user will want to hear what's being said now, not what was being said in the past, even if it means sacrificing some quality.

This is the simplest lossy scenario, because data only needs to be streamed out as quickly as possible, and if lost, no resending is necessary. You can think of it as a firehose—you let it spray data as fast as it can, and hope enough gets to where it needs to do the job.

This approach requires a lossy codec for your data. Luckily, there are a lot of good algorithms to choose from, since the telecommunications and cable industries have spent a lot of time and money developing them. Techniques like Linear Predictive Encoding are straightforward to implement and give acceptable results, although there are many advanced algorithms available for licensing.

Chat

Chat is a common scenario, and fairly easy to support. The messages must have guaranteed, ordered delivery. The bandwidth is not great. The logic is also fairly simple.

However, when you start targeting thousands or more simultaneous users, it becomes challenging—one has only to look at IRC to see the complexities there. But for your typical game of 10–100 players, chat is an easily solvable problem.

For chat, you can use things like LZW compression, Huffman encoding, and lookup tables with common words to reduce bandwidth usage. Human language is redundant, so compressible. It is easy to simply call zlib's `compress()` on some text before sending it or to look for common words and encoding their table index instead of the actual word.

In addition, because chat is not nearly as latency sensitive as game actions, it can often be sent when convenient instead of at top priority.

Gameplay

Gameplay is more difficult. Latency is very important. In a game like an RTS or an FPS, you only care about the most recent state—unlike chat, where knowing what people have previously said is nearly as important as knowing what they are saying now!

One exception is for the object that is being actively controlled by the player. Obviously, this is less of a concern for an RTS than it is for an FPS. Only sending the most recent state doesn't feel right when you have direct control. The solution there is to send frequent high-precision updates back from the server, and in addition, to transmit the move from each timestep to the server so that the player's character exactly matches on client and server.

Profiling Networking

Beyond looking at latency and other characteristics of a network link, what are the possibilities for optimizing your networking? How can you guide your efforts to improve the play experience most efficiently?

Well, first, make sure that your networking code is executing efficiently. You should carefully identify any bottlenecks or time sinks and optimize them away. Use benchmarks and careful measurements to identify areas of waste with regards to compute or memory. In most games, networking code takes up minimal CPU time compared to rendering, physics, and gameplay.

Second, expose what your networking layer is doing, especially in terms of number of packets sent and how bandwidth is spent in each packet. Adding accounting code so you can dump the average update size for each type of object in the game can be invaluable for identifying problem areas.

Often, one type of object will make up the bulk of your network traffic, either because it is extremely numerous in your game world or it is poorly implemented. To get better network performance, all you have to do is reduce the number of bits spent on that object type, either by sending fewer updates or by reducing the update size. This is where tricks like sacrificing precision or using more efficient encoding come in handy. Look for opportunities to avoid sending updates at all.

Third, be aware of situations when the client and server get out of sync. This is jarring to players and should be minimized, especially when their player character is concerned.

Finally, be aggressive about optimizing for perceived latency. Time how long it takes (with the aid of a video camera) between the user physically manipulating an input and the game reacting. It should take only a single frame to acknowledge input and start giving feedback to the user, if you want your game to feel snappy.

How to Build Good Networking into Your Game

There's quite a bit of complexity here! While any game that truly maximizes its networked potential will have to take it into account right from the beginning, a lot of the functionality is finicky, difficult to get right, and the same from game to game. In other words, a perfect job for a library to handle for you!

There are a lot of good libraries out there for game networking. We highly recommend OpenTNL (www.opentnl.org). It is open source as well as licensable from GarageGames for commercial use. And, one of your friendly authors worked on it!

Of course, that's not the only option. RakNet, ENet, and Quazal are also options. *Quake* 1–3 are all open source, and they all include their networking implementations. *Unreal* 2 and 3, Unity3D, and Torque have good networking, too.

As far as articles and talks, we can recommend the "Networking for Game Developers" (http://gafferongames.com/networking-for-game-programmers/) series by Glenn Fielder, as well as the "Robust, Efficient Networking" talk Ben Garney gave at Austin GDC '08 (http://coderhump.com/austin08/). Every game programming gems book has a few good chapters on game networking, too. The original "Tribes" networking paper is instructive (although the docs for OpenTNL subsume it), as is Yahn Bernier's paper on the networking in Valve's games (http://developer.valvesoftware.com/wiki/Latency_Compensating_Methods_in_Client/Server_In-game_Protocol_Design_and_Optimization).

If you do decide to do your own networking, we recommend designing it into your game technology from the beginning and testing heavily in adverse conditions. It takes a lot of work to build a solid networked game, and too many games have it tacked on at the end as an afterthought.

Conclusion

Bottom line: Networking in games is about building great experiences for your players. Optimization—minimizing latency and bandwidth and maximizing the feeling of control—is the order of the day. This chapter has outlined the major factors that go into building an optimal networking experience, discussed how you can optimize networking, and given you pointers to resources for integrating good networking into your own game.

CHAPTER 12

MASS STORAGE

Mass storage is where large amounts of data are kept. As you will recall, the memory pyramid starts with the register file, goes to cache, then RAM, followed by mass storage. Mass storage includes hard drives, CDs, DVDs, Blu-Ray discs, SSD, and Flash drives. On cartridge-based consoles, large ROM chips may even be available as "mass storage." Typically, you access mass storage via the file system API.

Mass storage is used throughout a game's execution. The game binary is loaded from the storage device at startup. DRM solutions often store keys and other identifying machines on the disk. Each level is loaded from the disk. Games with streaming assets are continuously loading from disk. And configuration and save games are written to the disk.

What Are the Performance Issues?

Mass storage is really, really slow. Not only is it slow, but it is unpredictably slow. Depending on when your IO request gets scheduled, the internal state of the file system, the rotation speed of the disk, and the location of the read head, speeds can range from "OK" to "abysmally slow."

On rotating media, like hard drives and optical discs, seek time is a huge limiter. Seek time is the time it takes for a disk head to move to the right position on the disk to read or write data. This can range from 2–20ms. There is also rotational delay, which is the time it takes for the platter to rotate such that the head can read from the disc. On a 7,200RPM drive, rotational delay can be as much as 8ms, although the odds that the drive will have to make an almost full rotation to read are low.

The final mass storage parameter is transfer rate. This is a measure of how long it takes, once the head and platter are in the right position, to actually read the requested data into a buffer in memory. This varies, but is on the order of 50–500MB/sec. You will have to determine your market segment to get specific numbers—high-end gamers with RAID arrays will be closer to the 500MB/sec range, while home users with aging desktop computers or laptops will be lucky to get 75MB/sec.

How to Profile

Profiling mass storage is pretty simple. Track how much execution time is spent in the mass storage APIs! You can do more specific measurements, like how many bytes are read/written, but for most game scenarios, the important thing is the time spent, not throughput. Similarly, the time the API spends waiting vs. doing real work isn't very important, unless the storage drivers are misbehaving to the point where they take a large chunk of the CPU.

Worst Case

What all this adds up to is a pretty terrible worst-case scenario. If you have data arranged on disk in the worst possible order (requiring a nearly full rotation and seek between each read), you might be looking at an 8ms delay between each block on the disk. If your file system works with 4KB blocks, then loading a 1MB file could take as long as two seconds (1024KB file/4KB blocks = 256 blocks. 256 blocks with a full seek is 256 blocks * 8ms/block = 2048ms = 2 sec.)! Loading a gigabyte file would take you the better part of an hour. (1,048,576KB file/4KB blocks = 262,144 blocks * 8ms/block = 2,097,152ms = 2097sec / 60secs/min = 34 min.) Your game would spend all its time waiting for the disk to spin, leaving you with a transfer rate of about 500KB/sec—not great for local storage. (NTFS for drives under 2TB use 4KB blocks; HFS+ for drives over 1GB use 4KB blocks; the default block size for ext3 is 4KB, too. That's why we use 4KB blocks for these calculations.)

Luckily, the worst case almost never happens. File systems are designed to keep data in some sort of order to prevent this sort of terrible scenario. Even a heavily fragmented drive will probably not hit this worst case, since fragmentation tends to be random. In addition, hard disk drivers and controllers try to schedule IO requests based on the disk's current rotation, which dramatically reduces seek times and increases throughput.

Best Case

If you can manage to get data in exactly the right order, what sort of performance could you see? Well, if seek time is zero (i.e., each piece of data is exactly after the preceding piece), then you are limited by the transfer rate of the disk. On average, this is about 75MB/sec (and going up every year). (See www.techarp.com/showarticle.aspx?artno=511&pgno=3.) So your 1GB file could load in as little as 13 seconds—a lot better than half an hour! Still much slower than RAM, though.

What About Fragmentation?

Disks are only of finite size. Files are written to the disk in blocks of a few kilobytes in size. The file system will try to store a file to contiguous blocks, as this will lead to faster access times, but it's not always possible. This results in fragmentation, where a file has to be broken into multiple fragments to fit into the free areas of the disk.

Fragmentation leads you a lot closer to worst-case scenarios. Every gap introduces a little more seek time, which eats away at performance. There is also more bookkeeping to keep track of where everything is located.

As disks get better and file systems more advanced, fragmentation is less of a performance scourge. Running a defragmenter used to be mandatory for good performance; now most computers do fine for long periods without one. Of course, if you can get your users to defragment, it's always a good idea, but you might be better off just convincing the developers on your project first!

SSDs to the Rescue!

Solid-state disks (SSDs) look like hard drives, but they do not use spinning platters for storage. Most commonly they use Flash technology, just like a USB thumb drive. This is a big win, because it removes seek times from the equation. Costs are generally fixed; writes are cheap and reads are cheaper. This determinism is a nice plus, because it means that fragmentation won't significantly affect performance.

SSDs have their own trade-offs, though. Writing and erasing data can be much slower, due to the nature of the storage media. They are also more costly (although the prices are tumbling). As the technology matures, they will become cheaper, more reliable, and more prevalent.

The Actual Data

Don't forget that once you have loaded your data from the disk, you will probably need to process it before it can be used. Images and sounds must be decompressed, script and XML must be parsed, and level data must be converted to runtime representations. A few milliseconds to get data off the disk leaves you very little time to process it before the user notices.

Bottom Line

The bottom line is that you'd better not be doing any disk IO in your inner loops. At minimum, a disk transaction is going to cost you milliseconds, and at worst, you could be sitting around for seconds or even minutes

Invariably, your game will be run on somebody's old, slow computer that has a 99% full disk and hasn't been defragmented in years. Don't assume that just because disk access isn't a problem on your computer that it will be fast for everyone.

A Caveat on Profiling

Because the path for mass storage is heavily mediated, be careful how far down the rabbit hole of disk optimization you go. File systems will optimize themselves based on access patterns. The disk itself will rebalance data based on load, sector failures, and downtime. The disk, disk controller, file system, and OS will all cache and reorder requests to try to enhance performance. User software may put itself in the path of disk access for virus scanning or backup purposes. Even a full reboot with power cycle won't reset all this state.

The best policy is to focus on big wins and test on fresh computers from time to time. Getting really reproducible disk benchmarks is not worth the effort.

What Are the Big Opportunities?

File access opens a huge can of worms. More than almost any other API you can touch, the performance downside of touching mass storage is almost unbounded. That said, there are a lot of things you can do to keep your game smooth even during heavy IO.

Hide Latency, Avoid Hitches

Basic IO operations can be slow. So don't do them in your inner loop! At the minimum, try to limit disk access to specific times during execution. Ideally, these times will be the loading screen between levels and the save screen. Users are trained to tolerate slowness at these times, but if the game starts hitching during intense action because you're blocking disk access, they won't be happy.

Operations like listing a directory can take quite a while. We highly recommend avoiding operations of this sort.

Minimize Reads and Writes

What's the difference between reading a gigabyte a byte at a time vs. a gigabyte in one request? A performance gain of 2^{10x}!

When you do hit the disk, make it count. Don't get data piecemeal. It's much better to get it all at once and then process it in memory, as the test data shows in Figure 12.1.

As you can see in Figures 12.1, 12.2, and 12.3 (the performance difference is so great that we broke it up into three ranges), only once you exceed a read size of 16KB does the cost of making the request become less than the cost of reading the data.

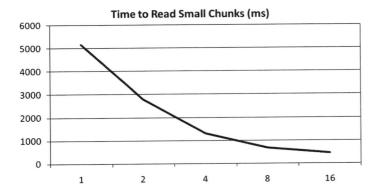

Figure 12.1

Reading a gigabyte of data in different size increments. At 1-byte chunks, it takes ~5,000ms, while at 16-byte chunks, it takes 500ms, a 10x speedup.

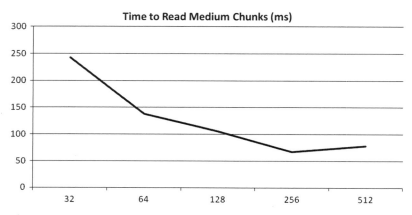

Figure 12.2

Reading 32-byte chunks takes 250ms, while 512-byte chunks takes 75ms, a 4x improvement. Notice that 512 increment is slightly slower—one of several hard-to-explain interactions between different parts of the disk subsystem.

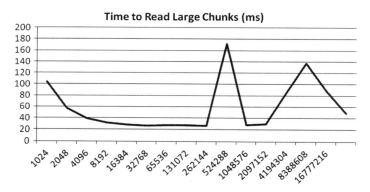

Figure 12.3

Performance gains increase until 256KB chunks, after which behavior becomes somewhat erratic.

There is a performance loss when you get to read requests of 1MB or greater, but it doesn't scale with the size of the read. In general, the best policy is to read data in the largest chunks possible. Often, it's smart to read the whole file in one go, because it gives the best information on what you are trying to do to the OS and disk. This can break down if you have lots of small files.

Asynchronous Access

The best way to hide the performance hit from disk access is to have a secondary thread that waits for it to complete. This is a several fold win.

First, it means that the user won't perceive any hitching. Your game can fire off a request and continue being interactive while the OS services the IO. If it takes 100ms for the file to read, it's not a big deal.

Second, since waiting for disk access means the CPU isn't doing anything, the thread will be spending 99% of its time waiting. This is a cheap cost to pay for smooth execution.

Third, you can use the standard POSIX file APIs that everyone else uses. If you try to have asynchronous IO on a single thread, you typically have to use a secondary set of IO functions provided by the operating system. These may or may not work very well. However, the standard APIs are always going to work right, because everyone uses them all the time.

Fourth, if the system can handle it, you can have background threads put multiple reads up at once. You'll want to test, but this can help performance by giving the disk driver something to do when it would otherwise be waiting for the disk to rotate.

If you go for asynchronous loading/streaming content, you will want to determine a strategy to deal with resources that aren't available yet. We'll discuss this in "For Those Who Stream" at the end of this chapter. We look at multithreading and disk performance in Figures 12.4 and 12.5.

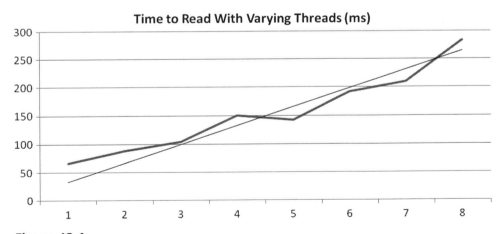

Figure 12.4

Multithreaded IO performance scales better than linearly. Each thread performs the same amount of IO (i.e., one thread reads N total bytes, two threads 2*N total bytes, and so on), but eight IO threads only take ~4x the time to execute.

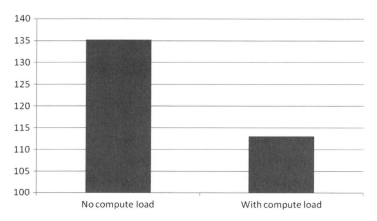

Figure 12.5

Left column shows how long it took to perform IO and computation in same thread. Right column shows how long it took to perform IO and computation in different threads.

We ran some tests comparing background threads to foreground IO, with the results shown in Figure 12.5. The first axis of comparison is background thread to foreground thread. All of these are performed with a computation load (the mandelbrot set) running to simulate the game's processing. As you can see, the background thread makes performance almost 3x better than doing loads in between processing.

You can also see that with multiple background threads, as shown in Figure 12.4, performance does not decay linearly. Going from one to eight threads only quadruples running time. This is because the disk has more opportunities to service IO because more requests are queued at the same time.

Optimize File Order

If you can control where data is written on your media, you can optimize based on your knowledge of your game. This typically applies to games shipped on optical disks, since it's very difficult to control where data is written on a user's hard drive.

The basic idea here is to order the data on disk to reduce seek time. The most frequently read data is put on the rim of the disk (since the disk rotates at a fixed angular speed, so linear speed is faster on the perimeter and reads are faster). In addition, data is ordered so that most reading is done in linear order to reduce seeks.

If you are on a file system with slow directory listing, or you have a lot of very small files, it can make sense to bundle many small individual files into a larger package. Most games nowadays use some variant of the ZIP format for this purpose, although early on very simple formats like WAD were used.

Optimize Data for Fast Loading

The big trade-off for game files in disk is space on disk vs. time to load. For instance, a JPEG compressed texture might be small on disk, but costly to decompress. On the other hand, storing the image in an uncompressed format like DDS that can be directly loaded will be a lot faster to process once in memory, but represents more data to transfer from the disk. Which one is faster?

In our tests, loading DDS images from disk was faster than JPEG with decompression. We loaded the Lena image, 512px by 512px. Times include both load from disk and decompression time. We used stbimage to decompress the JPEG. As you can see in Figure 12.6, the overhead of decompressing the JPEG is significantly more than the cost of loading the extra data for the DDS.

A format like XML is very convenient for editing, but it's overkill for runtime because in most games you already know most of what the format is telling you. It can make sense to convert from a more flexible format to a less flexible format when speed is more crucial. For instance, you might convert from XML to raw structs for fast loading.

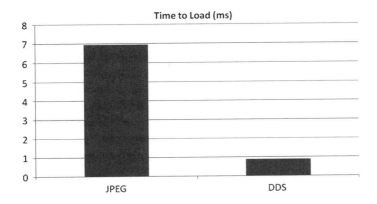

Figure 12.6

Despite its larger size on disk, the DDS format does not require any complex processing to load, and thus takes much less time.

We did some simple tests comparing the cost of parsing numbers printed in decimal form versus reading them directly into memory. Since most XML solutions would use `scanf` or a `scanf` similar function to convert raw strings from the XML parser into usable data, this forms a conservative test. As our results show in Figure 12.7, the `scanf` parser is a great deal slower. (For this discussion, we group `sscanf/scanf/fscanf`, as they differ only in the source of their data.)

Using XML or other human-readable formats can make a great deal of sense in terms of gained productivity, but not for performance. You will want to balance your team's need for usability against the application's need for performance. A useful technique is to convert human-readable data to binary data on load, so that loads of unchanged data are fast.

Loading binary disk data directly into memory is a powerful and venerable technique. The standard C library includes `fread` and `fwrite`, which are designed to directly read/write arrays of structs. Platform executable formats (COFF, ELF) are typically designed to be loaded directly into memory and executed. DOS overlay programming (which was not a new technique even then) was a technique for loading new executable code and data on the fly into the existing memory space as a program was running.

However, with dynamic memory management, endian issues, security issues, and changing internal structures, it's not feasible anymore to simply load data directly from the disk into memory. Instead, some abstraction is needed. XML is

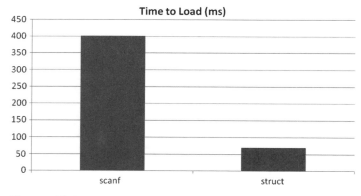

Figure 12.7

Parsing even simple human-readable text is slow; directly loading structs and doing pointer fix-up can be nearly an order of magnitude faster.

one such abstraction, and it is probably the most robust option for easy-to-manipulate data storage. But it is costly and bloated, compared to binary data.

A powerful technique is to serialize data directly from structs but store enough metadata to identify what type each field is, where it is in the file, etc. From this information, it is possible to do endian conversion at load time. Pointers, which normally would not be valid across serialization, can be stored relative to the start of the file. The data in the file can be loaded into a single buffer, and the starting address of the buffer can be added to every pointer field. The single-buffer load is both faster from the disk and also good for memory since it reduces the number of small allocations. Finally, the format can be versioned by comparing the metadata in the file describing the data structures to the application's actual working versions of those structures, and fields can be added or removed accordingly.

This fix-up naturally takes some time, but it is quite a bit simpler and faster than XML. In addition, if performance is needed, the format can be cooked to a greater or lesser extent. For instance, if you were shipping the data for a specific console, before preparing the final version of the data, you could endian-convert and match structures for all your data files to maximize loading time. However, our memory traversal performance numbers suggest that this wouldn't gain much.

Granny, by RAD Game Tools (www.radgametools.com/), implements a very mature version of this approach for its data format, and Dave Moore, the current maintainer, was kind enough to provide the information we used for this section. While Granny is ostensibly a 3D model loader and animation system, it has most of the building blocks of a good 3D engine in it. If you're working on a game project with a budget, we highly recommend reviewing Granny.

The file system itself imposes a lot of overhead. Opening and closing files is a good example. Is it worthwhile to group files in order to reduce the overhead? Our tests indicate that there is a big win here. The results from a test where we opened 100 random files and read one int, versus opening one very large file and reading 100 random ints (see Figure 12.9), shows that it's about 100x faster to go with the big file route. Performance did not change when varying the number of files in the folder from 100 to 1,000,000 (see Figure 12.8.)

Listing files in directories is also somewhat costly, but it scales linearly with the number of files in the directory (see Figure 12.10). So unless you have many thousands of files, it shouldn't be a big problem (although you won't want to do it frequently).

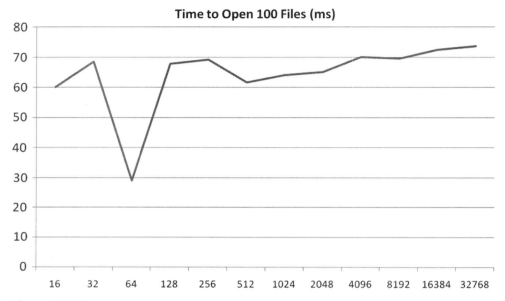

Figure 12.8

Time to fopen( )100 files as the number of files in the directory is varied. As you can see, even a large number of files in a directory doesn't adversely affect performance.

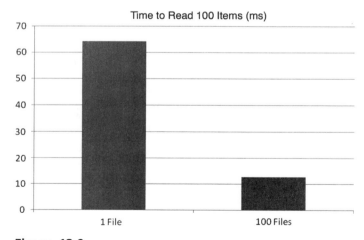

Figure 12.9

Loading 100 ints from a single file is about 6x faster than loading one int each from 100 files.

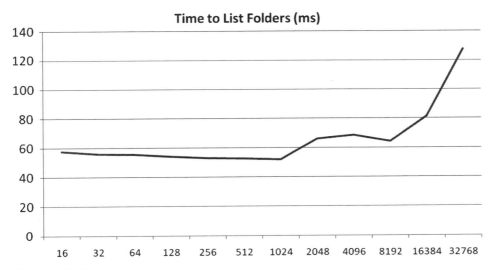

Figure 12.10

Time to list files in a folder. Notice that the X-axis is logarithmically scaled. It is scaling sublinearly.

Tips and Tricks

Bottom line: There isn't that much you can do about disk performance at runtime. Either you read data or you don't. Either you perform accesses in an efficient manner or you don't. Either you do it asynchronously or not.

If you are configuring your own hardware, there is a lot you can do, and not only a lot of literature, but a lot of companies that would love to help you build a super-fast storage node. If you are running content on consumer hardware, however, you have little to no control, and must simply tolerate whatever performance is available. Consoles are nice because you get very consistent behavior, so you can at least take everything you are given.

Know Your Disk Budget

Every game has an upper size limit. Maybe you are doing a downloadable game with a cap of a few megabytes. Maybe you are working on an AAA title spanning multiple optical discs with many gigabytes of space. Either way, make sure to sit down and figure out what your storage budget is.

The biggest resources will be videos, followed by sound and image data. Next come geometry and script files, and last but not least, the actual game binary.

Table 12.1 gives some useful rules of thumb for estimating resource sizes. For things like compressed image data (GIF, PNG, JPEG), game data (XML, binary

Table 12.1 Data Rates for Different Kinds of Data

Resource Type	Data Usage
CD-quality compressed audio (256KB MP3)	1MB/minute
CD-quality raw audio (44.1kHz @ 16-bit stereo samples)	10MB/minute
DVD-quality compressed video	1MB/sec
HD (1080p) compressed video	12MB/sec
1MP JPEG	200KB
1MP PNG	1MB

data), and executable code, the compression settings and context have so much influence it's hard to guess without doing tests for your particular situation.

If you have a disk budget, you'll know when you need to explore better compression or procedural techniques in order to keep your game to the right size. It also helps you plan for distribution and guesstimate your loading times.

Filters

File access is commonly hooked by third-party programs. For instance, anti-virus programs will typically scan disk IO for malicious activity. Even before A/V apps became commonplace, users ran disk extenders that would compress/decompress data on the fly to trade CPU time for storage space. These are particularly hard to profile or plan for, because they do nondeterministic operations inside the normal API calls.

The best defense is to make sure you are treating the API well. Do reads as big as you can, as infrequently as possible. Make sure that things degrade gracefully when performance is less than expected. Test on crappy fragmented hard drives with lots of AV software running.

Support Development and Runtime File Formats

Artists (and coders) benefit from rapid iterations. If they can tweak a texture and see the change immediately, it helps them build better art faster. In addition, it may be slow or complicated to produce files crunched down for runtime use. Files that load fast are often slow to edit.

For internal builds, it's much more important to make it easy to modify the game than it is to load quickly. Make sure that you can support file formats that are easy for the artists to work with. There are libraries to load Adobe Photoshop files, as well as many other formats (one such is OpenIL, found at http://openil. sourceforge.net/). This leads us to our next point.

Support Dynamic Reloading

One of the features that artists like best is being able to change a file on disk and have it update in the game in real time. If you build this into your game from the start, it's pretty easy to support. Adding it after the fact can be a huge pain.

To do this you need two pieces. First, you need a directory watcher routine that can look for changed files—by contents or by modification time. Second, you need a way, internally, to refresh the things that are using a resource.

Allowing artists to quickly and easily modify art while it is visible in the game lets them get more iterations in the art in the actual game environment. It's a small thing that can directly lead to better and higher quality art.

Automate Resource Processing

If resources need to be processed before they can be used or for optimal performance, it's a good idea to have them automatically generate as part of your build process. Resource builds, like all builds, should be done without human interaction in order to keep them consistent.

For smaller projects, all that might be needed is a quick script to look for everything in certain folders or with certain extensions and run a conversion tool. For larger projects, there are several large art management packages like Alien-brain that are specifically targeted for game artists.

Centralized Resource Loading

Only load things once. The best way to be sure is to have a centralized resource manager. Keep a dictionary with all your resources in it and check if something has already been loaded before you grab it from disk again. This can save you a huge amount of memory! It also gives you global visibility of load requests and loaded resources so that you can make more intelligent choices about what to load and unload.

Preload When Appropriate

If you know a resource is going to be needed, start loading it as soon as you can. For instance, you could start loading resources that the game will need as soon as execution starts so that by the time the player gets through the menu, everything is already loaded. Or you might just cache certain resources in memory all the time.

For Those Who Stream

If you're going to stream resources from the disk on-demand, make sure to have something to fill in the gaps until the resource is available. For instance, for a sound, you might keep the first second in memory all the time and load the rest when needed.

For textures, keep a few of the smaller mip levels in memory. This can also help reduce pressure on a streaming resource system, as you can defer loading until the resource is close enough to need the detail. With DXT compression, you can fit a couple of mip levels in only a few bytes. (DXT and related block compression schemes take 4px by 4px regions and convert them into 64-bit or 128-bit values. So you can store mipmap level 2 for only 4 or 8 bytes—just the right size for a header or object description structure.)

For geometry, it can make sense to have low and high LODs. In *Grand Theft Auto*, there are low-res models of the world that are always loaded, and high-res data that is paged in as the player moves. But even for quite a large, dense game world, only a few levels of LOD are used, instead of any sort of continuous method. This technique was used in *Grand Theft Auto: San Andreas* and in *Grand Theft Auto IV*.

If you are streaming, make sure to distinguish data that is needed for gameplay from data that is just for appearance. For instance, you may need to keep collision data loaded almost all the time, while everything else is optional.

Downloadable Content

If you are dealing with a game that must be downloaded to be bought, then download size is often more important than super fast load times (plus the total data size is smaller, so decompressing data won't be a big bottleneck). For AAA games on DVD, it might make sense to use uncompressed formats like DDS and heavily optimize for load times. For a smaller casual game, going with JPEG/PNG or even GIF and keeping your download small will pay off.

Conclusion

The best thing to do with disk access is to avoid it. Mass storage can take tens or hundreds of milliseconds to get your data. You should keep data in RAM if you can, or minimize its size on disk if you do need to load it. Put disk access on another thread so that waiting for data to come back from the disk does not block execution. And access data in big blocks and perform minimal processing on it so that loading stays fast.

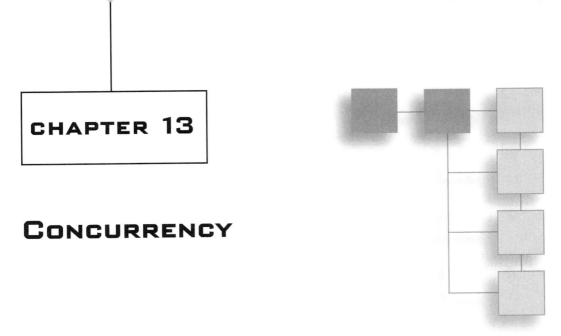

CHAPTER 13

CONCURRENCY

For years, we've heard about the need for multi-core processing and the promised benefits of implementing multiple threads as a means for doing more work in less time. If this is true, then why isn't everyone embracing multi-threaded algorithms? Even more perplexing is the lackluster returns many see when implementing multiple threaded algorithms. The legends of mythical, many-fold speedups have many asking: "If multiple threads on multiple cores are so great, then why does my single-threaded implementation run faster than my multi-threaded?"

The answer lies under the surface. Creating a thread is easy. Creating multiple threads is easy. Getting significant performance from multi-threaded applications can be very hard. The biggest risk is parallel code inadvertently becoming serialized, although there are other problems to overcome.

First, we're going to look at why multi-core CPUs have become so popular and the basic physical issues behind multi-threading that make it both so powerful and challenging to use well. Then we'll present the basic vocabulary of threading as it relates to performance. Finally, we'll give some practical examples of performance tuning concurrent code. This chapter isn't going to make you a threading expert, but it will give you the knowledge you need to make your threaded code perform well.

Why Multi-Core?

Why scale to multiple cores? Isn't it better to build single core chips that run faster and faster? To answer this, we have to look at the physical limits involved in manufacturing a microprocessor.

What are the ultimate limiting factors for a single processor's performance? One limit is the speed of light. To date, no one has figured out how to send a signal faster than the speed of light. This becomes a major issue. As chips get bigger, chip designers run into significant timing issues because signals take time to propagate. In addition, transistors, the building blocks of chips, take time to switch. There has to be time for signals to propagate and potentially many transistors to switch every clock cycle. Ultimately, even the speed of a transistor is limited by the propagation delay due to the speed of light.

So we want everything to be as small as possible for maximum speed. But there are limits to size, too—and light is largely at fault here as well. The photo-lithographic process that is used to "print" chips relies on a light source, and the wavelength of that light determines the minimum size of any individual piece of the chip. An electron charge sent through a wire will not travel faster than the speed of light by any means understood today. The limit of the speed of light becomes more noticeable as the size of chips increases.

While technology keeps improving, there are other factors that get in the way of increasing performance by increasing frequency. One is power consumption. As we increase frequency, we also increase power consumption. Unfortunately, this is not a linear correlation, so more and more power does not lead to higher and higher frequency. We have lots of power to spend, but all that power has to go somewhere, and a very dense chip runs into power dissipation issues very quickly.

In addition to all this, the chip requires that the rest of the system keep up with it. Latency to memory limits performance, as does the responsiveness of every other piece of the system. Another issue is the wall we hit from fetching memory. Going back to our earlier analogy in Chapter 6, "CPU Bound: Memory," which compares a CPU to a sports car and memory to a stoplight, reminds us that increasing frequency would only speed up the sports car and not the stoplight.

When architects build a city, they don't build one tower a thousand stories tall. Instead, there are many buildings of different heights, built appropriate to their purposes. It is a lot easier to build many cores that work together than it is to build a single core that can move the world. By adding more cores and decreasing frequency so that the additional cores don't use more power than we can provide, we can get a lot more performance per watt.

This is great news for laptops. And even before laptops were popular, the Voyager, Viking, and Galileo space probes (among many other projects) used networks of CPUs to get greater performance, reliability, efficiency, and flexibility.

Concurrency In Space!

In the aeronautics world, multi-core systems have been the standard for over four decades. Voyager 1 and 2 effectively ran three RCA 1802 chips at 1.6MHz. Viking and Galileo had larger processing networks. These networks gave higher reliability, and enabled real-time control of the probe's systems even with the very limited computing resources available. Take a moment to reflect on what it must be like to write a control routine to drive a billion dollar mission in 8-bit assembly!

Of course, progress is not going to stop tomorrow. Transistors will continue to decrease in size and increase in speed and efficiency. Frequencies will rise. Power dissipation will improve. Basic performance of cores will continue to rise for decades to come.

Before we dive into multi-threaded development, we can thank hardware, compiler, and OS developers for doing an awful lot of work for us. Instruction level parallelism gives us limited concurrency without any involvement on the part of the programmer. Multiple cores help reduce the pressure that multi-processing puts on a system without any effort from application writers.

However, in most situations, the best way to scale an application to multiple cores is with multi-threading. Either across multiple processes or within the same process, each thread can run independently on its own core. This allows the total system to achieve performance far in excess of any single computing element.

Why Multi-Threading Is Difficult

This title may be more suitable for a chapter or a book, but for now, we will cover the most fundamental reasons why multi-threaded programming is difficult. The issues lie in the understanding of the basics of your operating system and its relationship to a thread.

Here is a quick refresher on threads. Simply put, a *thread* is the smallest element of execution in a functional unit of an operating system. There are different ways to create threads, depending on which threading API you use. Some APIs are high level and abstract the finer details, such as OpenMP or Intel's Threading Building Blocks; other APIs, such as Windows Thread API and POSIX, enable low-level control.

Threading happens in two broad varieties: preemptive and cooperative threading. Cooperative threading is simplest. When a thread is ready, it yields execution to another thread. However, this has problems scaling; every thread has to know about every other thread in order for the scheduling to be fair. If a single thread fails, then the whole system grinds to a halt.

Modern operating systems implement preemptive threading. A scheduler monitors execution, and based on various rules, it switches executing threads so that each gets a turn to work. This switching process is called a *context switch*, and involves copying the thread's entire state—including registers, stack, and OS context—and replacing it with the next thread's state.

Preemptive threading is at the root of threading difficulty. Context switches can happen at any time, usually when it is least convenient. Preemption can happen right in the middle of a line of code, and it usually does.

The unpredictability of context switches gives us bugs that are not deterministic, given some set of user interactions. If you are lucky, the bug submitted by QA will occur every time you follow the sequence that created the bug report; if you are unlucky, that bug may only occur one every hundred or thousand times, or not at all if you are not on the tester's hardware.

Every thread programmer knows about the synchronization primitives—mutexes, semaphores, conditional variables, and the like—that allow us to ensure correct functioning. However, by adding synchronization logic, we all too often create performance problems.

Finding the minimum amount of synchronization that guarantees proper functioning is a fine art, and one we hope to introduce you to over the course of the rest of this chapter.

Data and Task Parallelism

Allowing a job to run in parallel requires that the job be broken down into pieces so that different hardware can operate on the job simultaneously. This process, known as *decomposition*, is achieved via two methods: data parallelism and task parallelism.

With data parallelism, you can achieve parallelism by dividing data and processing each segment independently. To compare data parallelism to a real-world example, consider an envelope stuffing session for a campaign. To perform the task in parallel, the envelopes and flyers (the data) are split between the volunteers. Each volunteer then independently opens envelopes, stuffs them, and closes them.

Data parallelism includes both a scatter and gather phase. Using the envelope stuffing session as a metaphor, the scatter operation occurs when you pass out the envelopes. The gather occurs as each envelope stuffer places an envelope in a bin to send to the post office. Often, the scattering of data is easy, but when it's time to gather the data, complications occur since threads may need to communicate closely in order to work correctly. In our example, if the volunteers don't communicate correctly, then they may end up filling a bin until it overflows.

To understand task parallelism, let's take the same circumstance and reorganize the group. This time, we will divide tasks among each volunteer and create a paradigm more like an assembly line. The envelopes will arrive at the first volunteer who will open it and pass it to the second volunteer who will stuff it. The envelope will continue down the assembly line until the overall task is complete.

This distinction works well, but in practice, more complex algorithms will be hybrids. Modern graphics pipelines are a good example of data and task parallelism at work together. For example, a GPU distributes data across its many cores and processes it in parallel. The vertex, pixel, and rasterization tasks a GPU performs are examples of scatter/gather. Through synch and ordering primitives, the work is split up and passed out across multiple cores, and later it is gathered. For instance, pixels from multiple draw calls can be in flight, but you have to make sure that they appear in the correct order when you blend them so the image is consistent.

Performance

For some, seeing is believing, and many don't see the performance increase they expect in their multi-threaded implementation. There are many potential causes, but most threading performance problems are due to three main causes: scalability, contention, or balancing.

Scalability

Problems of scalability prevent you from seeing continual increases in performance as you increase threading and/or cores. Many multi-threaded algorithms will not continually show an increase in performance as you add threads and cores. Developing an algorithm that will scale indefinitely can be quite daunting. Problems that can scale indefinitely are called "embarrassingly parallel." Graphics/pixel processing is one such problem, which is why GPUs have been so successful at increasing performance.

For a long time, we pointed to Amdahl's law when trying to describe one of the typical scalability issues. Amdahl stated that the maximum speedup from parallelization depends on the portion of the task that is serial. The serial portion often occurs where communication between processors exists or when a gathering of information occurs. Using our letter stuffing campaign as an example, serial execution occurs when the letter bin is full and everyone stops adding letters to the bin until the old one is gone and a new bin is in place.

Amdahl's Law reads:

$$1/(1-P+P/S)$$

Where P is the proportion of the program we are speeding up and S is the factor by which we've sped that part up. Let's take a look at what happens if we can take 80% of our program and parallelize it.

As you can see from this graph, ultimately the speed of the app is limited by the part that *isn't* parallelized. In other words, the limit to scalability is the serial portion of our app. Of course, in our example, we still made the whole thing X times faster. But that's assuming that the parallelized part has no serial portions and that the code runs in complete isolation from the rest of the system until it's synchronized.

In 1988, Gustafson came up with his own law, which offers another solution to the calculation of predicting scalability.

Gustafson's Law reads:

$$S = a(n) + p * (1-a(n))$$

Where $a(n)$ is the serial function and p is the number of processors. Gustafson states that the significance of the serial portion becomes less a contributing factor as n approaches infinity. In other words, according to Gustafson, if the size of the job of the parallel algorithm can grow to be larger and larger, so can our returns of being parallel since the serial part does not necessarily grow linearly with the parallel part.

For an example of how Gustafson's Law plays out, let's look at image processing. There is a serial part (loading and unloading the buffers holding the image) and a parallel part (running the processing kernel on each pixel). The more complex the kernel, the bigger the speedup from parallelization because it will overshadow the cost of copying data into/out of the buffer. In this example, increasing the size of the image can improve performance gain, as long as your processing time per byte is greater than your transfer time.

To add to the confusion, Shi suggests that there is, in fact, one law and the two equations are actually equal (Shi, 1996). Shi states that determining the concept of a serial percentage of a program is misleading and that Gustafson's definition of p is different than Amdahl's.

Computer scientists continue to cite and dispute the methods for predicting parallel performance increase. But there is one thing they won't dispute: Serial execution in a parallel algorithm is bad for performance. When designing a parallel algorithm, consider what elements of your algorithm will cause serial execution and do your best to reduce or remove them.

Contention

In a perfect world, we would be able to write programs that could be entirely parallelized with no serial portion at all. But practically, we run into a major issue related to our desire for our program to execute correctly and in a reliable and consistent manner. This limiting factor is called *contention*. Contention occurs when one or more threads attempt to access the same resource at the same time.

Imagine each resource as an intersection. Cars (threads) pass through it in several directions at once. If cars go through with no regulation, then eventually there will be a wreck, either a literal crash or incorrect program behavior.

There are many ways to tackle this problem. They vary in complexity, performance, and effectiveness.

The simplest solution is to put up stop signs. Threads use the resource on a first-come, first-served basis. You can implement this by using a mutex. This approach requires each thread to lock the mutex while they're using the resource, and you're set. You'll often see this approach used to quickly make a subsystem thread-safe—for instance, a memory manager will often have a global mutex.

Another option is to replace the intersection with separate, nonintersecting roads. For instance, we might give each thread its own local heap, instead of making them contend over a single global heap. But in some cases, this isn't feasible. For instance, memory usage by threads might be so great that there isn't enough to reserve for each thread's heap. Or the shared resource might need to be common between all threads in order for correct program execution, like a draw queue.

Even though a resource might need to be shared, it doesn't need to be exactly in sync all the time. For instance, the draw queue might only need to be double buffered rather than shared, reducing the number of potential contentions from hundreds a frame to one.

A third option is to look for more efficient synchronization. In the context of the intersection, this is like installing stoplights and allowing turns on red. Sometimes, you can break up a single resource into multiple parts that can be accessed independently, for example, do finer-grained synchronization. Other times, you can use hardware support to make synchronization operations faster. In yet other cases, it may be possible to remove extraneous synchronization checks.

Synchronization primitives (mutexes, locks, semaphores, atomic operations, etc.) are essential for correct functioning. But each one holds the possibility for your threads to fall back into a serial mode and lose all the performance gains you get from concurrency. Serial operation, as we noted in the previous section, is a major limiter for performance of multi-threaded implementations.

Balancing

Balancing workload is the final third of the thread performance picture. Just as the whole computer must have a balanced workload for maximum efficiency, your various computing tasks need to be balanced among the different hardware elements that can run them. It's no good having a multi-threaded application that uses one core completely and leaves the rest untouched.

We already have a powerful set of techniques for measuring this, which are the same profiling techniques we have been discussing throughout this book. Look at the CPU utilization of the cores on your target system, and if they are uneven, determine what factor is preventing them all from being used evenly. Likely causes are starvation (not enough work to keep them all busy, or an artificial limit preventing work from being allocated properly) or serialization (for example, dependencies between tasks that force them to be executed in order rather than in parallel).

The rest of this chapter goes into more detail on strategies for keeping workloads balanced.

Thread Creation

When we create a thread, we also create the structures required to manage a thread. These structures include thread local storage, kernel stack, user stack, and environment block. Creating threads involves some overhead and memory, and as you saw in Chapter 6, "CPU Bound: Memory," dynamic allocation of small amounts can lead to memory fragmentation. To use threads efficiently, you should create a thread pool and reuse threads instead of frequently creating and destroying threads.

So how many threads should you create? A common piece of advice, in regards to thread count, is to create one thread per core. But a quick look in the Windows Task Manger will yield numbers in the range of 500 to 1,200 threads, depending on how many processes are running. Does this mean that we need 500 to 1,200 cores to meet performance expectations? Technology moves fast, and although Intel suggests that we should be thinking in hundreds or thousands of threads (Ghuloum, 2008), we aren't there today on the CPU.

The 1-to-1 ratio of thread to core is a good general rule, but like any general rule, the reason for the popularity is probably more due to its simplicity than its accuracy. The 1-to-1 ratio is not necessarily for every case. For example, threads that are running as a lower priority or aren't performance sensitive do not require a 1-to-1 ratio. Threads that are often blocking on the OS can also be run at a higher density without problem.

The reason a 1-to-1 ratio works so well is due to the hardware support for concurrent processing. For example, consider the synchronization of six threads on a four-core machine. Since hardware only supports four threads, then only four threads can synchronize; the other two must wait for their turn on the core. We've now increased the time it takes to synchronize. We examine this point in the section "Example" at the end of this chapter.

Thread context switching is another part of the overhead of having many threads. It can take the operating system many cycles to switch from one thread to another. In many situations, it is cheaper for a thread that has completed a unit of work to grab another piece of work from a job queue rather than for it to switch to another thread or (worse) terminate itself and later start a new thread.

Thread Destruction

Since you shouldn't create threads during runtime, it probably follows that you shouldn't destroy them either. There are no real concerns for thread destruction and performance; however, you must ensure that all threads are finished before closing the application. If the main thread doesn't close all remaining threads successfully, the process will still exist, and you will likely need assistance from the operating system since you probably don't have an interface to shut down that dangling thread.

Thread Management

Sheep may appear to move in a semi-random way. Herders introduce other elements such as fences, dogs, and whistles; and although we can't control the sheep directly, a watchful eye ensures that the sheep don't go astray. Thread management, implemented with synchronization primitives, gives you the same capability not to directly control the OS, but rather manipulate it to do what you want.

Semaphore

Years ago, Edsger Dijkstra invented the semaphore, a primitive with two operations: acquire and release. Operating systems implement semaphores differently, but all synchronization objects share or decompose to the underlying concept of the semaphore. (A *mutex* can be thought of as a binary semaphore.)

```
class Semaphore
{
  // member functions
  unsigned int m_Current;
  unsigned int m_Count;

  //member functions
  Acquire();
  Release();
  Init( int count );
};
```

A semaphore acts as a gatekeeper for requests for threads. Consider the following, not so sanitary, analogy.

Often, when you need to use the restroom at a gas station, it is locked. Asking the store clerk yields some form of key, with a brick, hubcap, or some other object to deter you from stealing the key. Imagine if a particular gas station has 10 restrooms. If no one is using the restroom, the clerk has 10 keys; when the first person arrives, he/she is gladly handed a key. The clerk now has nine keys to pass to people requesting a key. If 10 people are currently using the restrooms, there are none available to give. The 11th person must wait until any of the other ten returns.

To compare the previous analogy to the class in question, m_Current is the total number of people using a restroom and m_Count is the number of restrooms. Acquire is similar to asking the clerk for a key and Release is akin to giving the key back. The people are the threads.

This simple structure is the basis for manipulation of the threads. Different operating systems implement this simple structure in different ways, so understanding the concept of the semaphore gives you a foundation for understanding every OS implementation.

Win32 Synchronization

Since many games use the Win32 thread primitives, we will spend a few sections discussing them specifically. All of the APIs we discuss here are valid from Windows 2000 on, and are likely to remain part of the core Windows API for many years to come.

Critical Sections and Mutex

A critical section and mutex have similar functionality with different implementations and performance implications. A critical section is a userspace anonymous mutex, and a Win32 mutex is an interprocess named mutex. There can be any number of either critical sections or mutexes. The functionality provides the easy ability to place an enter-and-leave call before and after a section of code that you want to protect from access by more than one thread or (in the case of the Win32 Mutex) process at a time.

Imagine two lakes connected by channels wide enough for only one boat. If any boats (threads) want to navigate to the other lake, they must first determine if the channel they want to use is empty before entering. This channel, where only one boat can fit at any time, is similar to a critical section or a mutex.

When a thread enters a critical section or takes a mutex, any other thread wishing to enter the critical section or take the mutex will contend for that space and block, until the occupying thread leaves the section or releases the mutex. Contention, as noted previously, is a cause of serial operation and a limiter of performance increases.

In Windows, the difference between a critical section and the mutex is the level at which the synchronization primitive is visible. The critical section implementation is only visible within an application; the mutex implementation is visible between applications as well. A mutex will be slower on average than a critical section, because it must deal with more complex scenarios. In most cases, you only need to synchronize between threads in the same application, so the critical section will be the most commonly used option.

The critical section and mutex, in Windows, share a similar interface. A critical section will use the syntax of Enter and Leave to specify areas of code where only one processor can enter at any given moment. A mutex will use a wait-function to enter the protected code and a `ReleaseMutex` call to exit the protected call.

Critical sections and mutexes are powerful and easy to use; unfortunately, they are also easy to abuse. For performance considerations, developers should not think of these two synchronization objects simply as a means for preventing multi-threading problems. Since contention is expensive, and noncontention is not, developers should create their algorithms with the goal of naturally reducing contention. If you design this way, you can use critical sections and mutexes as a failsafe in the unlikely event that two or more threads attempt to enter the same area at the same time. Reducing contention as much as possible is ideal.

Semaphore

Windows has a traditional semaphore implementation. A windows semaphore object uses `ReleaseSemaphone` to increment the semaphore and a `WaitFor*Object()` to decrement it.

Events

An event in Windows is a binary semaphore. So instead of being able to increment an event, it only has two states: signaled and nonsignaled. They are marked as signaled by using `SetEvent()`.

WaitFor*Object **Calls**

WaitForSingleObject, supplied with a handle to an appropriate object, and WaitForMultipleObjects, supplied with an array of handles, are two calls you can use to block these objects. For example, you can call WaitForSingleObject on an event handle to create an OS implemented blocking system to keep a thread waiting efficiently for another thread to signal the event. The wait function also has a parameter for setting a time-out interval. This time-out can be set to INFINITE, which implies that the function will wait indefinitely to control the semaphore, mutex, or event, or you can set a millisecond value that specifies a wait time before "giving up" on the wait and moving on.

```
HANDLE mutex = CreateMutex( NULL, FALSE, NULL );

DWORD dwWaitResult = WaitForSingleObject( mutex , INFINITE );
If( dwWaitResult )
{
   //critical code
   ReleaseMutex( mutex );
}
```

Multi-Threading Problems

So why are we doing all this synchronization? What would happen if we just let the threads run as they seem fit? Are there parts of our hardware that cause contention, or is this merely a software problem? Are there any problems other than performance that can occur if we use synchronization objects? These questions are answered when we examine race conditions, false sharing, and deadlocks.

Race Condition

In a typical race, the winner is the person who arrives first. In a race condition, the winner may be the thread that gets to a memory address last.

A race condition creates incorrect data due to unexpected interactions between threads. The classic example is two threads trying to increment the same variable. The interaction should go something like this:

1. Thread A) Read the value from memory into a register.

2. Thread A) Increment the register.

3. Thread A) Write the register to memory.

4. Thread B) Read the value from memory into a register.

5. Thread B) Increment the register.

6. Thread B) Write the register to memory.

If the value started at 1, now we have 3. But depending on the order of execution, the following could occur:

1. Thread A) Read the value from memory into a register.

2. Thread B) Read the value from memory into a register.

3. Thread A) Increment the register.

4. Thread A) Write the register to memory.

5. Thread B) Increment the register.

6. Thread B) Write the register to memory.

In which case, we end up with 2. Whoever writes his invalid data last has won the race and broken the program.

Sharing/False Sharing

A race condition creates incorrect results due to the issue of order; false sharing describes an issue with one or more cores using a memory address at the same time (or very near to the same time). It cannot happen in single core execution for reasons that will become clear shortly.

From the earlier chapter on memory, you should understand that memory utilizes a hierarchy of registers, caches, and DRAM. As the cache hierarchy transfers data, there is the potential for data to get out of sync. For instance, if one core reads some memory into cache right before another core writes to the same memory, there is the potential for the first core to have old values in its cache. When two or more cores share a cache line, the memory subsystem may force serial updates of the shared line to maintain data integrity. This serialization, known as *sharing*, creates an overhead that the program can do without. Figure 13.1 further explains the process in steps.

Consider two cores, 1 and 2, that read the same cache line from DRAM into the L2 cache and L1 cache (A). So far, coherency is maintained. If core 1 changes a value in the cache line, a coherency issue occurs (B). This type of issue is common

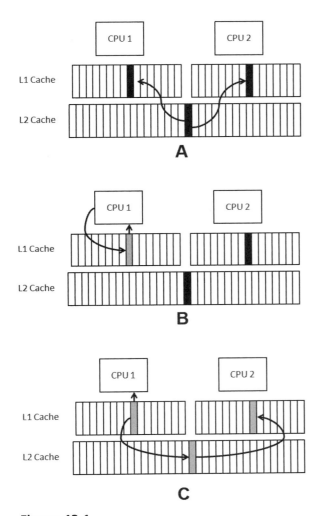

Figure 13.1

A shows the same data being loaded into two CPU's caches. B shows CPU 1 writing to the shared data. C shows corrective action being taken by the system to propagate the change to CPU 2's cache.

for a single thread, the discrepancy of the value in core 1's register is temporary and eventually the value of the register will copy to the cache and back to the DRAM. In this case, however, there is another discrepancy that exists between the register in core 1 and the register in core 2. This discrepancy is unacceptable and could lead to inaccuracies.

The hardware solves this problem the only way it can—by blocking core 2 from proceeding and forcing an update to occur that ensures the values in core 2's register match the L1 caches, the L2 cache, and core 2's registers. This comes at a cost of the update and time lost for the synchronization to occur. (When a CPU does this, it will also drop any predicatively executed results so that code runs consistently.) This update process is known as *sharing*.

False sharing is similar, but a bit more obtuse. Since the synchronization occurs when sharing cache lines, this type of synchronization can occur when core 1 and core 2 are working with completely different variables. The usual suspects are member variables or global variables being acted upon by two different cores at the same time.

In the worst case, false sharing can result in every core in the system running in serial, since each updates a cache line in turn and then blocks until every other core gets a chance to process the update. This results in a ping-pong effect because each processor runs in a serial mode updating the other.

Sharing of the same variable should be avoided; it is likely also a race condition. While false sharing will not result in a race condition, it still incurs the performance penalty of sharing. In the case of false sharing, the solution is easy: ensure that variables that are frequently updated by different threads are not on the same cache line.

```
struct vertex
{
  float xyz[3];   //data 1
  float tutv[2]; //data 2
};


vertex triList[N];
```

Let's use a vertex as an example to discuss the possible solutions. Let's assume that core 1 is working with data 1 and core 2 with data 2. We could pad the shared variables so they aren't on the same cache line, and although this would work, we have greatly bloated the size of the array.

We could reorganize the implementation to have core 1 operate on all even vertices and core 2 operate on the odd. This case will work well if the vertex is 64-byte aligned and 64 bytes in size (which is actually a popular vertex size). If it is close, padding by four bytes or so is probably an acceptable trade-off.

A better solution would be to convert the array of structures to a structure of arrays. The data is now separated and each core can access its data linearly, as opposed to periodically, a requirement of the prior structure.

```
struct vertices
{
  float xyz[3][N];    //  Core 1
  float tutv[2][N];   //  Core 2
};

vertices triList;
```

False sharing is not ideal; however, it's not as bad as it once was. Cores on the same chip often have shared caches, which removes the need for them to synchronize by writing all the way out to DRAM.

Deadlock

A deadlock occurs when two or more threads are mutually blocking. A deadlock is similar to a stalemate in chess—nothing wrong occurred per se, but the game is over and no one can move. Deadlocks can occur for many reasons, but typically, they are the result of faulty logic causing interdependent synchronization objects.

Let's start with a simple example. Let's take two threads, X and Y, and two critical sections, CSa and CSb. A deadlock would occur if the following order of events were to occur:

1. Thread X acquires CSa

2. Thread Y acquires CSb

3. Thread X blocks on CSb—thread X blocks indefinitely

4. Thread Y blocks on CSa—thread Y blocks indefinitely

Thread X waits indefinitely for Y's release of CSb, and thread Y waits indefinitely for X's release of CSa—they will wait forever. Deadlocks aren't performance concerns that you can optimize; you just need to remove them.

Deadlock occurrences are measureable statistically, meaning they can occur on a spectrum of having a high-to-low probability. A deadlock that has a one-in-a-million chance to occur is very hard to debug and chances are that there is a lot of shipped software with deadlocks in this probability. To combat this problem, there are tools that can perform a statistical analysis of your code and report where deadlocks may occur. One such program is Intel's Thread checker.

The previous example, if performed in a different order, would not have triggered a deadlock. If the OS created context switches in the following order, the code would proceed:

1. Thread X acquires CSa

2. Thread X acquires CSb

3. Thread X releases CSa

4. Thread X releases CSb

5. Thread Y acquires CSb

6. Thread Y blocks on CSa

7. Thread Y releases CSb

8. Thread Y releases CSa

Balancing

Resource contention can be an issue, but it's usually possible to avoid it with good design. For instance, if you are going to be doing a lot of disk IO, you might want to have a worker thread that services disk requests instead of having each thread do its own IO and potentially overloading the disk. Or if two threads are going to access the same section of memory frequently, they might benefit from having their own copies of the data.

Practical Limits

If you're writing useful programs, you'll have to deal with contention issues. In the last section, we talked about some situations where contention comes up and some ways to deal with it. But what are common reasons for contention to be needed?

Hidden locks can be a big performance hog, because they typically aren't added with performance in mind. Third-party code can sometimes have synchronization primitives in it that cause problems. For instance, a memory allocator might have a lock to access a shared heap. If you have threads that are frequently allocating or freeing memory, this can completely kill performance, effectively reducing the threads to serial execution. The hardware can sometimes enforce synchronization, too, for instance if two threads are trying to write to the same area in memory.

How Do We Measure?

At a basic level, you can spot threading performance issues by looking for lost time, time spent idle or waiting on synchronization primitives. If you see that 80% of your thread's time is spent trying to acquire locks, you know that something is wrong. Make sure that you have a profiler that supports multiple threads!

Look for normal API calls that sometimes take much longer than expected, as this is a sign of hidden locks or other forms of contention. If `printf` starts taking up 50% of your time when you add a second thread that prints, you should check whether it has a lock in it.

There are a few considerations to keep in mind when measuring threading performance. Look out for "heisenbugs," which are problems that disappear or appear when you try to observe them. Sometimes, the profiler can alter execution sufficiently to change your performance bottlenecks. Make sure that you test with a real workload; threading is indeterminate, so your numbers may change dramatically, depending on the situation.

Looking at it from a positive perspective, when you add threading, you should be measuring overall time for your benchmark. It's helpful to be able to execute in both a single-thread or multi-thread mode; then you can quickly do A/B comparisons to see where you're at performance wise. Sometimes, all that's needed for this is to force CPU affinity so that the program only runs on a single core. Additionally, you should be looking at the utilization of the resources that you intend to be using (for example, the other cores). When running with multiple threads, you should see much more even distribution of load.

Setting CPU affinity can also help identify some race conditions. If you force everything to run on one core, it has to be run in serial. Doing this lets you remove simultaneous access of data as a potential cause of problems.

In the case of using a thread to manage a slow resource (like disk access), you probably won't see a spike in utilization. Instead, you'll see a reduction in latency spikes—i.e., more regular and even frame times.

Solutions

First, look at your threading approach from a high level. Amdahl's Law is useful here; you can determine some theoretical limits on performance. Be aware that Amdahl's Law requires full knowledge of the system to be entirely accurate. If you only model part of the system with it, you may not be properly estimating available performance. For instance, sometimes you can get super-linear speedups because the hardware is better utilized by multiple threads.

Then you can use the usual process. Grab a multi-thread-capable profiler, identify the biggest performance loss, and fix it. Measure and repeat.

The best tactic for optimizing concurrent applications is removing sources of contention—attempts to lock mutexes, semaphores, etc. You must be careful that you don't sacrifice the correct functioning of your program. From there, it's very similar to optimizing a serial application.

There are some new tactics you can use. Try to keep high-use resources thread-local. If your thread is going to be allocating a lot of memory, give it its own local buffer of memory to use, so it doesn't have to hit the global heap all the time.

Depending on your hardware, you might be able to use so-called lockless algorithms, which can be much more efficient because they bring the granularity of synchronization down to single elements in a data structure. They require specific hardware support, so you have to be careful not to rely on functionality that only some users will have.

Finally, try to defer synchronization, if synchronization is costly. For instance, let a thread buffer several work elements before it merges them into the final result set. If you are doing lots of little tasks, this can save significant amounts of overhead.

Example

To better understand the challenges of writing fast multi-threaded code, we will step through an example using a multi-threaded implementation of parallel streaming data. This example would be a useful implementation for someone looking to read from an asynchronous resource or to parallelize a stream of messages and their associated data. In Chapter 16, "GPGPU," we will use a similar example to see how the GPU could also process this data. Most of the concepts from this chapter are used in the following examples.

The example demonstrates feeding data between two or more threads. Half of the threads will perform writing operations that will push an integer into an input/output buffer that we call a ReadWriter. In a more practical example, the reader operations may perform processing operations and then end with a reduction to a single value like you would in a MAX function, but for simplicity, this example will end with reading the data, a stream of integers, from the buffer. Efficiently

Example   277

reducing the buffer is an equally challenging problem. Luckily, the tips you will learn from this example with provide you with the understanding to solve that problem. Figure 13.2 illustrates the flow of execution in this example.

Using this example, we will review the concepts we've discussed thus far in this chapter.

Naïve `ReadWriter` **Implementation**

The simplest (incorrect) implementation of the `ReadWriter` would be to have a shared variable that threads could access. A writer thread could write to a variable and then a reader thread would read the value. Writing variables is not guaranteed to be atomic, so if one thread is writing to the memory, the reading thread may perform a read on a partially written value. This partial update is known as *tearing*, an occurrence you must protect against.

If you were to make the shared variable's reading and writing atomic, say by surrounding the shared variable with a critical section, or by using atomic operations (for instance, `InterlockedIncrement` on Win32), then the transaction would be safe; however, this is not optimal. In the best case, the two threads would behave serially, with a ping-pong-like transaction involving one thread waiting for the other to exit the critical section.

You might assume that two cores running at 50% give a similar performance to one core running at 100%, but that is not the case. Switching from one thread to another involves overhead in both hardware and in the OS. So in this implementation, two threads taking turns in lockstep is not as fast as one thread running without the overhead of thread switching.

In Figure 13.3, you can see that while one thread is running, the other is waiting—each thread is running in lockstep. In the multi-thread visualization, each core is

Figure 13.2

High-level concept of this example. Multiple threads will write to a `ReadWriter` that manages the handoff and sharing between a writer and reader thread.

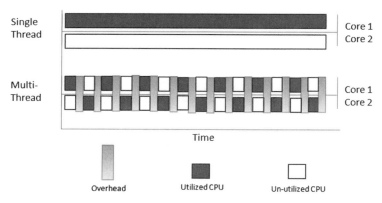

Figure 13.3

Visualization showing how a single-threaded implementation with no overhead achieves better utilization than a dual-threaded implementation that causes costly overhead due to the switching that occurs when two threads execute in lockstep.

spending nearly as much time waiting as it does running, and each switch comes at a cost that limits the overall utilization.

How bad is the overhead of switching cores? Well, let's run an experiment to find out.

We are able to create this lock-step behavior using the PerformanceHarness example `threading/writeReader` and defining `THREADSTREAM` to 0 at the top of the file.

Running this code on our test machines and using Intel's Thread Profiler yields statistics about the active time for the two threads. By examining a 500-millisecond section of execution during the writing and reading, we find that thread 1 is active, meaning not in a wait state, for about 370 milliseconds and thread 2 is active for about 300 milliseconds. This yields a combined total of 670 milliseconds or 67% of the total 1,000 milliseconds possible (2 threads × 500 milliseconds). Of the 670 active milliseconds, 315 milliseconds are spent in serial operations attributable to the critical sections used to implement the synchronization. This inefficiency leads us with only 355 (670-315) milliseconds of real processing. So to summarize, we are only utilizing the processor for 35.5% of the total that is theoretically possible for this time span.

Running this test 10 times provides an average time that we can use for comparison with later implementations. When tested, the benchmarks average for 10 tests is around 2.422 seconds. It should also be noted that the number of contentions is so high, that the Thread Profiler takes quite some time to visualize them all.

Example   279

Array Implementation

For the next optimization, let's increase the single variable to an array, similar to the visualization in Figure 13.4. At each array point, we will have a space for a value and a synchronization primitive.

You can re-create this example by defining the preprocessor value THREADSTREAM to 1. This implementation has some significant advantages over the single variable approach in the previous attempt. The likelihood of experiencing a contention is significantly reduced since, instead of a guaranteed contention, the program has the potential for contention, meaning that it doesn't always contend. The more you increase the ARRAY_SIZE defined value, the less likely you are to contend.

Intel's thread profiler confirms this approach and the utilization is high. Using the previous implementation, both threads are nearly 100% utilized. We are able to move through 1,000,000 integers in roughly 106 milliseconds, which is a 2,179% performance increase.

Earlier in this book, we discussed the three levels of optimization: system, application, and micro. Those lessons transfer well to optimizing our algorithm. By reducing the contentions, we have increased the utilization, which is a step in the right direction.

But a high utilization doesn't automatically mean that we have the fastest algorithm. If you sit behind your desk all day at work and search the Internet, you might be busy, but your productivity is horrible. To optimize, we must

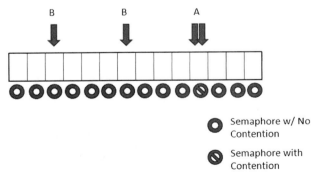

Figure 13.4

Contentions could dramatically be reduced by switching from a single variable to an array. In case A, a contention occurs. In case B, a contention does not.

have both high utilization and efficient processing. That leads us to our next optimization.

Batched Array

For our final implementation, we will build on the array approach by reducing the number of critical section enter-and-leave calls by maintaining a mutex for each section of the array. Figure 13.5 shows the approach.

In the array implementation, we have an enter-and-leave call for every read or write. By using an array-of-arrays instead of one big array, we can have a lock per row. This reduces the overhead of enter-and-leave calls and uses more of our processor for processing data. You can re-create this example by setting the preprocessor define THREADSTREAM equal to 2.

Utilization is great, and now the processing is more efficient and takes advantage of the CPU's ability to step quickly through linear memory. Our implementation is now running in 9.9 milliseconds, an appreciable performance gain.

For a test, we implemented a single-threaded version of the reader writer and compared it to the multi-threaded version. The results are not incredibly

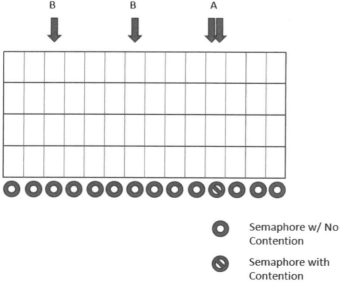

Figure 13.5

Notice that no contention occurs except at point A, where two threads try to access the same data at the same time.

Example   281

impressive; the single-threaded implementation achieves nearly 11.5 milliseconds, which begs the question of why so much work was done for such a small increase and the potential for such bad performance.

The answer lies in scaling. The delta between these two implementations improves performance as we increase the number of integers. By upping the ITERATION to 10,000,000, the threaded version becomes nearly twice as fast in total execution time instead of just slightly ahead. By increasing the thread count to four, the average time moves to 6.9 milliseconds.

Thread Count

Conversely, increasing the thread count to six reduces performance to 9.1 milliseconds. Why? Executing more intensive threads than cores will create over-utilization, a term that defines a condition in which we are using more software threads than the number of simultaneous threads in hardware. There are many references that suggest the optimal thread ratio is 1:1 cores to threads, but there are very few examples of why.

We found that the biggest contributor to this is not overhead caused by having too many threads. We do not believe that the OS will increase context switches by shortening time slices and the processor doesn't manage threads, so it has no say in the matter as well. (Even in the case of Hyper-Threading, the CPU doesn't schedule. It just allows two threads at a time to run on the same core.)

A key issue is synchronization. Synchronization is slower when there isn't a one-to-one relationship of thread to hardware. Four threads can synchronize nearly instantly on a four-core machine. When we run six threads on a four-core machine, only four can synchronize concurrently. The remaining two will require a thread context switch from the other threads. The serialization of these threads can be significant, especially if the OS is switching to other threads in-between the serialization.

If synchronization is the issue, then algorithms with larger concurrency-to-synchronization ratios should see less of a performance problem. This data is presented in Figure 13.6.

Sharing, Balancing, and Synchronization

Lastly, the source code for these tests provides us more information on sharing, balancing, and synchronization primitives.

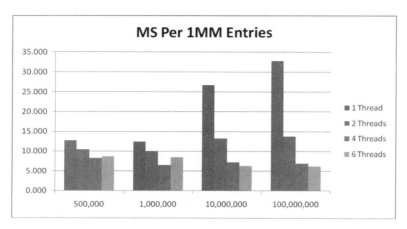

Figure 13.6

Elapsed time, normalized for 1,000,000 entries, for varying numbers of entries and threads. On our four-core test system, four threads gave the consistently best performance.

Several variables in the source have the `__declspec(align(64))` preprocessor directive (not cross platform). This is because the variables nearby have the possibility to incur performance hits due to false sharing. By forcing 64-byte alignement, the variable will have its own cache line, eliminating any opportunity for false sharing.

To experiment with balancing, try allocating an uneven number of readers and writers. By default, the program allocates one reader for every writer.

Finally, there were many efforts taken to increase the performance of synchronization primitives. Events provided a faster implementation for signaling from one thread to another. In this algorithm, events were much faster than implementing spinlocks with volatile Boolean variables.

Conclusion

In this chapter, we covered the basics of threading from the perspective of performance. While not always easy, multi-core, and therefore multi-threading, is here to stay.

You control threads indirectly, meaning you don't tell threads what to do like the OS does, you just provide the means for directing and synchronizing them by using synchronization objects.

There are many barriers to achieving performance through multi-threading. First, you must understand what tools you have; then you must learn how to use them. Contention should be minimized, as well as all areas of serial execution. You should strive to reduce serial sections of your algorithms since they contribute significantly to the potential of performance increase.

Lastly, we presented an example that demonstrated how an algorithm can evolve from having a lot of contentions and a very low degree of parallelism to having very low contention and a very high degree of parallelism that is scalable.

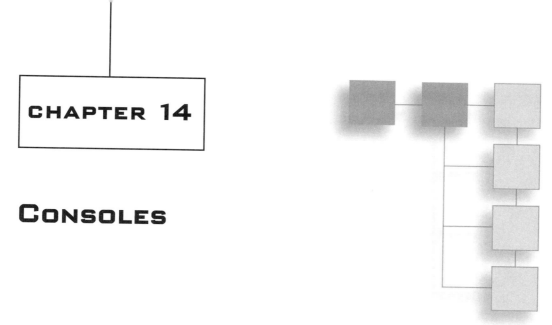

CHAPTER 14

CONSOLES

On the surface, consoles look a lot like any other platform. The first Xbox was nearly identical to a mid-range gaming PC of the era—even down to its size. The PS3, Wii, and Xbox 360 behave a lot like the computer on your desk. They download software updates, run applications, allow you to play media, access the Internet, and a lot more. In some cases (such as with XNA or the Net Yaroze or less legitimately with homebrew), it's possible for users to run their own applications on them.

Don't be fooled. Deep down, a console like the 360 has a lot more in common with an NES than it does with your desktop. Consoles build off of 30 years of hard-won game development knowledge. They may have operating systems and mass storage instead of on-cartridge hardware and satellite modems, but they resemble consumer PCs as much as an Ariel Atom resembles a Honda Accord.

This chapter will cover the key differences between console performance tuning and the PC-oriented optimization techniques we have discussed up until now. Fundamentally, the same basic techniques of profiling, identifying the bottleneck, and tuning still apply. But consoles let you get a lot closer to the hardware and build code that takes better advantage of what the hardware can do.

A quick disclaimer: The console world is highly NDA'ed, and as a result we cannot give code samples, performance numbers, or development information beyond what is publicly available. All of the performance tests and optimization techniques from the rest of this book still apply, of course. But you will have to run tests with your own development hardware to get real-world numbers, and read and review the documentation from the console vendor in order to learn the details of what its hardware is capable of.

Know Your Console

What are the defining characteristics of consoles as far as performance goes?

- **Low-level hardware access:** On the NES, you had direct access to the rasterization chips. On a 360, you have direct access to the internal data structures on which the GPU operates. Abstraction layers that are mandatory when you have to support 10 different hardware manufacturers become superfluous on a console.

- **Fast bus:** Consoles routinely achieve memory transfer rates far in excess of PC games. When you have limited hardware, the best way to maximize it is to push as much data through it as possible.

- **Fast memory:** Memory is expensive, and when you are only running a single app, lots of memory isn't a big win. Consoles tend toward small amounts of fast memory so they can get the most out of it (see "fast bus").

- **Specialized hardware:** The NES had specialized processing via chips on the cartridge. The PS3 has Cell processors. The Xbox 360 has an extended Altivec instruction set. The Super Nintendo had a custom audio synthesis chip. Consoles wouldn't be consoles without specialized hardware.

- **Homogeneous:** Every console has the same capabilities and hardware. You don't have to worry about supporting 10 different driver versions or eight different GPU vendors. There is one GPU, one set of drivers, and while there may be updates, a major part of the console promise is that it will run all games correctly even if the internals are updated.

- **Contractual quality:** Console vendors are the gatekeepers. Only software they approve gets out to the market. The value proposition of a console is as much due to its quality standards as its underlying hardware. As a result, console vendors require you to meet certain quality and performance standards before they will allow you to ship your game.

All of these factors combine to make console development a unique beast. Naturally, if you are a good PC developer, it will not take too long to pick everything up. But you have to be willing to rethink your assumptions and start from zero if you want to really learn the system and get maximum performance.

Keep Your Fundamentals Strong

While many assumptions change on consoles, a lot stays just the same as it does everywhere else. You might want to review the first four chapters of this book, but let us stress a few things. First, there is no substitute for careful profiling before you start any optimization. For every clever PC performance hack, there are 10 more on consoles. Focus on the big problems first.

Second, do your homework. Consoles come with a lot of performance-oriented documentation explaining all their cool features. Use this as a starting point to see what is possible, but do your own tests to make sure that real-world wins match the theoretical claims. The guys doing this performance work are smart, but you can never tell for sure until you try it in your own situation. Documentation can be outdated, wrong, or just inapplicable to your situation.

Finally, keep your eye on the goals of the project. Figure out your performance budget early on—both in the context of what the game needs as well as what the console vendor requires—and make sure you stick to it.

Push It to the Limit

You can walk on the razor's edge of performance when you do console development. While there will be some limits, they are a great deal more generous than you get on PC development. You can rely on using 100% of a console's capabilities, instead of having to cater to the lowest common denominator as you must in the PC market.

Because you have low-level access, you can also cut corners in ways that aren't an option on the PC. Console games have historically done all sorts of strange things, like keeping memory images on disk, and loading them, pointers and all, in a single IO request, or running important bits of game logic on sound controllers, or using spare space in system data structures to get a few extra bytes of RAM.

This is probably the biggest difference between PC and console development. By making everything permissible, modest hardware can achieve as much or more than much more capable systems. All it takes are the skill and insight to squeeze out the last bit of performance from a fixed target.

Do your research and use everything you can.

Trimming It Down

Consoles give you low-level access to the hardware. As a side effect of this, while they have limited OS and driver APIs, they are typically cut down compared to consumer offerings. Many features are removed entirely. Other features are simplified to fit the console's focus or to enhance performance.

Every consumer system runs a complex operating system designed to shield programs from each other and protect the hardware and user. Software may be poorly written or malicious, and as a result a lot of error checking must be done so that the system continues to function correctly. Even well-written software has to share resources, adding layers of virtualization and indirection to common operations.

On early consoles, there was no OS. The NES, for instance, booted and directly executed code without any intermediate layers at all. Since only Nintendo could manufacture the cartridges that held the games, the physical interface acted as DRM to prevent untrusted code from running. In addition, since the hardware didn't preserve state across resets, it was very difficult for games to do any permanent damage even if they did do something unexpected.

On modern consoles, there is a lot of complex software that runs to give the user a pleasant shell experience. In addition, there is an OS that runs underneath the game to provide useful services. DRM is also a big concern, since games can be downloaded off the Internet or loaded from other media. Optical discs make it a little challenging to make your own copies of games, but disc burners are cheap, so the OS and console hardware always have to validate that games are trusted and allowed to run.

However, unlike a desktop, the OS is tuned to run one application—your game— with maximum performance. Typically, this means that extraneous OS services are removed, and often the game is run with elevated privileges so that fewer security context switches are required. The scheduler is tweaked for the single-app scenario.

Virtual memory is usually the first feature to go. While it can save a lot of trouble when multitasking on limited RAM, in a single application system like a console, it gives added complexity whose only benefit is enabling a very slow failure mode. It's better for games to monitor their own memory usage and cap their allocations so they fit into physical RAM.

Often where there are multiple APIs with similar functionality, the console manufacturer will choose one—usually the lowest level—and drop the others. In addition, only common usage patterns may be supported. Nonessential or infrequently used modes are often dropped.

In order to meet security or feature requirements, the console APIs may have added complexity. For instance, there are often strict requirements about what network services a console may access, so additional handshaking steps may be enforced by the OS. Audio may be required to support a variety of output scenarios (headphones, Dolby, THX, 2, 2.1, 5.1, 7.1, etc.) and therefore may only accept the richest format and down convert. Mass storage access may involve mandatory validation to prevent security risks from user-modified data. Or it may be removed entirely and access only allowed through strict APIs tailored for individual situations, like save games.

Functionality that normally happens behind the scenes is often much closer to the surface in a console. For instance, with a fixed amount of memory and limited processes, heap management doesn't really need to be in the OS at all—it can give you all the available memory and off you go. The distinction between OS and user code also becomes weaker. Some consoles run game code in the same kernel ring as the OS, which greatly reduces the cost of context switches.

Some things—like functionality that would normally be in the graphics driver—will be provided as normal user code that you compile into your application. This is great because, if that code becomes a bottleneck, you can really tune it to do exactly what you need for good performance. Compare this with waiting for a new driver update from a vendor!

The effect of these changes is to make console development lean and mean. Focused, fast APIs lead to focused, fast games. Sometimes, you have to give up a few niceties, but the trade-offs are worth it in terms of stability and performance.

Mind the Dip: Middleware

In *The Dip*, Seth Godin talks about the idea that things often get worse before they get better. The dip in an endeavor is how much worse things can get before they improve. An important part of planning is to figure out how deep the dip is— if it's too deep, you won't be able to make it across to the point where things are good again.

Really taking advantage of a console can take a lot of R&D. This is the dip you have to contend with when you are looking at implementing a video codec or a physics library or a sound engine or another complex piece of functionality on a console. If you have 18 months to ship your game, can you afford to spend 12 months writing an optimized character animation system? It will probably be really good when it is done, but if it is harder than you expect or it takes longer than planned, your game is in real trouble—never mind that you would be losing that much extra time to spend on gameplay or graphics.

Today's consoles are very complex. Sony does not expect people to fully take advantage of the PS3 for years to come, despite it having been on the market for some time now. The games at the end of the PS2's lifecycle are nearly unrecognizable as being on the same hardware as the launch titles.

In general, if you have the budget, using middleware is a good choice. Especially on consoles, the gulf between a naïve implementation and a really good one can be vast. You will want to do your due diligence, of course.

In fact, good middleware is so essential that many console vendors develop middleware and libraries for common scenarios and give it away as part of the development kit. For instance, the D3DX library that comes with a 360 is enough to implement a basic game unaided. But this is not going to solve the same problem that, say, Havok does.

More and more middleware is available under open source licenses. For instance, Bullet is a good physics library that has optimized kernels for Cell and other specialized console features. It even receives development time from Sony researchers.

You do not want to fritter away your game's budget on third-party software, but a few strategic investments might save months of intense development, debugging, and optimization work.

Support Exists

One of the best parts of console development is that the support, compared to PC development, is really good. The console manufacturers really wants you to succeed because they receive a royalty on each copy of your game that is sold, as opposed to PC development, where the connection is more tenuous between sales of game and sales of OS/hardware.

Typically, a certain amount of support will be stipulated as part of the development contract. In addition, console manufacturers are usually very interested in fixing bugs in their APIs and core system code. Between those two factors, you are already way ahead of the game compared to, say, developing an OS X game.

Obviously, developing your game is ultimately your own responsibility. But watching some presentations and reading the library of documentation that comes with the SDK will help quite a bit, as will lurking on the mailing lists and forums that are available for console developers on your platform.

Understand the Contract

Consoles are all about consistent, reliable play experiences. If there were 10 variants of the NES, each with different capabilities, Nintendo would not be a household name today. A big part of the process of developing a console game is conforming to the standards for that console.

When you sign a contract with a console vendor, the company will typically specify certain technical requirements that you must meet in order to ship a title on its console. This can range from minimum frame rate to network usage restrictions to the size, color, and appearance of menu UI buttons to how translated text for localizations must be encoded. These are enforced by the QA process, and represent a big part of the value of a console game—that it *is* tested, that it *does* run correctly, and that it *meets* performance requirements.

Make sure that you understand these constraints fully, and that you budget time and engineering resources to meet them. Sometimes they can be onerous, but it is worth it to deliver a great product. From an optimization perspective, they should fit into your budgeting as hard constraints.

RAM and the Bus

Consoles have limited resources, but these resources are fast. In particular, RAM and bus speeds are very high. This leads to some interesting possibilities.

For instance, on the typical consumer system, it is slow to read VRAM. Since consoles have extremely fast RAM<−>VRAM access, this opens up a wide variety of techniques that are too costly elsewhere, such as heavy texture streaming or frequent readbacks from the framebuffer. We will discuss some of these in the GPU section that follows.

Consoles often have more involved memory hierarchies. This adds some labor for the programmer but can lead to huge performance wins. For instance, the

PS3 uses the Cell architecture, which provides each Cell processor with a small amount of chip-local, very fast memory. Designing algorithms that leverage this memory result in major speedups. Similarly, the 360 includes a small amount of very fast RAM that is used for rendering, separate from the normal VRAM (http://en.wikipedia.org/wiki/Xenos_(graphics_chip)).

Console GPUs Are Crazy

GPUs have all kinds of interesting low-level features, but they cannot be exposed via a higher level graphics API because they are wildly incompatible with how other cards or even the API itself work. Most console GPUs let you manipulate video memory directly, including the internal structures that the GPU uses for rendering. This can be a huge time-saver because you can stream data directly from disk into VRAM, in exactly the format needed for rendering. You can directly do what would otherwise require a lot of gyrations.

The memory interconnects on consoles are reliably fast, too. On a PC, a graphics card might be on one of several different busses with order-of-magnitude variations in speed. Since many applications may be using the card at the same time, performance can suffer due to factors entirely outside your control.

On a console, you know exactly how many MB/sec you can transfer, and it will be the same on every version of that console in the world. Immediate fast access to VRAM leads to some interesting possibilities. On the PS2, it was possible to read back from the framebuffer and do deferred shading on the CPU. This was very useful because of the very limited GPU capabilities on that console.

More recent consoles have significantly better GPU capabilities, reducing the appeal of this technique, but it's certainly still feasible (http://research.scea.com/ps3_deferred_shading.pdf) for some consoles. For an algorithm like SVT (http://www.silverspaceship.com/src/svt/) or tone mapping that involves reading back data from the framebuffer, fast busses lead to significant performance gains.

Console GPUs often expose interesting special features, like custom texture formats or specialized shader instructions. Find these and take advantage of them.

Pushing the Algorithms

There is a certain level of performance tuning that is counter-productive on consumer hardware. Consumer hardware will vary by quite a bit, so you cannot make assumptions that are too specific. Assuming a fixed cache size or specific timings is unwise. Spending a lot of time tweaking your algorithms for performance on a single CPU or GPU is a waste after a certain threshold because it will cost you performance on other varying hardware.

But consoles are, by definition, fixed hardware platforms. So you can actually dig down and really get extremely specific. There is still some variation just between different product batches and different revisions of the console, but this is usually manageable, and in addition, big changes will generally be planned and documented (for example, the vendor might reserve the right to completely change the optical drive in future revisions, requiring you to use only established interfaces).

Fixed Output, Tuned Data

Consoles originally targeted CRT televisions, which ran at one of two fixed resolutions. With the advent of HD, this became more variable—now there are a dozen possible target resolutions with the option of upscaling/not, interlaced/progressive, etc. ranging from 640×480 to $1,920 \times 1,080$. Nevertheless, consoles will typically focus on a fixed target. For instance, most Xbox 360 content will target $1,280 \times 720$ with upscaling to $1,920 \times 1,080$, while Wii content will run at 640×480.

The vendor will generally require a certain minimum frame rate on the game. These two parameters can help you limit the resources that you need for simulation and rendering. You can do a lot of preprocessing in order to cap texture size to the maximum size that will ever be needed.

As the game gets closer to being done, you can do things like tightly limit resource usage with hard caps. With consoles, there are no variations of the system to scale up/down for, so you can precisely budget your resources and use everything available to you.

Specialized Tools

Consoles are their own specialized world, so it only makes sense that they have their own special tools. Most console tools require a special version of the console hardware known as a development kit that has extra capabilities to make it easier to develop, debug, and measure.

Because the hardware is more open to the developer on a console, the profiling capabilities are generally much more powerful than the equivalent tools on consumer hardware. PIX was originally an Xbox 360 tool, and on its native environment it is a much richer tool than on the desktop. While most consoles don't have a developer experience that is quite as polished as PIX, they all include utilities for analysis and tuning of rendering and other activities.

The compilers for consoles are customized. At the low end, they might just be a build of GCC that exposes certain intrinsics and hardware features. At the high end, Microsoft developed a whole new compiler for the 360, and there are several vendors who maintain compilers for PS3.

Many of these cutting-edge developments trickle back into the PC space, but it's definitely worth your while to review the tools available on your console.

Conclusion

Consoles are homogeneous devices with specialized capabilities targeted at a fixed gaming experience. Because of this, it is possible to tune your game to the very limit of its performance. Consoles expose a great deal more power to the game developer, since they are not constrained by PC concerns like compatibility or upgradability.

The legal and technological issues around consoles present a unique set of challenges and advantages. If you are a long-time PC developer, approach them with an open mind. Regardless of your experience level, always profile, optimize, benchmark, and repeat in order to focus your time on what's worth optimizing. The same basic rules apply to console optimization, even though there is a great deal more freedom in how you get your performance.

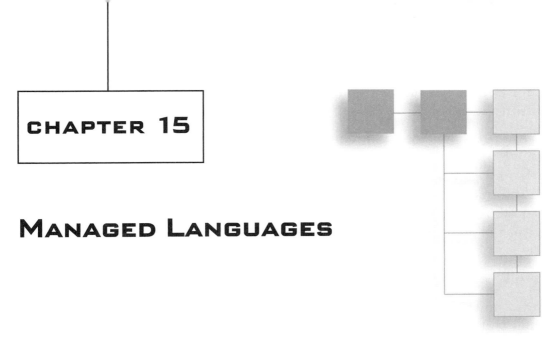

CHAPTER 15

MANAGED LANGUAGES

Microsoft originated the term "managed" to refer to languages that run on their Common Language Runtime (CLR)—C# especially, but many other languages and language variants as well— and the term "native" or "unmanaged" to refer to code that targets a specific CPU architecture and runs via the usual operating system facilities. The CLR provides a suite of foundational language features, like a garbage collector, a just-in-time compiler (JIT), a portable bytecode format (IL), a large standard library, debugging/profiling infrastructure, and a lot more.

In this chapter, we use the term "managed" to include any language that is cross platform and requires a runtime. Python, PHP, Java, Perl, JavaScript, Action-Script, C#, Ruby, Lua, and many more all fit in this category. "Native" is used to refer to any code that is delivered as a binary containing machine code, C/C++ being the best example.

Why have a chapter on managed languages in a book that focuses on performance? Two reasons: first, because video games have traditionally relied on scripting languages. Gameplay can be costly and time consuming to implement in native code, so most games end up with an embedded language that is used for menial tasks like managing inventory, specifying game missions, and so forth. Lua is popular for this, although Java and C# are also used, as are a wide variety of proprietary languages.

Second, more and more products are being written entirely in a managed language. If you work with a technology like Flash or Unity, you'll write your whole game in C# or ActionScript, respectively. Web development is often done entirely in PHP, Java, Python, Ruby, or JavaScript, with no native code being written at all.

Most of the content of this book applies to managed languages in the same way as it does to native code. Find the biggest bottlenecks and remove them—this works just the same in PHP as it does in C or assembly. However, many assumptions have to change when you are working with a managed language, and those changes in assumptions are similar across all the managed languages, which takes us to the heart of this chapter.

Characteristics of a Managed Language

Disclaimer: Every language is a little different. Even official Microsoft languages that target the same version of the CLR use slightly different features in slightly different ways. As a result, you will need to check the feature set of the language you are working with against the features we outline here. We do not intend to present a bulletproof definition. We want to point out areas that may be relevant or trip you up.

There are characteristics common to most managed languages. We'll focus on the ones that are important from a performance perspective.

Managed languages do not allow direct allocation or access of memory. Typically, everything is stored by reference, and there are no directly accessible pointers. This leads to more random access and less opportunity to optimize your memory accesses. You are also more limited in your allocation strategies, although there are still a few options that we'll discuss later in this chapter.

Some languages are better about memory than others. For instance, C# lets you use a struct to directly store data in a block of memory, and ActionScript 3 tries to store values instead of references when it can, as opposed to always putting values on the heap. If you are working with an embedded language, you could write some native code to do fast, intelligent data management for a specific case and let the managed code call the native code. Or you might be able to leverage a language feature. For instance, strings are usually stored as bytes adjacent in memory, so you might be able to pack frequently iterated data into a string. Or you might know that integers in an array are always stored adjacent in memory and use that to your advantage.

Memory in a managed language is usually garbage collected, removing most responsibility for proper memory management from the developer. This removes a lot of bookkeeping work and streamlines development. Of course, even with a

GC, you may still want to manually manage memory at certain times, and there are tricks to do this that we'll cover a little later in the section titled "Dealing with the Garbage Collector."

Most managed languages use a platform-neutral bytecode. Java is probably the best example of this, but nearly every managed language takes this approach. This means that you can distribute bytecode rather than source files, which is helpful. A few languages directly interpret their source code, but this is rare (and slow since it tends to lead to reparsing the source code all the time).

Bytecode isn't bad, but it is intrinsically slower than native code, because every bytecode instruction requires many native operations to run it. As a result, many languages support just-in-time compilers (JITs), which convert bytecodes to native operations with varying levels of quality. A good JIT can get you in the ballpark of native code performance, which is really useful. It's unlikely that JIT compiled code will outperform well-written native code, but most of the time, the things that managed languages are doing (like implementing gameplay) don't need to be blazingly fast. The important thing is that they avoid being really slow, and almost any JIT will get you there.

Unlike native code, which is directly run by the hardware/OS, managed languages require a runtime. Sometimes (like for C#), this is a standard set of libraries and binaries that is installed by the user, and other times (like for Lua or JavaScript), it will be embedded in an application, like your game or a Web browser. This can affect application size, and some features must be built into the runtime to work (like debugging or profiling).

Concerns for Profiling

The biggest difference when it comes to profiling managed languages is that there is more going on behind the scenes. In your typical native application, accessing an array will be pretty cheap and consistent in terms of performance cost. In C, for instance, it's an add operation and a memory load. In a managed language, array accesses may involve a lot more. For instance, in ActionScript, arrays are implemented via a generic data structure, so every array load means hitting that data structure and querying it. You can also override the array access, potentially running an arbitrary amount of user code on each access. Suddenly, at minimum, you are doing several function calls to do what you might do in a few cycles in native code. On the CLI, you can create objects that dynamically resolve their fields, have getters/setters, and introduce other overhead.

Most mature managed languages have profiling tools. In the C# world, JetBrain's profiler is a good option. There are others, including nProf, SlimTune, and the one built into Visual Studio. ActionScript has a profiler built into Flash Builder. Languages like Lua and Python have profiler solutions, too.

If you are assigning data to the array, then there may be a memory allocation, in which case the GC can fire, and there may be an arbitrary amount of work that happens while it is processed. A GC collection can take hundreds of milliseconds or longer (although there are many techniques to mitigate this, as we'll discuss in the section, "Dealing with the Garbage Collector"). The result of all this behind-the-scenes action is that it can be harder to accurately profile your code.

In addition, in managed languages with JIT support, the JIT can affect your measurements. Because it is a just-in-time system, it is active at runtime, and will compile code on demand. Like the GC, this tends to be difficult to predict and liable to happen in the midst of other work. Unlike the GC, once the JIT compiles a piece of code, it won't usually process that code again. Some language runtimes will compile code the first time it is encountered, while others wait until a certain amount of time has been spent executing a block of code before it is compiled by the JIT.

Another major factor is that the managed language may not have high-accuracy timing information. This can be the result of two things. First, its standard library may not expose high-accuracy timers. Second, even if you can get the timing information, the cost of getting it may be so high that you cannot do it very often without bloating your code execution time.

Why would you use timers directly for your profiling? Well, many managed languages do not have good tools for profiling. This is especially true if you are using a homebrew/proprietary language, but many mainstream managed languages only have limited profiling tools. JavaScript, for instance, does not have profiling capabilities on many browsers. Be sure to check before giving up hope because it's better to use a tool designed for the purpose of profiling than it is to hack up your own solution.

These are the main new causes of error when you profile managed code. But every language has its own quirks, so the best policy when you start working with a new runtime is to spend a little time profiling basic operations. As in the rest of our chapters, we include a set of performance tests to help you with this. In this case, we chose ActionScript 3 and Flash because it runs on most major platforms, is widely supported, and it has a free SDK. It is a decent baseline to work from, and it is not as heavily performance-tuned as the .Net languages, but it is better than or equivalent to most other managed languages.

Change Your Assumptions

As we established earlier, the costs of basic operations in managed code can be much more varied than in native code. They also tend to be higher, sometimes a lot higher. This makes developing a good set of basic performance data even more important, since doing so helps you know what to avoid.

For instance, constructing new objects is very costly in AS3. A useful work-around is to keep a list and put objects in it when you're done with them. Then, instead of creating a new object of a given type, you can just grab one from the list. This requires a little care to make sure you're not "leaking" state from one use to another, but the performance wins are big—5x for a basic type like a Point and 80x for the more complex Sprite type. (We got our numbers from Michael Baczynksi's excellent Flash blog: http://lab.polygonal.de/2008/06/18/using-object-pools.)

Many managed languages do not store data on the stack, but only on the heap. This means that temporaries have a much higher cost than they do in C/C++, since they require getting memory from the GC, which must be freed later. Suddenly, reusing your iterators can make a lot of sense. That's overstating things a bit—most of the time, it doesn't matter, but for inner loops, allocations can be a huge issue. This can be a concern even in native languages, but it's much more pronounced in managed languages.

The cost of strings can be unexpected as well. Some languages have very naive string management, and as a result, even fairly simple C string management will out-perform them. Other languages implement complex string management strategies and achieve performance that is hard to match, even in native code. Do some tests to figure out which kind of situation you're dealing with.

A final issue is numerical precision. Some managed languages play games with their numerical representations. For instance, some proprietary languages tend to convert things to strings during processing, and as a result, you lose precision sometimes. In AS3, floating-point numbers get stored on the heap, but integers (smaller than $2^{**}32$ or so) get stored directly in the reference, saving a lot of overhead. Usually, if there are issues of this type, they are well documented, and most managed languages bias toward more precision than less.

What *Should* Be Implemented in a Managed Language?

A lot of applications will run great in a managed language. Anything where proper functioning is more important than speed is a good choice, since features like GC, exception handling, and no direct pointer access lead to code that is much less likely to fail catastrophically. Nearly all gameplay fits into this category. The last time you profiled your game, how much time was spent in gameplay logic vs. physics or spatial queries or rendering?

Another place where managed languages shine is server-side. You typically want high reliability there, and since it's over the network, users can tolerate a certain amount of irregularity in processing time (as a GC collection might introduce).

Managed languages are good at interfacing with fast, native-code-implemented functionality. The best practice when you're working with an embedded language is to write as much as you can as quickly as you can in the managed language and then start hoisting things out into native code as you find there are bottlenecks. You might find that scanning for finished objectives is slow, but it's likely there is some inner loop that is causing the slowdown, like a spatial query implemented in managed code. Move the slow inner loop to native code, and you will see a huge performance benefit.

Marshalling data can have a cost. Depending on the technology you are using, a costly serialization routine might be invoked, or extra memory copies might happen. If you are aware of it, it's easy to spot in the profiler. You will find that even a null function call will have a cost in some situations.

JITs raise the bar for what code needs to go from the managed to the native side. Say the JIT makes functions on average 4x faster (as Lua's JIT does, according to its site: http://luajit.org/luajit_performance.html). That's that much less code that you need to worry about being slow enough to require a native replacement.

What *Should Not* Be Implemented in a Managed Language?

Speaking of native code, take advantage of standard libraries and built-in functionality as much as you can. While in the native code world this can be a big pain, it's generally a win in the managed world. Of course, you want to profile to make sure that the convenient ways really are faster. Grant Skinner's performance testing harness compares different AS3 iteration methods. In C#, some iteration methods introduce overhead.

If you have the option, it can make sense to implement focused, specific pieces of functionality in native code so that it can be driven from your managed code. For instance, writing the core of your 3D renderer in native code might make sense because it can have more efficient access to the underlying APIs. By implementing a few basic services in native code, you can more easily write the rest of your game in managed code. Some platforms do this for you; for instance, C# has XNA, which wraps the DirectX APIs.

This approach allows you to leverage the strengths of each language. C/C++ is great for implementing focused, fast routines. But they aren't as good as most scripting languages at implementing loose gameplay code, which mostly revolves around lots of one-off checks and dictionary lookups written by people who are not primarily programmers. Naturally, there are times when you have to do the "wrong" kind of tasks in each language, but if you can give your designers an easy-to-use scripting system, you'll be able to avoid a lot of pain and trouble. More importantly, you will be able to do more in less time, because maintaining gameplay code in script is cheaper than the same code in C++.

Some languages offer specialized computing APIs. For instance, Adobe is starting to adopt OpenCL-like capabilities into Flash so you can spin certain computations into a thread or onto the GPU. Python has NumPy, which is a library for fast scientific matrix operations. C# has native parallelization primitives. Look for these possibilities and take advantage of them when you need to.

Dealing with the Garbage Collector

Vendors like to claim that their garbage collector technology is fantastic and that you'll never have to worry about performance. While it's entirely possible to coexist in peace with garbage collection, it's by no means the natural order of things. Using a GC incorrectly can result in huge slowdowns, despite the best efforts of the vendor.

Garbage collectors come in many shapes, sizes, and flavors. The purpose of this book isn't to be an in-depth discussion of garbage collection technology, and some of our generalities won't hold up in every scenario. If you find that you are spending a lot of time working with GCs, it's worth it to spend some time on

Wikipedia getting familiar with generational garbage collectors, write barriers, and related concepts. This site, www.javaworld.com/javaworld/jw-01-2002/jw-0111-hotspotgc.html, is also a good introduction. If you really need to dig deep, *Garbage Collection: Algorithms for Automatic Dynamic Memory Management* by Jones and Lins is an excellent resource.

Under Pressure

With manual memory allocation, the big concern may be how much total footprint you introduce, or how much fragmentation is happening, or how slow cleaning everything up is. With a garbage collector, the biggest issue is memory pressure, which is the amount of memory that is being allocated over time.

Most GCed languages limit what data can be stored on the stack, so you end up allocating temporary objects that stop being used almost immediately. These could be strings, objects, scope information, or other data. The side effect of actively running code is a level of continuous memory allocation. Careless code might burn through megabytes every second; careful code might do a lot less or even none at all.

Most garbage collectors are configured to "collect" whenever a certain amount of memory has been allocated. For instance, if the amount of in-use memory after the last collection is 50MB, the GC may have a rule that says, "Do another collection when the amount of in-use memory has doubled." Your code runs along at 1MB/sec in allocations. In less than a minute, you have 100MB of allocated memory, and the GC is running again.

The diagram in Figure 15.1 shows two programs' memory usage. Notice the characteristic sawtooth pattern. As code runs, it allocates temporary objects off the heap. When the heap reaches a certain size, the GC runs and brings allocated memory back down to the amount that is actually in use/referenced at that point in time. Each time the GC runs, there is a performance hit, which means that the user is likely to experience a short hitch. Program A has higher memory pressure, so the GC is running frequently and has to process more memory when it does. Program B has lower memory pressure, so the GC has to run less often, and processes less data when it does run. The end result to the user will be that Program B feels smoother and more responsive.

If you program without regard for memory pressure, allocation rates of 10MB/sec or even higher are not unheard of. With those kinds of rates, you might see a

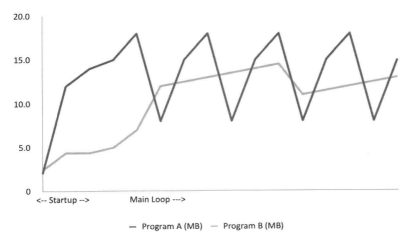

Figure 15.1

Consumed memory (Y-axis) over time (X-axis). Each time the line moves downward, the GC runs. Notice that Program A causes the GC to run much more often than Program B.

collection happening every few seconds, causing big performance problems. Even multiple collections per frame are not unheard of with poorly written code!

Pressure can also cause your program to have a bigger memory footprint (since the GC may let in-use memory grow more than normal if it is running frequently) and hurt cache efficiency (if you have lots of small objects that are scattered all over the place).

A secondary consideration for GCs is the total working set of memory. To perform a collection, a GC must basically traverse every pointer (or sometimes every byte!) in memory to determine what is free and what isn't. If you have a gigabyte of objects with many references, this can take quite a while. So reducing memory usage in general can have benefits. (GCs like MMGC and Boehm GC operate this way; see www.hpl.hp.com/personal/Hans_Boehm/gc/gcdescr.html under "Mark Phase.")

Usage isn't as huge of a deal as pressure because most GCs are incremental or generational. An incremental GC will do little bits of work at frequent intervals so you don't have to sit and wait for a complete collection to run. Instead, collections happen as a byproduct of the GC being used. If memory pressure is high, then the GC will be forced to do an "emergency" collection and do all that work at once to try to free some memory.

A generational GC will track how long memory has been around. Older objects are stored in a separate portion of memory and checked for potential collection less frequently than new objects. This works out pretty well because most new objects are temporary and can be freed almost immediately. It also helps reduce the amount of memory that must be checked at once, reducing GC performance impact. However, you must be careful to treat memory properly so that the GC will do the right thing.

The Write Barrier

Some GCs use a technique called a *write barrier.* This is an optimization that helps keep the GC from reprocessing data that has not changed. However, it also incurs a penalty whenever you write to memory. (Some systems will only incur the penalty on writing a reference; others may have the penalty on every write.)

Because of this, writes can be slower than expected. While writes are required for correct functioning of the program, some algorithms (developed in situations where writes are cheap) will write the same value to a memory location many times. In these situations, you can get a substantial speedup by checking if the value is different before writing it.

Strategies for Better GC Behavior

What can you do to keep the GC happy? From the last section, you know you should reduce the amount of allocation you do, and secondarily, try to minimize the total amount of memory in use. This section will discuss some techniques for this.

One option is to get data out of the GC's hands entirely. For instance, you might keep data without pointers in a big array rather than storing it as individual objects on the heap. Instead of storing a bunch of Points with X and Y members, for instance, you might just have a big array of floats and store alternating X and Y values. Some languages also give you explicit opportunities to do manual memory management. For instance, Alchemy in Flash lets you access a ByteArray as if it were system memory, allowing you to do your own memory management. C# and other languages can access native code, which can do its own allocation.

Another more general-purpose option is pooling, as discussed in Chapter 6, "CPU Bound: Memory." Keep a list of free instances of a type and reuse them instead of allocating more. This can dramatically reduce memory pressure, and as a result, the amount of work the GC has to do. It also takes advantage of generational

GC behavior, since the pooled items will get marked as an older generation and checked less often.

Pooling doesn't just reduce memory pressure; as we described previously, it can also reduce a lot of overhead from the language itself.

Another option is to reuse temporaries. For instance, if you need a `Matrix` object for some temporary calculations, you might want to store one as a static member on your class rather than allocating new ones all the time. Remember that you have to balance that against the memory cost and risk of side effects.

Dealing with JIT

Many more popular managed languages feature a just-in-time compiler, a compiler that is used as runtime converts bytecode to (hopefully faster) native machine code. Since one of the biggest problems with an interpreted language is that every instruction of interpreted code requires multiple native instructions to execute, this can give a significant win.

A JIT can introduce a lot of overhead, so different runtimes will use them in different ways. For instance, Java running in a server environment will often be set to aggressively JIT everything right at startup to maximize performance during the server's (hopefully) long up time. However, for client environments, Java tends to run the JIT only after a function has been run several times in order to keep startup snappy.

JITs walk a fine line between trying to produce maximally optimized code and finishing fast enough to keep your application running smoothly. A normal compiler has thousands or millions of milliseconds and gigabytes of RAM to burn on producing optimal code, while a JIT might have just one millisecond and very limited memory. Knowing when and how your runtime will activate the JIT is an important piece of the performance puzzle.

When Is JIT Active?

While a compiler processes every piece of code in your application, a JIT is often more selective. JITs tend to only do a function (or less!) at a time. For instance, often only routines that are run frequently will get compiled by the JIT. This can be a crucial piece of information to be aware of when you are running performance tests and profiling!

In addition to performance considerations, the JIT may be disabled in other contexts. For instance, constructors are often left out of JIT processing because they are run relatively infrequently and can contain difficult cases for the JIT to handle. Do your homework on this one! You might need to put your heavy-duty initialization code in a helper function instead of the constructor.

Certain language features can also factor into JIT behavior. For instance, in AS3, providing typing information can give a huge performance gain. Using the right kind of iterator can be very important (and tends to vary). Function calls are often never inline, so manual inlining can give a much bigger performance gain than you might see in the C/C++ world.

A JIT may not be available on every platform. Make sure that even your lowest-end platform has JIT support. Otherwise, you're going to have to really scale back your performance expectations!

Analyzing the JIT

When a JIT is available and running properly, you can get some very significant performance gains. For inner loops, JIT compiled code can approach the speed of unoptimized native code. However, there are some caveats.

Because a JIT must respect all the language's original semantics, it must often introduce extra checks and function calls for what would be simple operations in a native language like C or C++. In dynamic languages, fetching a property from an object may require a complex lookup. Even though the JIT has produced native code, the best it can do may be to call the same lookup function that the interpreter uses. Some runtimes detect code that operates on similarly structured data and optimize access in those cases. (See the Google V8 design notes: http://code.google.com/apis/v8/design.html#prop_access.)

If you really need to figure out what's going on, the best thing you can do is compare the input bytecode and output native assembly. The mapping from the managed language to actual assembly can be very surprising—some things that look simple end up being incredibly inefficient. However, most of the time, profiling will get you where you need to go.

Be sure that the profiler and the JIT interact properly. Often, debug runtimes will not have the JIT enabled. As a result, when you are profiling you will be gathering data that is not relevant for your end users.

Practical Examples—ActionScript 3 and C#

Most of the performance guidelines in this book are likely to stay the same for years. While rendering gets ever faster, most of the trade-offs and decision points are pretty consistent. CPUs get better every year, but the chip manufacturers work hard to make sure that fast code stays fast.

For interpreted languages, which are less mature, there is a high possibility that even a minor version can introduce tremendous changes to the performance landscape. Look at the enhancements to JavaScript performance in FireFox, Chrome, and Flash in the past two years (2007–2009) for a good example of this.

All this is to say that of all the performance discussions in this book, this section is the most likely to be outdated by the time you read it. If you are working on a managed language project, make sure to do your homework—check online sources for the latest performance guidelines, and do your own tests to make sure that you aren't tripping over any hidden performance rakes in the grass.

The AS3 examples here are from work done by Grant Skinner and released under the MIT license (www.gskinner.com/blog/archives/2009/04/as3_performance. html) and the C# discussion is from an article by Jan Gray on MSDN (http:// msdn.microsoft.com/en-us/library/ms973852.aspx). You can find Grant Skinner's AS3 performance tests alongside our C++ performance tests for convenience, but the latest version is on Grant's site and definitely worth a look.

Watch Out for Function Call Overhead

Figure 15.2 shows a comparison of four methods of calling functions in ActionScript 3. Notice that three of them (`anonymousRef`, `method`, and `reference`) are all pretty fast. What's happening in `anonymous`? It's doing this:

```
for (var i:uint=0; i<loops; i++)
    (function() { var a:Number = 10; })();
```

This is a good example of the kind of performance issues you can run into with a managed language. In this example, there's no reason why the runtime couldn't generate the anonymous function once and reuse it for each call. In fact, the `anonymousRef` test does this manually for a huge performance win.

What is happening here is that the runtime is making a new `Function` object (so you get the overhead of allocating from the GC) each time through the loop.

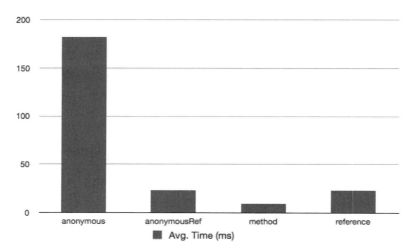

Figure 15.2

Relative times for different types of function calls in ActionScript 3.

In addition, it is probably grabbing a copy of the scope chain in case the function references something in local scope. Only after this is done is it executing the do-nothing code inside the function body. There may also be performance penalties due to lack of typing information (the return value of the anonymous function is not specified).

No doubt that as the JIT and VM mature, this sort of scenario will be dealt with more efficiently. Certainly there is a lot of performance left on the table, and this sort of thing is less of a problem with languages like C#. In general, managed languages are less mature, and have more "uneven" performance than native languages like C/C++, so you need to be more aware of performance.

Language Features Can Be Traps

Sometimes a convenient feature can be a performance trap. The `with` statement has been that way for years across multiple languages. It lets you do property lookups in the context of a parent object, in order to simplify your code. For instance, compare these two code snippets:

```
// Snippet 1
with (shape.graphics) {
    for (var i:uint=0; i<loops; i++) {
        lineTo(i%100*3,i%200);
```

```
    }
  }
// Snippet 2
var g:Graphics = shape.graphics;
for (var i:uint=0; i< loops; i++) {
    g.lineTo(i%100*3,i%200);
}
```

This is another instance of code that should run with very similar performance. However, the second snippet beats the first by a factor of 7!

AS3 isn't the only language with `with` problems. Visual Basic 6 tended to have performance problems with `with`, too.

Boxing and Unboxing

In C#, passing primitive data generically requires that it be boxed. That is, if you have an `int` that you want to pass through a data structure that deals with objects, the `int` must first be placed on the heap and then a reference stored and passed around. When you want to get that `int` back, you have to unbox it. This can introduce a significant overhead. Boxing data is about $10\times$ the cost of simply writing it to an array, and unboxing it is $2\times$ the cost of reading it from an array. Using generics helps quite a bit, because data can be processed entirely as its native type rather than requiring boxing.

Conclusion

You can get good performance out of managed languages. But you have to pay special attention to the JIT and GC behavior, the latter of which can eat a huge amount of performance if you are careless. Leverage the runtime and native capabilities of the environment to get maximum performance.

The same basic optimization techniques apply to managed languages that apply to native languages. However, the same things that makes managed languages attractive (powerful built-in functionality, automated memory management, and flexible typing) also add a layer of complexity that must be taken into account when you are optimizing. More often, you will have to figure out the right code to make the runtime do the right thing, as opposed to writing fast code to begin with.

In the end, managed languages are a major asset because they allow game code to be written in a more flexible and maintainable way. By reducing the cost of developing and maintaining gameplay code, the overall cost of the project, in terms of time and money, is reduced.

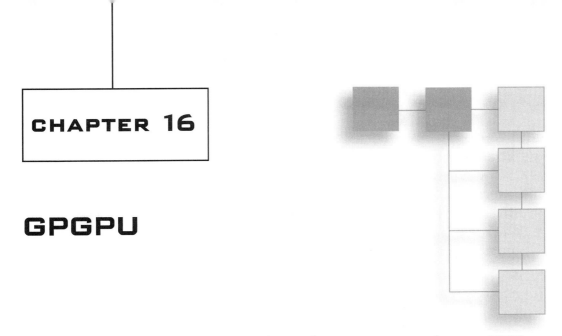

CHAPTER 16

GPGPU

Commonly referred to as *GPGPU* (general purpose computing on GPU) or GPGPU, the architecture and techniques we'll discuss in this chapter take advantage of the strengths of GPUs while providing the flexibility and generality of CPUs. For certain problem domains, GPGPU is the best of both worlds.

What Is GPGPU?

GPGPU is the logical conclusion of the evolution of GPU development. Every generation of GPUs for the past several decades has had more generalized capabilities. High-end GPUs have had more and more parallelism, thus greater total computing power. With the latest Shader models (4 and beyond), fully general computations can be performed at good speed.

Initially, researchers realized that they could use GPUs to offload some calculations from the CPU. For instance, certain financial and scientific calculations required operations on large matrices. By storing the matrix's data in a large texture and evaluating a pixel shader, the work could be massively parallelized, resulting in a major speed gain.

This led to the term *GPGPU*, since the GPU was able to do general-purpose work. Under this banner, developers gradually accrued a library of techniques for getting GPUs designed for image rendering to produce accurate numerical results. While effective, it was anything but simple to get a calculation up and running reliably. But once up, if it was a good fit, the performance was up to three orders of magnitude better than traditional CPUs could achieve.

GPU developers focused on GPGPU as a way to sell more hardware, especially to the lucrative scientific and commercial markets. Small clusters of GPUs could act as desktop supercomputers, enabling computations that would otherwise require a modest data center. In the consumer space, middleware packages began offering GPU-accelerated processing. Proprietary APIs came out from NVIDIA and ATI that provided convenient languages and interfaces for doing general computation on GPUs.

At the same time, IBM launched its Cell processor, which is used in the PS3. While not GPGPU, it supported many of the same concepts and provided similar performance. The main downside was a lack of good tools and languages for targeting the Cell's hardware.

Subsequently, with ATI's acquisition by AMD, Intel's development of Larrabee, and NVIDIA's release of ARM system-on-a-chip, there was convergence of GPU and CPU technology. In this time frame, common, vendor-independent APIs for GPGPU were also released by Apple and Microsoft. This allowed the development of GPGPU code that could be run reliably on multiple vendors' GPUs.

That's as far as development has progressed by the time of this writing, but it is clear that this process of convergence is not yet fully completed. The main changes we foresee will be the trickle-down effect as GPGPU becomes available to the vast majority of users, enabling its use in more applications, and maturation of the APIs, languages, and tools that enable GPGPU. Bottom line? GPGPU is here to stay.

There are only a few major languages for doing GPGPU. Most of them are C/C++ derivatives: CUDA, Sh, OpenCL, DirectCompute, and Brook all fall into this category. They strongly resemble the shader languages discussed in Chapter 10, "Shaders." As you have probably noticed by the name, they are tied closely to an API.

When Is It Appropriate to Process on the GPU?

There are not many PC games taking advantage of GPGPU processing outside of physics APIs. A quick Google search will return many more results for scientific applications, such as medical visualization or fluid dynamics modeling.

But the raw horsepower of GPU computing is available for more than just academic research. In many cases, games are missing out. Pontificating on the opportunity losses the game industry might be missing leads us to ask the question: "When should you use the GPU for more than just rasterization?"

The answer is obvious at the system level. If the CPU is highly loaded and the GPU is not, it makes sense to move work to the GPU. For games that are CPU bound, this can be a big win, or it can enable new features that would otherwise be infeasible.

Offloading work to the GPU can also make sense when it is a good fit. Even when an application is GPU bound, it doesn't make sense to move rasterization over to the CPU, because CPUs are so much less efficient at rasterization. Similarly, if you have a task with GPU-friendly memory characteristics and high computation demands, it might make sense to move it over regardless. In other words, when an algorithm maps well to the GPU's design for processing, moving it onto the GPU can provide double- and sometimes triple-digit performance increases.

You should consider using the CPU over the GPU when your algorithm has many divergent branches—branches which, when run in parallel on many threads simultaneously, do not resolve to the same condition for a given conditional. While the GPU does support branching, it does not excel at it. In some cases, a GPU compiler can perform tricks to reduce performance degradation, or you, as developers, can organize the traversal so that threads of similar conditions execute in batches; in absence of those tricks, a CPU is probably a better tool.

A GPU is not a good processor if you would like to perform one calculation and block until it returns. The round trip path to the GPU is long and unless you are working on a machine that has fixed paths to DRAM (like the Xbox 360), then you do not want to incur the round trip performance implications involved in the path from CPU memory to the GPU. The preferred approach is to batch calculations together, submit them, and retrieve the answers later asynchronously. This reduces the overhead per calculation.

Finally, GPGPU processing will be more acceptable for mass market when Shader model 4 becomes a minimum spec for your game. If your users are not using 4 hardware, you may find yourself writing both a CPU and a GPU version and choosing the correct path based on the user's hardware profile. There are some caveats to this suggestion, however. There are particle system and skinning animation implementations on hardware as old as Shader model 2. These algorithms are useful and perform well, but obviously are not general solutions. Only more recent hardware makes it easy to implement GPGPU solutions for general computation.

How Fast Is the GPU for Things Other Than Graphics?

So is the GPU really able to deliver on all the hype promised by GPU advocates? If it didn't, we probably wouldn't spend so much time writing this chapter and the Kronos group, NVIDIA, and Microsoft probably wouldn't work so hard trying to build APIs that interface with the GPU.

Let's take a look at a benchmark that shows how well the GPU can perform on general processing.

Stanford's Folding@Home program highlights the GPU's potential. Folding@Home's algorithms, which measure how proteins fold, is implemented for many different processors including Intel, PowerPC, ATI GPU, NVIDIA GPU, and the Cell Processor in the PlayStation 3. The value measured is performance in terraflops per second, or 10^{12} floating-point operations per second. For an apples to apples comparison, Stanford scientists converted the GPU flops into x86 flops since GPU flops are often lower than x86/PPC due to specialized floating-point hardware.

Using data from Stanford's Website as of September 13, 2009, GPUs represented 4.9% of the total processors used in their experiments but delivered an impressive 67.1% of the total teraflops.

GPUs were able to achieve these numbers with a very low price per theoretical gigaflop. For example, using prices as of June 2009, an NVIDIA GTX 280's cost is $0.41 per theoretical gigaflop while an Intel Core 2 Quad Q9650 costs about $6.45 per theoretical gigaflop. This comparison isn't strictly apples-to-apples because GPU theoretical performance typically counts the floating-point operations of the multiply-add instruction, which is able to deliver two flops in one cycle; yet, the staggering price difference between the GTX and the Core 2 allows for some wriggle room.

More evidence of how well the GPU can perform is evident simply by looking at the literature published by NVIDIA, ATI, and independent developers. There are many white papers discussing how an algorithm can be brought to GPGPU. Typical wins for GPU-friendly algorithms range from 10–100x.

GPU System Execution

GPUs, graphics processing units, might be misnamed. Looking back, launching this technology for gaming may have been more of a tactic than a strategy— maybe gamers are simply a means to an end? GPUs are semi-conductors, and while their architecture helps to define your rasterization pipeline, at their core, they are throughput-focused processors that provide hardware support for data parallel processing on concurrent streams of data.

Let's decode that last sentence by examining a model of the round-trip communication required of GPGPU processing. Figure 16.1 shows this visually; it may be useful to refer to this figure during this section.

The journey is long. First, the CPU submission passes the data and an executable program. The CPU passes the program to the hardware drivers, which passes the data to the expansion bus, which transfers data across to the GPU. Now that the data is in GPU memory, the GPU can fetch it, process it, and store it back to GPU memory. The drivers, upon notification, can return the data back to the CPU, after data transfers back across the bus where it will reach its final destination in the CPU's system memory.

With this long journey, how does the GPU achieve faster rasterization than the CPU?

The answer is throughput. Even though the GPU's latency, when looking at a single operation as a round trip operation, is poor, the throughput that is possible is impressive. The GPU, its design, and the efficient use of this design reveal efficiencies that do not exist on the CPU.

The GPU does a lot of work to ensure that the process stage, listed previously, is as parallel and coherent as possible; this is essential to achieving the throughput. This processing is both highly concurrent, which increases the rate of processing, and coherent, which increases the speed of memory fetching and storing. That is, the processing does many of the same instructions at the same time (concurrency), and the data is arranged, fetched, and processed linearly if possible (coherent). The goal of being concurrent and coherent is typical of many of today's processors; however, the GPU's implementation is significantly different

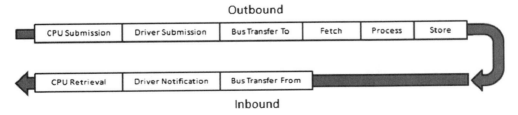

Figure 16.1

Lifecycle involved in a GPGPU computation.

in that there is more hardware for arithmetic than there is for speculation of memory or instruction fetching. In general, by using the GPU's approach, you, as programmers, give up some flexibility, unless of course the algorithm matches very closely to the architecture. We will cover more about the GPU's concurrency and coherency throughout this chapter.

Back to throughput. With the understanding of the importance of concurrency and coherence, let's dive deeper into the behavior of a kernel. A kernel, in its basic definition, is a small program or set of instructions. A kernel in GPGPU is analogous to a shader in a graphics API. Using the simple pseudocode that follows, let's examine how high latency can still deliver high throughput.

```
pChassis = GetChassis();//5 min
pFrame = BuildFrame( pChassis );//20 min
pBody = BuildBody( pFrame );//30 min
pEffects = AddEffects( pBody );//20 min
pFinishedCar = FinishedCar( pEffects );//10 min
```

If you were to measure how long it would take to make one car, you could very easily calculate the time by adding all the times associated with each action. In this case, you could claim that the total time, or latency, was 85 minutes. If you wanted to build two cars, would it take 170 minutes? Assuming that there was no concurrency, and each car must finish before the next one begins, then yes.

A more concurrent design would be to use the model of an assembly line. If you were able to begin the next car before the last car was complete, you would achieve better throughput. If you began the first car at time 0, it would finish at 85 minutes. If you began the second car as soon as possible, it would finish at 1:10 minutes. If you were to measure the rate of cars-per-hour, the first car's rate would be 1/(85/60), or 0.71 cars-per-hour. If you were to measure the effective rate of two cars, the rate would be 2/(115/60), or 1.04 cars-per-hour. You increased the throughput by 1/3 of cars-per-hour. If you add a third car, you would increase the throughput to 2/(125/60), or 1.44 cars-per-hour. In this simple example, you would get closer and closer to a theoretical rate of three cars per hour. The jump from .71 cars-per-hour to three cars-per-hour occurred without decreasing the latency. (In fact, since bottlenecks occurred at some stages, latency even increased to 120 minutes.) Table 16.1 summarizes these calculations.

This type of performance increase makes some assumptions. First, the assembly line needs to be full as often as possible. Starting and stopping the assembly line would greatly degrade the performance. It is the difference between 0.71 and 3.0

Table 16.1 Performance of Parallelized Car Construction

Cumulative Time (Min)	Car 1	Car 2	Car 3
0.00	GetChassis		
5.00	BuildFrame	GetChassis	
25.00	BuildBody	BuildFrame	GetChassis
55.00	AddEffects	BuildBody	BuildFrame
75.00	FinishedCar		BuildBody
85.00		AddEffects	
105.00		FinishedCar	AddEffects
115.00			FinishedCar
125.00			
Effective Rate Per Hour	0.71	1.04	1.44

with respect to throughput. Another assumption is that the system is able to supply raw materials quickly enough to reduce stalls at the beginning of the assembly line, at each task, or to store results. This is one reason why data coherence is so important.

A useful trait of this type of parallelism is that it is scalable without any intervention from the developer. Assuming that the system is able to provide data (raw materials in the analogy) quickly enough, you could clone this assembly line multiple times using the same set of actions for each thread. This is what GPUs do. This type of parallelism is referred to as *SIMT*, or single instruction, multiple threads.

Architecture

Understanding the performance capabilities of GPGPU requires an understanding of the underlying hardware. Thankfully, it will be familiar to anyone who has worked with GPUs before. We'll quickly run through the architecture and review its major performance characteristics. We'll generally refer to CUDA, although the same techniques apply across GPGPU technologies.

Unified Cores and Kernels

The introduction of DirectX 10 cards brought additional functionality and more efficient use of hardware. In prior generations, vertex processing and pixel processing occurred in separate hardware. In DirectX 10, there are shared computing elements that are allocated to tasks as needed.

This is the basis for GPGPU processing. Other parts of hardware, such as vertex assembly, raster operations unit, and framebuffer hardware are outside the bounds of most GPGPU applications. Understanding the core, and designing your algorithms to fit the architecture, is key to squeezing out the throughput defined here.

Next, let's discuss the execution model—how the runtime and drivers distribute work among the available processors.

Execution: From Bottom to Top

GPUs are designed to solve embarrassingly parallel problems, so they are geared toward concurrency from the transistor level on up. For our purposes, we'll start with threads and work our way up. A GPU thread is different from a CPU thread in that it is designed to begin and end frequently. Another significant difference is that many more GPU threads run at a time, and significantly more hardware is dedicated to each thread. An algorithm may utilize hundreds of GPU threads at once. Finally, groups of threads all execute the same code while CPU threads typically each have their own code to run. Figure 16.2 visualizes the relationship between blocks, grids, and threads.

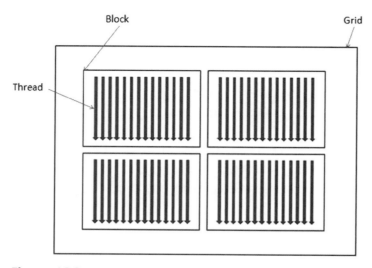

Figure 16.2

Visualization of the CUDA processing hierarchy.

Warps

For execution purposes, the SIMT unit schedules threads together into groups called *warps*. In CUDA, warps are currently groups of 32 threads, but you can query the API for the maximum your hardware supports via the warpSize variable. Warps execute the same instruction concurrently.

GPU support for branching affects the execution of warps. Flow control instructions (if, switch, do, for, and while) cause warps to serialize, executing branches that share the same value for the condition and temporarily disabling threads that are taking different execution paths. In some cases, the compiler may choose to write out both branches statically, using the condition variable as a predicate for determining which instruction should be ignored. In these cases, performance is sacrificed for correct functioning. Luckily, this performance drain only affects branches that diverge, so you can mitigate the cost by making sure that most of your threads will branch the same way.

Block

While the GPU executes threads in warps, a larger container, called a *block*, defines a higher level of similar functionality. Blocks will execute on one processor core, which ensures that, as a developer, you know that the execution of a block will have a locality for the block that doesn't require you to support cross-core issues; developing your algorithm as independent blocks also ensures that your algorithm is scalable. Block execution can occur at one, two, or three dimensions, which may assist developers in mapping their algorithm to the execution model.

Blocks also have a local memory. By taking advantage of memory that is shareable within a block, you are ensuring a reasonable locality for memory access. This shared memory is low-latency efficient, so taking advantage of storage per block can greatly benefit the execution time of a given block. The lifetime of this memory is equivalent to the lifetime of the block, so when all warps within a block finish, the scope of the block memory does not persist.

Thread synchronization is available at the scope of the block. In CUDA, if a kernel needs to synchronize data, it can do so using syncThreads(). The SIMT unit will schedule the warps and execute the block until each thread reaches the synchronization barrier. Once all threads reach the point, the scheduler finishes the execution of the block and moves on.

When the host (the CPU or client side) executes a kernel, CUDA enumerates blocks for distribution to the GPU's many multi-processors. When thinking at the block level, a developer should be aware that blocks may not require dependence; that is, blocks should be able to execute in any order without affecting the algorithm.

Grid

A grid is a collection of blocks, with the size specified by the programmer. A grid size of one is acceptable; however, memory constraints may require additional grids to provide another layer of subdivision.

Kernel

A kernel launches a function and specifies the grid dimension, block count, and thread count. Kernels operate serially, meaning that if a given application calls the kernels in order, they will execute in order.

An example will clarify things. Let's look at CUDA. To invoke a kernel in CUDA, you must first write the kernel and then call it. Calling a kernel is similar to calling a function with the exception of the <<< >>> operator, which defines the number of grids and block dimensions.

```
__global__ void MatrixMultiply( float A[N][N],
                                float B[N][N],
                                float C[N][N] )
{
    int i= threadIdx.x;
    int j= threadIdx.y;
    C[i][j] = A[i][j] + B[i][j];
}
int main()
{
    int numGrid = 1;
    Dim3 dimBlock( 4, 4, 1);
    MatrixMultiply<<<numGrid, dimBlock>>>( A, B, C );
}
```

In the example, the function MatrixMultiply will execute 16 times with all threads likely executing on one multiprocessor in the same warp. As an aside, the matrices A, B, and C are all stored in global memory, which isn't ideal. For maximum performance, the matrices would need to be placed in the right places in the memory hierarchy.

Bottlenecks

There are a few likely causes for performance problems in GPGPU applications. In the following sections, we will run through them and discuss solutions. The optimization techniques here build on concepts we have discussed in preceding chapters, especially Chapters 6, 7, and 10.

Host Communication

Similar to graphics programming, a major performance bottleneck tends to be getting data and commands on to and off of the GPU. There is a base cost to any compute job, and you have to make sure that the job you are providing is big enough to be worthwhile. Consider the following anecdote.

We recently saw a developer demonstrate the "power" of GPU computing by implementing a GPU-accelerated matrix transpose for 4x4 matrices. While a GPU can certainly transpose matrices quickly, the overhead of copying the matrix over the bus, preparing the kernel, and issuing the compute command are all significantly more costly—not to mention the cost of copying the results back to the CPU! At best, this is a slowdown of an order of magnitude compared to simply doing it yourself on the CPU.

However, as jobs become larger, the upside quickly rises. In addition, it is possible to pass data from kernel to kernel without copying it back to the CPU. So if a long chain of processing must be done, only at the first and last steps must data be transferred between the GPU and CPU. In addition, GPGPU computing APIs can interoperate with traditional rendering APIs, such as DirectX and OpenGL, in order to bring results (say, from a particle system or physics simulation) directly to your rendering code.

Memory and Compute

GPGPU exposes a more complex memory hierarchy than traditional GPU programming. This, along with explicit knowledge about how many threads are being run, opens the door for more careful performance tuning. If you can keep your computation's memory footprint in fast memory, there are significant performance gains. Conversely, fetching slow data frequently is a big performance drain, although the efficient scheduling on most GPUs can help hide the latency.

If you are working with local data, you have a lot of computing power to bring to bear on your problem. The biggest problem by far in GPGPU is determining how to structure your data for efficient processing. Once that is done, the GPU has no problem getting things done right and quickly.

Most of the considerations in the CPU, Memory, and GPU chapters apply to optimizing your GPGPU code. Look out for data dependencies and cache unfriendly access patterns. Optimize memory bandwidth usage.

Above all else, start with a good benchmark and some careful measurements. Identify your bottleneck and solve it. Then check that you got an improvement and repeat the process until you have acceptable performance.

Conclusion

If your problem is appropriate, GPGPU can give performance gains of multiple orders of magnitude. The main downsides are that it is not universally available and that not every computation task is a good fit. There is a clear trend towards embracing the GPGPU model of programming as a standard capability on consoles and PCs.

The performance bottlenecks that GPGPU development encounters will be immediately familiar to anyone familiar with optimizing CPU and GPU code. The three major bottlenecks are the transfer from CPU to GPU to issue and retrieve work, memory access, and computation. Thought and planning are required to manage these problems, but the rewards in performance make it worthwhile.

This is the last chapter of *Video Game Optimization*. We hope it has been helpful to you. By this point, if you were new to the subject, you have learned everything you need to start optimizing with confidence. If you were already an experienced developer, we hope this book has refreshed your knowledge and brought a few new details to your attention.

Remember, always drive your optimization with data. Establish a benchmark and measure it carefully. Identify the problem and then solve it. Check that you saw a real performance gain, and keep on going until you have met your performance goals.

Thanks for reading!

INDEX

Special Characters

Numerics

A